FLIP SIDES

Truth, Fairplay & Other Myths We Choose to Live By

⇅ ⇅ ⇅

Spot Cleaning Our Dirty Laundry

WISING UP ANTHOLOGIES

ILLNESS & GRACE: TERROR & TRANSFORMATION

FAMILIES: *The Frontline of Pluralism*

LOVE AFTER 70

DOUBLE LIVES, REINVENTION & THOSE WE LEAVE BEHIND

VIEW FROM THE BED: VIEW FROM THE BEDSIDE

SHIFTING BALANCE SHEETS:
Women's Stories of Naturalized Citizenship & Cultural Attachment

COMPLEX ALLEGIANCES:
Constellations of Immigration, Citizenship, & Belonging

DARING TO REPAIR: *What Is It, Who Does It & Why?*

CONNECTED: *What Remains As We All Change*

CREATIVITY & CONSTRAINT

SIBLINGS: *Our First Macrocosm*

THE KINDNESS OF STRANGERS

SURPRISED BY JOY

CROSSING CLASS: *The Invisible Wall*

RE-CREATING OUR COMMON CHORD

GOODNESS

FLIP SIDES

Truth, Fair Play & Other Myths We Live By

⇂↑   ⇂↑   ⇂↑

Spot Cleaning Our Dirty Laundry

Heather Tosteson & Charles D. Brockett
Editors

Wising Up Press

Wising Up Press
P.O. Box 2122
Decatur, GA 30031-2122
www.universaltable.org

Copyright © 2021 by Wising Up Press

Wising Up ISBN: 978-1-7324514-9-0

Catalogue-in-Publication data is on file with the Library of Congress.
LCCN: 2021938070

ങ൏ഠ඀

This above all: to thine own self be true,
And it must follow, as the night the day,
Thou canst not then be false to any man.
 —Polonius (Shakespeare)

The greatest revolution of our generation is the discovery that human beings, by changing the inner attitudes of their minds, can change the outer aspects of their lives.
 —William James

Man is born a predestined idealist, for he is born to act. To act is to affirm the worth of an end, and to persist in affirming the worth of an end is to make an ideal.
 —Oliver Wendell Holmes, Jr.

The talent for self-justification is surely the finest flower of human evolution, the greatest achievement of the human brain. When it comes to justifying actions, every human being acquires the intelligence of an Einstein, the imagination of a Shakespeare, and the subtlety of a Jesuit.
 —Michael Foley

Why do we call all our generous ideas illusions, and the mean ones truth?
 —Edith Wharton

ങ൏ഠ඀

ne Tools of Resist
Her Epiphany:
It Isn't Clear
You Think
BEHIND THE STORY
Sometimes You Belong
You Are Not as Specia
IT CAN'T CHANGE OVERNIGHT
BUT WE GOTTA START SOMEWHERE...
Anoth ime, Another Crisis
identity and the c of being an outsider.
An Excavated Voice
Race Gap Doesn't Stop
Inseparable
stening to the Past Is Kind of Perfect

CONTENTS

IV. FAMILY

AMBIGUITY

TRAUMA

ADDICTION

LOWELL JAEGER

HEATHER TOSTESON

FLIP SIDES:
Truth, Fair Play & Other Myths We Choose to Live By
↓↑   ↓↑   ↓↑
Spot Cleaning Our Dirty Laundry

Myths We Choose to Live by

We are not cynical. Even in our advancing age. Neither is our press—or the language that arises when we try to describe it, language that has an earnestness to it that occasionally bemuses, amuses, but which we also recognize as a gift, an insistence that, as Browning's artist-monk Fra Lippo Lippi says,

> . . . *This world's no blot for us,*
> *Nor blank; it means intensely, and means good:*
> *To find its meaning is my meat and drink.*

Actively committing to that search for meaning, good meaning, seems necessary in our increasingly polarized world where people find it more and more difficult to listen with a faithful heart to those whose values differ significantly from their own. We need to be able to hear that good far more clearly, not only in ourselves but also in each other: a good that is embodied, partial and fallible—essential and also contestable, and constantly being made and remade at both individual and the societal levels. We need to understand what it means to be faithful to it *and* to each other.

The idea for this anthology came in early 2020, before COVID, before the mass protests for racial justice, before contested elections, assaults on Congress, or recent gun massacres. It came before we had finally finished writing up and publishing *Sharing the Burden of Repair: Reentry After Mass Incarceration*, our account of an intensive listening project that looked at a surprisingly bipartisan effort of reform in Georgia, one of the most punishing states in our country, the state we have called home for the last fifteen years. We were exploring the role and the responsibilities that we, the apparently untouched and law-abiding, can play in repairing such a large, systemic injustice. Our radical contribution was to listen *in good faith* to all participants, from commissioners of corrections to men and women who had served forty years behind bars. The idea for *Flip Sides* came in tandem with the idea for another one, *Goodness*, which we edited and published some months ago, which did not separate goodness, the reality of it, from all this chaos, entrenched injustice, social and political grievance, rather anchored it firmly right there, in the midst, *our* midst, as equally real.

Flip Sides, however, is messier. It is all about complicity. *Our* complicity. Intimate complicity. With positive ideals. How we develop them, hang on to them, embody them. How we evade, smudge, qualify, and jettison them too. Why they matter. Why the dynamics by which we develop them—and qualify them matter.

The anthology was originally, and rather playfully, conceived as two. *Truth, Fair Play & Other Myths We Choose to Live By* was a response to an increasingly cynical world view that disavowed our best intentions. The other, *Spot Cleaning Our Dirty Laundry*, responded to an increasingly righteous reactivity in all of us that refuses to take responsibility for the harm we ourselves can cause. When I shared the ideas, our wonderful collaborator, Michele Markarian, suggested they were flip sides of the same coin. Thus the over-arching title.

Writers submitted to one category or the other, but as we read and selected the stories, poems, and non-fiction that spoke to us, we decided that it was far more interesting to immerse our readers in the dynamics of these value conflicts themselves and let you sort and categorize to your own satisfaction. We invite you into our *own* experience as readers, into a more intimate, not always comfortable, engagement with those two interlocked dynamics. Spot cleaning wouldn't be necessary if we didn't *have* beliefs and ideals—or if they didn't need to be continuously reconciled with the exigencies of raw life.

We have an evocative and thought-provoking collection here that allows us to explore many dimensions of these tensions—from our participation in systemic harms to the most intimate of ones, from dramatic instances to quiet, almost unnoticeable ones. We have organized them by the dilemmas they explore: race, nationality and culture, class and community, family dynamics, faith.

All of them explore these two essential questions:

- *Where do the positive values in our lives come from and how, why, and*

when do we live up to them?
- *What do we do when those values aren't met—by us or by others?*

These questions lead us, or at least they led me, to think more about the nature of moral emotions and the different ways of thinking, one logical and conscious, the other narrative, with a strong unconscious and visceral component, by which we register them. Also about self-deception, self-justification, harm and repair.

Positive Values and Moral Emotions

Jonathon Haidt and colleagues in the social sciences in their moral foundations theory have identified five, possibly six, primary moral emotions, which they think are common across cultures and form the basis of an "intuitive ethics." These emotions and values are associated with deep drives: 1) *Care/harm* is associated with our mammalian nature, attachment and nurture; 2) *fairness/cheating* is associated with reciprocal altruism (fairness has been modified to proportionality in later iterations of the theory); 3) *loyalty/betrayal* is associated with our being a tribal species and our sense of group identity; 4) *authority/subversion* is shaped by our being, as primates, deeply hierarchical; 5) *sanctity/degradation* is associated with the psychology of disgust and contamination; and another proposed one 6) *liberty/oppression* is based on the resentment people feel when they are dominated.

These first five emotions map easily onto the last five of the ten commandments, the ones related to our conduct as social beings, and on the basic moral imperatives found in other religions, like the Yamas or Vedic Restraints in Hinduism. These values are so crucial to human social functioning that they are each highly sanctioned by stigma. An important point that these scholars make is that not all societies—and not all individuals—put equal weight on all of these emotions—or even acknowledge them all. For example, when mapping onto political views in the U.S., they point out that most liberals use only two of the moral emotions—care and fairness (possibly also liberty), while devaluing the others—loyalty/authority/sanctity—that just happen to be more important for conservatives. Conservatives, because they ascribe value to each of the five, effectively devalue the core ones that liberals hold exclusively dear.

It is interesting as you read these stories, poems, essays and memoirs to see which values might be in play for different characters, and what value or values are so central to the story that they define what we feel is a coherent and satisfying closure to its central conflict—and determine whether we might put the story in the myths we choose or the spot cleaning category. For examples, stories that explore values and dissonance in our relations to systems and structures may rely far more on the conventionally liberal moral values of care and fairness, while the core conflicts within families and faith may turn far more on the questions of sanctity, authority, loyalty, liberty.

Moral Values: Received or Discovered

How we discover, experience, understand, and resolve our conflicts between values also differ, depending on whether we understand them as externally defined/received (commandments) or as something we have discovered directly from our own experience (beliefs). In general, the values we hold most close, that are most essential to how we understand ourselves, we have independently discovered and validated experientially, even if they also have also been taught. Concepts derived experientially are more easily modified by experience—they are accountable to life, not logic. They are also interesting because they come as story, as implicit action, thus with a sense of agency. They come as body states. So do the emotions that accompany their violation—shame, guilt, unease. These moral evaluations and our reactions to these evaluations come faster than thought. We know them, in ourselves and in others, before we can name them.

The use of the word myths that I instinctively chose to discuss these core values refers to this experiential potential. They take their real meaning from the stories they came from, the stories they create. I think everyone has an inner list like this—beliefs that have proved themselves experientially reliable, beliefs that we *can* act on, even if we don't always do so. Here is the list I jotted down for myself as I was thinking about this introduction. They each come with trailing sensory memories, story.

> *We are all created (existentially) equal.*
> *Life means and means intensely and means good. To find its meaning*
>   *is my meat and drink.*
> *So much depends on a red wheelbarrow.*
> *Do unto others as you would have them do unto to you.*
> *You <u>always</u> feed the baby.*
> *It's better to know.*
> *Words matter.*
> *People are more important than ideas.*
> *I am accountable for my choices.*

Hypocrisy stinks.
Life isn't zero sum.
Physical violence is wrong.

That's it. Seventy years, filled with great riches and blunders, and that's what I've come up with. I feel remorse, guilt, shame, exasperation when I don't meet those values, and I know that all of them are not shared, but I know having them and abiding by them as much as possible matters, helps me feel I am creating a world I want to be part of.

I think that I enjoy the Victorian writers so much because they understood that thinking the best of each other, acting our best, believing in our best *is* a choice—one that isn't always vindicated by its consequences, but even so is worth the effort. They saw cynicism as an essential enemy. Thomas Carlyle in *Sartar Resartus* describes that process as moving through increasing disillusion and despair until you reach a point where you reach The Everlasting No, that point where you say all right, the world really is going to the dogs, but not me, I stop here. In that reorganizing pause, which he calls The Center of Indifference, where you just sit without emotion, without labels, without purpose, something rises to meet you that he calls, The Everlasting Yes, where you are in tune again with your need for purpose, hope, and find you can say to yourself, "Be no longer a Chaos but a World . . ." Existentialism describes the same journey, but perhaps without the heavy breathing, the sense of stubborn striving. That striving, the raw effort of it, is truer to my own experience. For me, Fra Lippo Lippi's invitation is a visceral one that infuses and transforms thought, not the other way around. To some extent the very nature of the seeking is the finding.

Spot Cleaning Our Dirty Laundry: Self-Justification—Victims and Perpetrators

Which brings me to the next core question: *What do we do when our values, especially these profound, experientially essential values, aren't acknowledged—or lived up to, by others or by ourselves?*

The psychologist Jerome Kagan, exploring the differences between logical (semantical) and narrative/experiential (schematic) ways of knowing, asks an interesting question that addresses the question of spot cleaning:

> *Is human restraint on asocial behavior mediated by the visceral sche-*
> *mata for guilt, shame, anxiety, or remorse, or by the semantic networks*
> *for self that demand consistency between one's actions and the judgment*
> *of personal virtue?*

I would suggest that when we're spot cleaning, not making lasting change, we are far more interested in convincing ourselves and others that our actions can still fit under the semantic label good or at least justifiable, and, more importantly, *we* can still fit under the semantic label good people. As Daniel Ariely points out, we all are open to cheating, but not so much that it tarnishes our reputation or our self-concept. We need to be the heroes of our own lives.

But spot cleaning can diminish us because it prevents us from absorbing the multiplicity of consequences of our actions, the two-sided blade of our own agency. Most importantly, it minimizes harm. All this semantic juggling is more difficult—and less persuasive—when it is not just ourselves but other people we are betraying. When it is not just us doing the judging, but those around us. It is very uncomfortable to feel guilty or ashamed and we all do our best to avoid it. As Carol Tavris and Elliot Aronson wryly explain in *Mistakes Were Made (but not by me)*:

> *Self-justification is not the same thing as lying or making excuses. . . . That is why self-justification is more powerful and more dangerous than the explicit lie. It allows people to convince themselves that what they did was the best thing they could have done. In fact, come to think of it, it was the right thing.*

They also point out, more seriously, that the explanations we give for our actions in order to put them in a positive light can distort experience significantly.

> *The remarkable thing about self-justification is that it allows us to shift from one role to the other and back again in the blink of an eye—without applying what we learn from one role to the other. Feeling like a victim of injustice in one situation does not make us less likely to commit an injustice against someone else, nor does it make us more sympathetic to victims. It's as if there is a brick wall between these two sets of experiences, blocking our ability to see the other side.*
>
> *One of the reasons for that brick wall is that pain felt is always more intense than pain inflicted, even when the amount of pain is identical.*

In real life, at one time or another, we have all been both a victim and perpetrator. When the psychologist Roy Baumeister asked people to tell a story of a time when they had harmed someone *and* a story of when they themselves had been harmed, he found both types of stories were self-protective, but in different ways. When telling a "perpetrator" story, people reduced their cognitive dissonance by saying they did nothing wrong (either their actions were justifiable or not deliberate), or they acknowledged harm but told about mitigating or external circumstances. Half said they couldn't help themselves or blamed the victim for provoking them. If they couldn't deny the harm, they bracketed it—as atypical, a long time ago, or without lasting consequences.

Victims, on the other hand had the memory of elephants—and they felt their perpetrators were fully in control of their actions. Most interestingly, they couldn't, even years later, make sense of the perpetrator's motivation. What troubled them most was that the person who had wronged them couldn't *feel* the harm they had done—and they absolutely couldn't understand how that could be. Remember, the person telling these stories of victim and perpetrator is one and the same, but these roles are so different in their impact on us, we use completely different ways of understanding them.

Tavris and Aronson have an interesting metaphor for these divergences in understanding, which they call a pyramid of choice. We don't always start out to do something wrong, rather we are in an ambiguous situation and the right choice isn't clear, but as we make choices, we continue to justify them to ourselves even when their immorality is less ambiguous, so by the time we get to the bottom of the pyramid, we may be very far from our original choices—and our choices may not be comprehensible to those we stood close to at the top of the pyramid, who faced the same ambiguity and made very different decisions. We may now see each other as completely alien—and incomprehensible. *Categorically* different. Both parties can forget that there was a point when they stood very close together and could understand their similarities. A point where they could stand in each other's shoes. It is particularly difficult to stand in the *and* condition when trying to accept both our capacity for harm and our vulnerability to it.

This has personal and also systemic implications. Many of the stories and memoirs in this collection, especially in the first sections, struggle to reconcile the dissonance between the explicit social, systemic values they were raised with and which they have deeply internalized (we are all created equal; this is the land of liberty and equal opportunity), and contradictory, implicit ones that have shaped our society, and our own opportunities, equally profoundly and inequitably (white's best; not to be middle class is a matter of character, not circumstance; Americans are exceptional). At what point is there so much distance between a value and its actualization that it stops being aspirational and becomes hypocritical hype? If it becomes that for us, does that mean that others who still hold that belief are hypocritical? Or does it mean that they just have more hope than we do? If we don't share someone else's value, for hierarchy or group loyalty, for example, do we understand that our failure to comprehend that value, those choices of action, can in itself, be a kind of harm? As much as if they questioned our near primal need for care or a sense of existential equality?

Owning: Grounding and Expanding Our Story—Accountability and Forgiving

When you betray yourself, you are both perpetrator and victim. The person you are accountable to is yourself. But I'm not sure the nature of the forgiving that needs to go on is that different from that between individuals. A core dimension of forgiving is to be able to accept the reality of harm and to bear our capacity *for* harm. Desmond Tutu and his daughter Mpho Tutu in *The Book of Forgiving* write:

> *The boundary line between those who have caused harm and those who have harmed is not clear either. Each of us stands at one moment as the one who has been hurt, and at the next moment as the one who is inflicting the hurt. And in the next moment we straddle the boundary, lashing out in pain and rage. We all cross these lines often . . .*

The Tutus present sequences of actions for both the victim and the person in need of forgiveness—an essential part of each of which is claiming and sharing your story. A key part of releasing the role of victim is accepting that what has been done can't be changed or undone but that choosing to forgive can allow us to reclaim agency, to "move from victim to hero in our story. We know we are healing when we are able to tell a new story." For those of us who are in need of forgiveness—for harm we have caused others or ourselves in self-betrayal—two important steps are to acknowledge the wrong and *to witness the anguish and apologize.* This ability to witness the anguish, genuinely feel the pain, *to bear,* is probably the most difficult thing for any of us to do. Even if it is our own anguish, perhaps especially so. The acknowledgment of our capacity for harm and the reality of anguish are at the core of the golden rule: we need to act consistently as if we *all* matter because not to do so *hurts* us, not just as individuals, but also as a species.

But how, as the profoundly self-biased, self-aggrandizing species we are, do we get there? By acknowledging our capacity for harm as fully as our capacity for healing. Our capacity for error as fully as our capacity for clarity. By acknowledging that the difference matters, really matters. By seeing our story, as well as those of the people around us, taken in full, as healing ones, ones that move us mysteriously toward wholeness, not a blot, not a chaos, but a world that means and means intensely and means good. If that is a myth, for me it is a persuasive one, one I choose to live by.

What You Will Find Here

In the section Race, Johnny Townsend explores the many facets of the prism through which he has viewed race—a white southerner, a Mormon, a gay man, someone who has taught in black colleges—and how they intensify his commitment to racial justice. Leah Mueller examines her responses to the differential sentences given to the white and the black man convicted of her brother's murder, while the boy in Lucius Mark's story tries to explain why he used racial epithets on the playground, and in Lyn Steven's story, a mother frantically tries to reduce the consequences to her son of actions that have drawn him into the criminal justice system, consequences that are modified, however implicitly, by race.

The essays in the section on Nationality/Culture explore how we respond to challenges to our ideas of American exceptionalism, Maryah Converse looking at Abu Ghraib and Nanako Water, through the lens of dual cultures, the slave trade in Ghana. Karen Loeb's story about the various motivations of a woman going to be a foreign aid worker, and Frederick Yeager's of a young man tending his immigrant father's memorial to the fall of communism, introduce other layers of ambiguity, of motivation and consequence.

In Class/Community, where laundry as metaphor occurs most frequently, we see how variously the myth of class mobility expresses itself. Mark Pawlak's essay ponders why his parents find even the mention of their early poverty challenging to their current class standing, while C.W. Spooner's "Shoe Dog" explores how the economic pressures created by this myth pose other moral pressures as well. Terry Sanville's story "Driving Without Lights" looks at a time and place when, with class security, all these tensions could play out far more naturally and constructively.

The Family section is subdivided into various themes—ambiguity, trauma, addiction, personal responsibility. In each of these we find people struggling to find labels, myths, frames, for their complex experiences that will allow them to claim them, in their totality, as meaningful, redeeming. These moving poems and stories focus on the sensory density of personal experience, the values we have learned, often painfully, from the inside out. They also, in general, include moving from victim stories to something more resilient and agentic.

The Faith section explores how, as Jan Phillips describes in her essay

"The Power of Myths," we move from belief to faith, one received, the other discovered through our own experience and claimed by our own actions. In Hemlata Vasavada's story "Promises and Threat" the narrator relinquishes a superstitious propitiating of dread for something more faithful, while in Daniel Jaffe's story, a woman in a cross-faith marriage, alienated by what she saw as personal betrayal by her synagogue, returns and discovers that her attachment to her faith is based on something deeper and resilient that still seesaws briskly with rancor. Lowell Jaeger invites us to recognize and lift up our experiences of faith under many different names in many different settings.

REFERENCES

Ariely, Dan. *The (Honest) Truth About Dishonesty: How We Lie to Everyone—Especially Ourselves.* New York: Harper, 2012.

Browning, Robert. *Fra Lippo Lippi.*

Carlyle, Thomas. *Sartar Resartus.*

Kagan, Jerome. *Surprise, Uncertainty, and Mental Structures.* Cambridge: Harvard University Press, 2002, p.7.

Moral Foundations Theory. moralfoundations.org.

Tavris, Carol and Elliot Aronson. *Mistakes Were Made (but not by me): Why We Justify Foolish Beliefs, Bad Decisions, and Hurtful Acts.* Mariner Books, 2015. Direct quotations: self-justification—worse than lying, p.5; pyramid of choice, pp.43-45; self-justification—two stories blink of eye, pp.246-247. Summation of Baumeister, pp.248-252.

Tutu, Desmond and Mpho Tutu. *The Book of Forgiving: The Fourfold Path for Healing Ourselves and Our World.* New York: Harper, 2014, pp.4-5.

Additional Bibliography:

Frankl, Viktor E. *Man's Search for Meaning.*

Haidt, Jonathon. *The Righteous Mind: Why Good People Are Divided by Politics and Religion.* New York: Doubleday, 2012.

Hallinan, Joseph T. *Kidding Ourselves: The Hidden Power of Self-Deception.* New York: Crown, 2014.

Smith, David Livingstone. *Why We Lie: The Evolutionary Roots of Deception and the Unconscious Mind.* New York: St. Martin's Press, 2004.

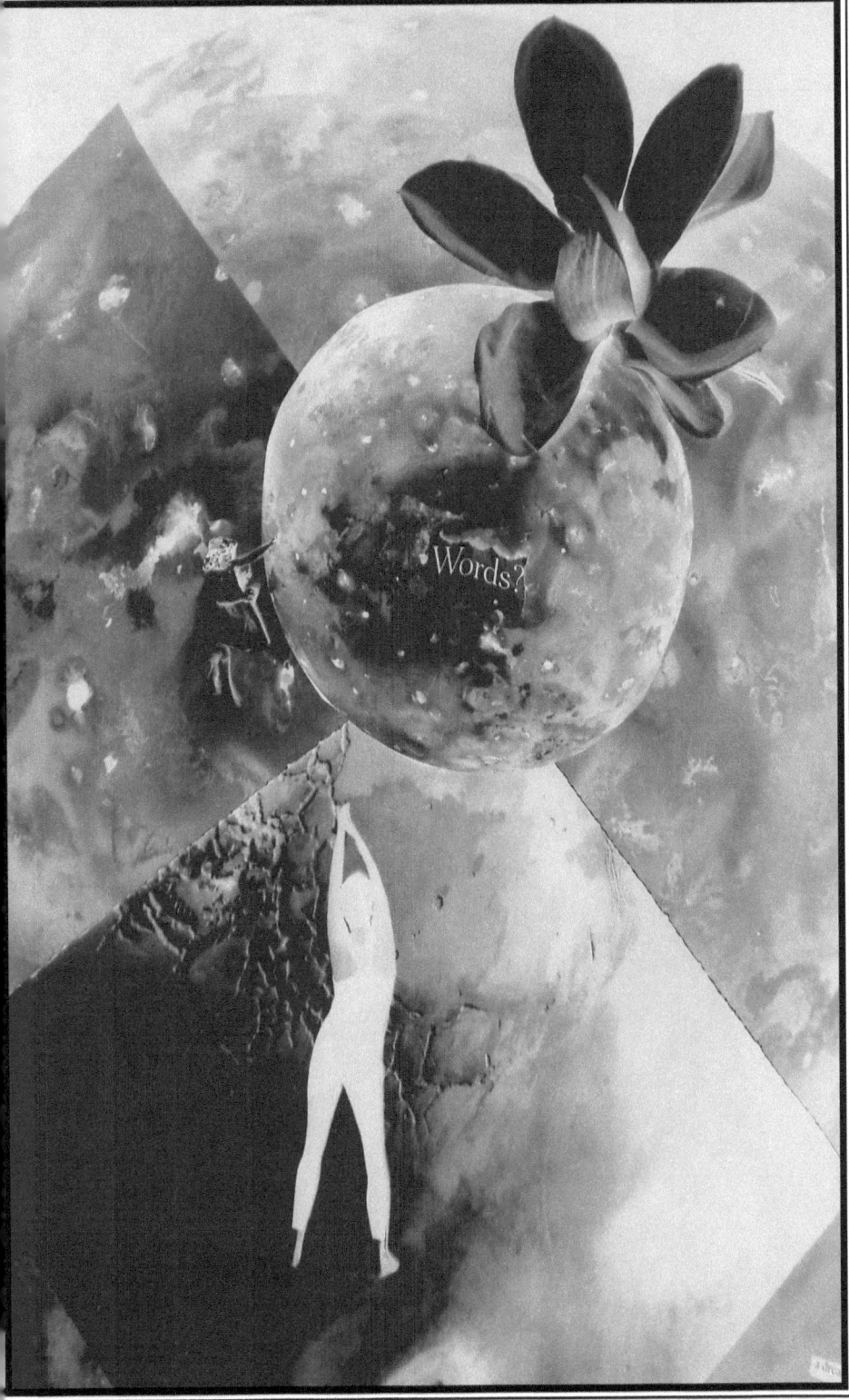

AN ELECTION
"This hurts my heart"
angst, re
ess by focusing attention
Is Still
ring Us
suppression
masks mandatory
'New normal' not even near normal
Close Your Eyes
She Is Seizing
The Selfie Generation
of Denial
ope for the
ntrol of Her
feel safe
after virus
reliably magni
Wait for J
hite suprem
Beauty
Cases surgi
A POWERFUL REASON

I
RACE

ಈಜಾರಿಸು

JOHNNY TOWNSEND

I THREW MY CONFEDERATE CAP AWAY

I just took an internalized bias test through my workplace for the third year in a row. The results? I show a "strong preference" for white people over black, just as I have on each previous exam. I threw my Confederate cap away decades ago, but it's not as easy to get rid of the bias.

As a child, visiting my grandparents in Mississippi provided some of my best memories. Making homemade ice cream on the back steps, picking blackberries, walking the cows in for milking, swimming in the creek, shelling pecans. But life on the dairy farm wasn't all fun and games. Sometimes, the news reported sightings of bears in the area or we'd be warned to keep an eye out for black panthers. No one in the family had ever seen one, but they were the mascot for the single high school in town, so we knew they were real.

Walking with my sister through a pasture the day we heard the latest alert, I saw her stop in fear and point. "I see something black!" she said breathlessly, fixated on something moving beyond the trees along the gravel road. "It has a yellow shirt on!"

It wasn't a panther.

So we relaxed and played among the flowers, a field of Black-eyed Susans, a name I didn't learn until I was almost an adult. We'd been taught to use a racial slur to describe them. "N-word navels."

We made occasional day trips to Vicksburg, the site of some of the heaviest fighting during the Civil War. Dad bought miniature Confederate flags for my sister and me, bought us Confederate caps. We ran up and down the steep hills, warned against wasting time with the Yankee monuments and encouraged to pay proper respect to "ours."

Back in Metairie, the middle-class suburb of New Orleans where we lived, my mother forbade me to watch the show *Julia* starring Diahann Carroll. I was also denied access later to the show *Room 222*. "It has a black person in it," my mother explained.

At one point, my mom wanted to move back to the country and placed an ad to sell our home, describing it as "Tara-style." It was a square brick box with brick columns, built in 1964.

One year, our family attended weekly meetings over several months to prepare for the Elks parade on Mardi Gras, the most prestigious day of the entire carnival season. We'd follow Rex down St. Charles Avenue and Canal Street. I was going to throw out beads and doubloons! The kids at school would be so jealous!

At the last minute, though, the group voted against participating. It was just too dangerous to be downtown with all those black people. They sometimes threw bottles at white people on the floats.

During my early years, Mom sometimes brought my sister and me to the French Quarter to tour the wax museum or the natural history museum. We ate beignets at the Café du Monde. We watched movies at the Robert E. Lee Theater on Robert E. Lee Boulevard, ate Italian sweets on Jefferson Davis Parkway. We passed a statue of General Beauregard on our visits to Storyland in City Park. Sometimes, we shopped along Canal Street. Those adventures all ended once there were "too many black people." My parents did permit me to go down to Lee Circle on Mardi Gras with my best friend and his mom, as long as I promised to be careful. Black people sometimes put razor blades on the tips of their shoes and kicked white people. Best if I wore boots for extra protection.

My suburban public school wasn't integrated until I reached fifth grade. By the time I reached ninth grade, my parents put my sister and me in a private Baptist school that banned blacks. "We're not prejudiced," the headmistress explained. "We just don't approve of interracial dating."

One of my classmates was a David Duke fan. The head of the KKK lived only a mile from the school. Several of my other classmates encouraged the rest of us not to elect the lone Hispanic girl in our class as one of the cheerleaders.

But at home I defiantly watched shows like *Good Times* and *The Jeffersons*. I wasn't prejudiced. Racism was stupid.

Though my parents had both grown up Baptist, we'd all converted to Mormonism in 1971, and in June of 1978, the Prophet announced a new revelation. Black men were now "allowed" to hold the priesthood. The only local news affiliate to cover the story was WDSU. "They're owned by blacks," my mom explained in a what-can-you-expect tone.

My mom sounds like a horrible person, and her racism was clearly destructive. But growing up with her was a mostly wonderful experience. That's a large part of why "good" people harboring terrible prejudices don't see themselves as "bad." It's almost as if racists like my mother have Multiple Personality Disorder. Ninety-seven of their personalities are good, upstanding people. It's the remaining three who are criminally insane. But it's too uncomfortable to rehabilitate those three, so the other ninety-seven simply go into denial.

It's not unlike what a friend of mine coping with schizophrenia has had to endure throughout her life, mean voices in her head telling her things that aren't true, making her and everyone around her miserable until she was finally able to start treating her disease.

When I turned nineteen, it was time for me to "serve" as a volunteer missionary for two years. Mormons have no say over where they're sent, so waiting for "the call" to arrive in the mail was excruciating. What if I were sent someplace boring? Or scary? One of my aunt's boyfriends had gone to Japan. The man she eventually married had served in Finland. When my letter arrived from Salt Lake, I ran upstairs and opened it.

When I came back down, my mother's brows furrowed. "Where are you going?" She frowned.

"It's someplace that has food you really like."

My mother's shoulders slumped. "Mexico," she said, shaking her head slowly. "You're going to Mexico."

"It's someplace *else* that has food you like."

My mother's eyes lit up. She started jumping up and down, clapping. "You're going to Italy! You're going to Italy!"

Everyone at church was excited, too. "Oh, you'll get to learn Spanish," they said.

"Uh, no, I think they speak Italian in Italy."

"Be careful with the water. You don't want to get sick."

Italy was wonderful and miserable and incredible and depressing, the negatives largely a result of the oppressive missionary lifestyle. Every moment of our lives was regimented, our actions constantly monitored. One of the songs we learned in Culture Capsule in the Missionary Training Center was "Zip-a-Dee-Doo-Dah" in Italian. My first four assignments were as companion to various district leaders, the position jokingly referred to as "District N-word." Told every day our lack of faith and success was a disappointment to God, I became suicidal for the first time in my life and wanted desperately to go home. Of course, doing so would have labeled me a failure among other Mormons for the remainder of my life. My mother, eager to help, wrote back after my latest unhappy letter. "If you want to come home," she said, "I'll hide you in the attic."

I plodded on, and my time in Italy became a transformative experience. I saw abject poverty for the first time. I witnessed a kidnapping near the train station in Rome. I was caught in a Camorra gang war in Naples. Teens threw heavy rocks at us because they hated Americans. I was spit on and kicked, chased with garden shears, had guns pulled on me. I was approached by dozens and dozens of "gypsies." A woman asked me to marry her daughter and bring her to the U.S.

I met folks from Ghana and Nigeria and Somalia. An African woman the sister missionaries were teaching was abducted. We never saw her again.

And then I returned to Metairie, struggling with culture shock in my conservative, white neighborhood as I began my sophomore year at the University of New Orleans.

When I saw a young man on campus I'd known growing up, I was surprised to realize for the first time that he was black. I'd always been confused at how different he looked from everyone else in the family, but it had never occurred to me he wasn't white until I saw him in a different setting.

I returned to Italy a year later, becoming engaged to a former Italian sister missionary I'd worked with who was a Communist. We agreed I should complete my degree in America before we married, and then I'd move back to Italy and teach English.

I absolutely loved literature. Jane Austen, Charles Dickens, Thomas Hardy, Edgar Allan Poe, Nathaniel Hawthorne, and more. I even liked Shakespearean sonnets and Middle English lit.

My Chaucer professor chastised the class one day for laughing at a story from the Canterbury Tales in which townspeople blamed the plague on Jews. "Medieval people were so stupid," a student said.

"You don't think people today bear illogical prejudices against certain groups?" the professor asked pointedly.

Years later, I wasn't surprised to run into my professor in a gay bookstore with his black partner.

At church, the first black man in our congregation was ordained a high priest, the most prestigious position at the local level. My father still used the N-word every time he spoke of the man, and he laughed every time I corrected him. I asked another high priest if he felt any of the others in the group were prejudiced. "No," he said. "We believe in equality."

"So you wouldn't mind if your son married Brother Alfonse's daughter?"

"Well, we don't approve of interracial marriage, of course, but that doesn't mean we're bigoted."

How blind, I wondered, could these people be? Thank God *I* wasn't biased.

I broke up with my fiancée after I realized I was always going to be gay. I came out while in grad school, was called to a Court of Love, and was excommunicated, my stake president and other members of the High Council telling me I'd denied the Holy Ghost and betrayed God. I was asked to remove my Mormon underwear.

But I felt free for the first time and soon met my first lover. We lived in a mobile home in St. Rose on the edge of the swamp past the airport. Everyone in the neighborhood lived in trailers and mobile homes.

Everyone was white.

Well, almost everyone. One day, two white neighbors stopped by our place. "We just told that guy down the street he'd better have that black guy staying with him move out or we'd burn them out." The men laughed. "What do you think about *that*?"

I could hardly say what I was really thinking: "Sure, the two faggots out here in the boondocks are thrilled to hear violent, bigoted threats."

We decided to move to the Marigny, just outside the French Quarter. There I noticed the neighborhood public schools always kept their classroom windows open in the sweltering heat and humidity. My elementary school in Jefferson Parish had air conditioning twenty-five years earlier, but schools in Orleans Parish still didn't. And I'd never known that until I was almost thirty.

Nearly every public school in New Orleans had a mostly black student body. Virtually every white public school student attended a magnet school for the "gifted." Nearly all the remaining white kids attended a variety of private Catholic schools or a single private school serving mostly Jewish students.

My first teaching job was at SUNO—Southern University at New Orleans. It was a public university, historically black like its sister campus in Baton Rouge. This was the 1990s, and the mostly black SUNO and mostly white UNO sat hardly a mile apart, two public universities still quite separate and not equal.

For the next ten years, I taught evening classes at SUNO, all the while thinking I wasn't prejudiced, every semester learning I still was. Some of that realization, unfortunately, didn't take place until years after I left campus. Looking back, I squirm at some of the things I did and said. I made a particularly awkward comment once in response to a general rebellion over the amount of homework I assigned. "We work during the day, Mr. Townsend. We don't have time to read all this stuff."

"You people," I said. I'd meant it as "you students," but boy, I sure learned something that evening.

Almost every semester, an angry student would meet with me after class. "You can't give me a D on this paper! I'm a high school English teacher!"

I was told by the assistant dean, "You're penalizing the students for being black. You need to understand the background of your students and take that into account when you grade." While three major grammar errors would fail a paper at the University of New Orleans, where I also taught, students could have fifteen at SUNO, and I was still expected to award a passing grade. But after I complied, the assistant dean called me back to her office. "You're trying to keep the students ignorant and keep them in their place!"

In class, we sometimes discussed current topics related to race, and when the Rodney King riots erupted in Los Angeles, one student defended an attack on a white woman, married to a black man, dragged out of her car. My student felt that every white person got what they deserved. When a young white woman, an American college student, was killed by a mob in a South African township where she'd been registering people to vote, one of my students said, "White people always think we need their help. They were right to kill her."

On my way to work one evening, I heard about the Oklahoma City bombing on the radio and upon arrival asked the assistant dean if she'd heard the news. She ignored me, so I thought I hadn't spoken loudly enough and repeated the question.

"Maybe the FBI did it!" she finally spat at me. I walked to my class stunned.

I received perhaps a dozen pieces of hate mail in my office mailbox one semester. One note simply declared, "The White Man is the Devil," but most of the letters were long rants. I tried comparing the handwriting on the notes with that of the essays by my students, but I could never find a match. I even compared the handwriting with that of the assistant dean, who'd told me flat out, "I think you're a racist, and I'm going to do everything I can to get rid of you." It wasn't her handwriting, either.

The moment the dean retired, the assistant dean got her wish, and I was no longer an instructor in the Evening and Weekend College. The truth is . . . the assistant dean was right about me. I have no doubt I said and did racist things I don't even remember now because I was unaware of their significance and impact. It never occurred to me to study racism because I was convinced I wasn't racist and therefore had no personal behavior or mindset to change. Even in an atmosphere that offered ample evidence to the contrary, I'd chosen to remain ignorant that such a thing as structural racism even existed, much less that I had an obligation to help dismantle it. At the time, I was relieved not to be rehired after the new dean took over. I'd no longer have to face feeling so uncomfortable every day.

Only I did.

The staff in a store on the "black" side of St. Claude refused to wait on me. Once, when I honked impatiently at a car taking too long to turn on Elysian Fields, the black driver made a U-turn and chased me for blocks. I gave up driving, recognizing my growing irritation with traffic wasn't going to improve. I soon found myself almost always the lone white passenger on public transportation. My family was aghast that I'd deliberately *chosen* to do something so reckless and dangerous. I only saw a single white driver in all the years I rode the bus around New Orleans.

A priest walking his dog one night two blocks from my Marigny apartment was shot and killed by a black man during a mugging. A woman jogging a block past that was shot by a black man during her morning jog. A tourist at a bed and breakfast two blocks in another direction was shot and killed by a black man. A friend of mine was murdered in his Marigny apartment by a black man. Another man was found tied to a chair in his apartment after a black man broke in. A man was seriously injured and his wife killed by a black man during a home invasion six doors down from me. Two of my friends were beaten in the French Quarter by black men. Another had his ribs fractured in a mugging Uptown. A white woman I knew was attacked stepping out of her car.

I understood by this point that white people had ensured a black underclass trapped in poverty with limited access to good education and decent jobs. But that didn't keep me from crossing the street when I saw a black man walking down the sidewalk.

Another friend was murdered by a white man during a gay bashing. But in my mind, the killer wasn't "white." He was a "religious homophobe."

One of my white coworkers looked hauntingly like Jeffrey Dahmer. I gasped when I saw him out on Mardi Gras day, leading his black lover around on a chain through the French Quarter.

Another coworker told me he was hoping to get into med school based on his minority status. "What minority are you?" I asked.

"I'm black."

One of my fuck buddies complained once about the extra layer of discrimination he faced as part of two oppressed groups. "What's the other group?" I asked.

"I'm black."

I'm not colorblind. I'm simply inattentive. I didn't even notice my husband had blue eyes until we'd been together two years. And in New Orleans, "black" covered a wide variety of skin tones.

Do I have any bias, any internalized white superiority?

Of course I do! How could I not? I recognize I must constantly and actively combat it every single day.

I learned in a History of the English Language course that the names of some towns in England are of Celtic origin, going back as far as 800 BCE. Some names still exist from inhabitants living on the British Isles even before the Celts. The residents since then have resisted any alteration in the names despite influxes of Angles, Saxons, Jutes, and Normans. "Place names are very resistant to change," my professor explained.

But a simple stroll through the French Quarter of New Orleans showed me that change was possible. Ursulines Avenue used to be named Calle del Arsenal. Governor Nicholls bore the prior name of Calle del Hospital. Decatur Street had previously been named Camino Real y Muelle at one point and Rue de la Levee at another. And Jackson Square had first been Plaza d'Armas.

Working on my genealogy as a teen, I learned the 1850 census was the gold standard for information. I was confused at first to discover that the area my ancestors had lived in almost since their arrival in Mississippi had originally been named Lawrence County. I'd only known it as Lincoln County. Obviously, it would not have been named that before the Civil War. Yet despite my family's continued racism, no one seemed to suffer unduly because of the renaming.

Mormons do genealogy so we can perform "proxy work" in temples and baptize our ancestors posthumously. In a university library, I discovered a letter from one of my great-great-grandfathers who fought at the battle of Vicksburg, in which he petitioned his commanding officer to transfer him away from the fighting because of his hemorrhoids. We were all so happy to know he was now Mormon in heaven.

Andrew Jackson was the president who'd signed the Indian Removal Act of 1830, opening the land now known as Mississippi to my ancestors, who all arrived within the following decade. The capital of Mississippi is, unsurprisingly, named after him.

Many among my family and friends talked of Confederate symbols as part of their "heritage." But since the Confederacy only existed for five years, what they're really celebrating is the white supremacy that both pre- and post-dated the Civil War.

Almost all of my white friends and family, like me, never felt they were prejudiced. Some still adamantly deny it. But if we can't make the most minor effort to change the names of a few streets and university buildings, relocate a few statues to museums, and agree that naming military bases after traitors was a mistake that must be both repudiated and rectified, then our "lack" of prejudice doesn't mean very much.

The problem, of course, is that most white conservatives *don't* think the Confederates were traitors. I'm well aware of how these folks *do* treat traitors.

And I can guarantee they're not waxing nostalgic over me.

After Hurricane Katrina, I relocated to the Pacific Northwest, but on a return visit to New Orleans, I heard the daughter of one of my friends talk about her work with the National Guard immediately after the storm. She was assigned to make sure everyone evacuated. "This one old black man wouldn't leave," she said. "He wanted to stay in his house." She shook her head. "He told me, 'You can't make me leave,' so I told him, 'I can shoot you if you don't.'"

She thought this was a funny anecdote.

After several weeks of Black Lives Matter protests, after taking several more online courses on bias and diversity through my employer in addition to the in-person workshops I participated in over the two preceding years, I was unhappy to discover that my latest internalized bias test still showed I have a "strong preference" for white people over black. If I keep taking this test every year for the rest of my life, I'm not sure the results will ever change much. Maybe, if I continue to work at it, my score may eventually evolve to, "slight preference."

The least we can do as "good" white people, and I mean absolutely the very least, is remove monuments to racism from public spaces and rename the streets, university buildings, and military bases honoring those who caused so much suffering and death to our fellow citizens.

If farmers in Mississippi, middle-class churchgoers in Metairie, and so many other white people can still feel the sting of losses incurred over a five-year period more than 150 years ago, can we not manage to feel the slightest empathy for folks who have suffered continually for more than 400 years?

We must make this small token of repentance immediately so we can move on to dismantling more serious aspects of structural and institutional racism.

But that's the reason for so much resistance to taking *any* step, isn't it? We want to think we've already arrived at our destination, and we dread acknowledging we haven't, because the rest of that road looks steeper than a hill in Vicksburg, and we know there is no place to rest along the way.

Our journey doesn't have to be a Trail of Tears, though, or a Middle Passage. It can be a Path to Reconciliation, a double-lane highway to both secular and religious morality.

While the road to Hell may be paved with good intentions, the signs pointing the way are posted by resentment and a refusal to accept the truth.

So let's choose to march—humbly, haltingly, boldly, however we can—up the Road to Peace. Throwing away our bias may be harder even than losing the weight we gained eating Grandma's homemade pecan pie.

But justice is a choice. And we can make it.

Lessons in Survival
provokes
Echoes the Past
Inequality by Degrees
focus on new essentials
Survivors Plagued by Problems
A Reckoning Over Objectivity
HING STILL COMES WITH A GRAIN
We just looked the other way.
It is one thing to understand people's desperation and quite another thing to be its victim.
at Lies Beneath
Competitor of conscience

LEAH MUELLER

RACISM AND REASONABLE DOUBT: WHY OUR ENTIRE CRIMINAL JUSTICE SYSTEM IS A SHAM

Like many people who grew up during the 60s and 70s, I have hazy memories of the civil rights movement. After Martin Luther King was shot, my adored third grade teacher described his murder as "very sad." She was a severe woman of Germanic descent. I don't recall whether she elaborated further.

In 1968, I lived in Chicago with my pregnant mother, stepfather, and baby brother Danny. Folks referred to our area as "mixed", which meant it wasn't comprised solely of white people. The streets overflowed with boisterous Puerto Rican and black families. They stayed up late and partied on their front steps until the wee hours of the morning.

My parents, Gil and Polly, belonged to a local block club. The club intended to "clean up" the neighborhood. Everyone had white skin. Members gathered in living rooms and spoke angrily about street crime. Their unstated objective was to make the neighborhood as white as possible.

After King's assassination, several of the members decided to arm themselves against the ensuing riots. Someone gave my mother a pistol, though she had never shot a gun in her life.

In the midst of the violent clashes, our family's washing machine broke down. Danny's diapers began to pile up and smell. Polly needed to do two things that fell outside her comfort zone—operate coin equipment at a laundromat, and pack heat on the streets of Chicago.

She lugged her heavy baskets of soiled laundry into the crowded facility and deposited the receptacles on the floor. As she fumbled in her purse, searching for coins, the new pistol tumbled out. Lacking anything as sophisticated as a holster, my mother had simply tossed the gun into her purse, figuring she could access it if necessary.

Instead, the metal projectile hit the linoleum floor and skittered towards one of the washing machines. Polly watched it travel across the surface, marveling at its velocity. The black and Puerto Rican patrons stared at the pistol with horror. Then the group leaped to its collective feet and ran like hell from the laundromat. My mother had managed to get the whole place to herself, without even trying.

This story became one of Polly's favorite anecdotes. Over the years, I pondered its meaning many times. Had she really expected to use that gun? The poor woman was mired in her housewife role. During the next two years, she helped elect Richard Nixon, gave birth to two more children, and moved to the suburbs.

Strangely enough, both of my parents identified as liberals. My mother expressed sadness about King's assassination. Though she and Gil spoke disparagingly about people of color, they both voted for McGovern in 1972 and cheered Nixon's resignation two years later.

A militant hippie teenager, I often wore a denim hat with a "Free Angela" button to middle school. It felt good to piss off my less enlightened classmates. I never thought of myself as a bigot, and I'm certain my parents never grasped the depths of their own racism.

Danny was first diagnosed as hyperactive, then later as schizophrenic. The intervening years were not pleasant ones. Gil killed himself in 1978. Afterward, Danny did time in juvenile detention, foster care, a Mexican mental institution, and finally prison. By the time he turned twenty-six, my brother had spent nearly half his life in some sort of lockup facility.

In 1992, he was able to rent an apartment in a shabby building, thanks to the combined largesse of the federal government and Washington state. I'd spent several months trying to get him into an SSI program, so he wouldn't need to live with me. I already had my hands full with a toddler and an alcoholic husband, and Danny's continuous presence would have sent me over the edge.

Once Danny found his niche, I spent as little time with him as possible. He was an adult, after all, and entitled to his privacy. Besides, his long, rambling conversations with God and Satan wore me out.

One February night, shortly before Valentine's Day, Danny fell into the companionship of two men, Samuel and Robert. The three of them met at a party in the building next door to my brother's dwelling. Samuel was black, the son of a well-to-do local preacher. Robert was white, the son of an impoverished ex-con. Both men had been arrested before—Samuel once, and

Robert on multiple occasions.

The three men decided to continue the party at my brother's apartment. Danny had bragged about receiving his SSI check. He wanted his two new friends to come over and look at the stereo he'd just bought at K-Mart. Samuel and Robert also had some low-grade cocaine to sell, so they needed to relocate to a more private setting.

At Danny's apartment, everything went haywire. One of the men hit Danny in the head with a toaster oven, then stabbed him repeatedly. As my brother bled to death on the floor, the two assailants made off with his stereo, television, and several bags of food bank items.

The cops arrested Robert first. For several weeks, he remained in custody, loudly insisting that Samuel had been with him on the night of the murder. Eventually, the cops connected the dots, picked up Samuel and tossed him into the local jail.

After some prodding, Samuel admitted to accompanying Robert to Danny's apartment. Then the finger-pointing began. Robert claimed Samuel had suddenly leaped to his feet and attacked Danny for making a racist comment. Samuel first hit Danny with the toaster oven, then began stabbing him over and over. Though Richard tried to stop him, it was too late. Afterwards, he helped Samuel steal Danny's possessions because he was afraid for his life.

Samuel, on the other hand, claimed that Robert was the assailant. Robert left the apartment briefly to grab some cocaine, returned with a weak facsimile of the drug, and tried to pass the goods off on Danny. When Danny tasted the coke, he became irate and claimed that Robert was trying to cheat him. Robert, enraged, first hit Danny with the toaster oven, and then stabbed him to death. Samuel helped Robert steal Danny's possessions because he was afraid for his life.

On the surface, both explanations sounded equally plausible. Danny had picked up some alarmingly racist ideas in prison, and he could well have said something incendiary to set Samuel off. On the other hand, Robert was already an accomplished petty criminal and small-time coke dealer. He had a reputation for both thievery and violence and had assaulted his girlfriend several times.

The court offered Robert a plea deal—second-degree murder charge in exchange for the opportunity to testify against Samuel. Robert appeared in the courtroom a couple of days later, disheveled and weeping. He expressed remorse for his part in the murder but pinned the stabbing on Samuel. "I was there, so I deserve to go to prison," he insisted. "But I did not kill that man, your honor."

His story certainly sounded convincing. The all-white jury felt similarly and gave Robert fourteen years. A mid-range sentence, due to my brother's vulnerable mental state. Samuel was charged with first-degree murder, and the long, arduous process of conviction began.

Polly made her presence felt at every court session. Sobbing loudly, taking long sips of Rescue Remedy, my mother was impossible to ignore. Meanwhile, Samuel's father rallied the congregation, and scores of churchgoers packed the small courtroom, offering support for the preacher's son.

Why were they so convinced of his innocence? None of it made sense to me. I didn't possess the emotional tools to deal with the trial, and as the mother of a toddler, I had good reason to avoid it. After Robert's confession, I stopped attending entirely. I never pondered why Robert had been offered a plea bargain and not Samuel. The ugly, racist connotations of the court's decision were completely lost on my traumatized brain.

Samuel's trial dovetailed exactly with the Rodney King riots. As the defense and prosecuting attorneys duked it out in a small town courtroom, huge protests erupted in Los Angeles and other cities across the United States. The four cops responsible for King's beating had recently been acquitted. They struck him over fifty times with batons and burned his leg with a stun gun following a high-speed chase through the streets of Los Angeles. A nearby bystander caught it all on camera.

King himself seemed shocked by the intensity of the protests. "Can't we all just get along?" he famously lamented. Obviously, the answer was no. The demonstrations raged for five days. 63 people were killed, 2,383 sustained injuries, and 12,000 were arrested. Property damage costs soared to over one billion. Much of the blame fell to police chief Daryl Gates, and he resigned in disgrace.

I watched in horror as the events unfolded on television. Polly paid little attention, wrapped up as she was in the trial. My mother's usually submerged racism had already bubbled to the surface, and I tried my best to quell her rage with palliative words. I pleaded with her not to hate all black people because of Danny's death. It never occurred to either of us that Samuel might be innocent of murder. Folks in town corroborated our suspicions. That was all the proof we needed.

Samuel's trial ended in a hung jury. No one wanted to convict a black man so soon after the Rodney King riots. The court set a new trial date for October 1992.

This time, the hearings progressed more swiftly, and a second jury found Samuel guilty of first-degree murder. They sentenced him to twenty-four years in prison, and the guards led him away in handcuffs. The congregation wept. My mother went home to Arizona, and I settled back into my normal, unhappy routine.

During the ensuing years, I never questioned the official narrative surrounding my brother's murder and Samuel and Robert's subsequent convictions. Justice had been served, and there was nothing left for me to do except mourn the dead. Every February 12, I revisited the horrible incident and then pushed it out of my mind. I felt guilty for being reluctant to help Danny. Shouldn't I have allowed him to live with me, instead of casting him to the wolves?

Meanwhile, despite Rodney King's high-profile media exposure, police beatings and murders of black people continued, unabated. If anything, the incidents increased and became more severe. People of color fell prey to violent cops on a regular basis, brutally murdered for little or no reason. Trayvon Martin. Tamir Rice. Sandra Bland. Michael Brown. Ezell Ford. Botham Jean. Only a few of many. As a result, Black Lives Matter burst upon the scene, forcing comfortable white liberals to confront their own racism.

Even as I write this, I have trouble saying, "our own racism" (or heaven forbid, "my own racism"). "Discomfort" is a mild word for what I experienced as I plunged into the depths of my hidden biases. How could I, a person whose closest friend was black, possibly hold racist attitudes? Racists were those people in the South who screamed at children for desegregating schools. Not me, the girl with the Angela Davis pin.

Oh, but there was no denying it. I cringed every time I unearthed my hidden, dark chunks of anger towards people of color, or remembered times when I'd inflicted emotional pain on them without provocation. Many times, I had crossed the street when I saw a couple of black men approaching. I recalled countless incidents when I expected to be treated well simply because I was white. I didn't know any better at the time, but that was no excuse.

One night in 2018, I couldn't sleep, so I decided to surf the internet. This behavior was nothing unusual, but that particular evening took me in an unexpected direction. I googled Samuel's and Robert's names and tried to ascertain what had become of the two men.

I'd already heard that Samuel had received a shortened sentence for good behavior. Twenty years in prison instead of twenty-four. Still an enormous chunk of a young man's life. Imagine being put away for first-degree murder when you're only nineteen, not even old enough to legally drink.

The local paper had archived most of their stories about the trial. I pored over them with increasing fascination, mixed with horror. Suddenly, I experienced an uncomfortable epiphany. Why had the authorities offered Robert a plea bargain, especially since his rap sheet was so much longer—and more violent—than Samuel's? Both men's stories were equally plausible. It didn't make sense that the court believed Robert's account, and not Samuel's.

Except that it DID make sense. The courts are made up of racist judges and racist juries. Black men are sentenced to prison at a rate five times higher than white men. That's IF they actually make it into the courtroom and aren't murdered by law enforcement first. Why had I believed Samuel's case was any different?

Obviously, my role as Danny's sister made it difficult for me to be objective. At the time, the word on the street insisted that Samuel was the killer. But we live in a racist society, and the streets overflow with bigots. Maybe Samuel murdered my brother. But maybe the court convicted him because he was black, like his father's congregation believed.

I didn't resist this epiphany nearly as much as I would have only a couple of years earlier. Black Lives Matter had inspired a considerable amount of soul-searching in me—painful as hell, but necessary.

I continued to scour the internet for information about Samuel's and Robert's post-incarceration lives. Apparently, Samuel had been a model prisoner, because he was granted work-release and a reduced sentence. Despite extensive searching, I could find no further information about him, which struck me as a good omen.

Robert, on the other hand, had just been arrested for the umpteenth time, after eluding a outstanding warrant for domestic violence. Prison hadn't changed him a bit. The article mentioned a pattern of arrests, including a murder dating back to the 1990s. Why had the court assumed he hadn't killed my brother? Why had they given him the gift of a plea bargain?

By then I'd figured out the answer. I sat with my new realization for a while and concluded that my entire worldview around Danny's death had officially been blown to bits. I will never know for sure who killed him on that horrible night in February 1992. Still, I strongly suspect the real story might be quite different from the narrative I was fed. That narrative put a black man in prison for twenty years.

Two years later, our nation erupts in flames, both literally and figuratively. The brutal police murder of George Floyd has proven a catalyst for pent-up, collective rage that boiled for many years beneath the surface. Furious protesters swarm city streets, throughout all fifty states and around the world. Twelve days and counting. The crowds continue to expand. These folks don't fuck around.

Despite considerable property damage, most demonstrations remain peaceful. At least, most of the protesters are non-violent. Cops, on the other hand, have ripped off their masks to reveal the depth of their tyranny. They run amok in the streets, assaulting protesters at random. Everyone is presumed guilty. This behavior has exposed the sham of our criminal justice system. Of the entire foundation that our country is built upon, really. The truth is even more hideous than we imagined.

Donald Trump is terrible, but he's a tiny part of a much larger problem. The whole rotten edifice will need to be dismantled, and a new one erected in its place. Everything else is a Band-Aid, a panacea. Shit keeps happening, while white folks continue to defend and uphold it. After each new televised murder, we roll over and go back to sleep.

We no longer have the luxury of slumber. During the past couple of years, we've racked up more dead, black bodies in our country: Pamela Turner. Dominique Clayton. Atatiana Jefferson. Christopher Whitfield. Christopher McCorvey. Eric Reason. Michael Lorenzo Dean. Breonna Taylor. And now, George Floyd.

Say their names. Then say them again. Because this time, we can't forget.

MARK LUCIUS

WHAT DID YOU HEAR, WHAT DID YOU SAY?

> I never said an ugly word.
> —Robert Louis Stevenson, *A Child's Garden of Verses*

You and the guys play ball at lunch hour whenever the weather is good, and it's oh so good today, no jackets nowhere. Oh, so good to be running to the baseball diamond dropped at the edge of school property, where a culvert and alfalfa field square off. All your thoughts of morning classes, history, math and civil rights civics, as far removed as the streaky clouds in a high, high sky.

But wait, the ball field is full up. Mr. Schoolman, phys-ed volunteer, leading third and fourth graders in a game. Mr. Schoolman, father to Barbara, prettiest girl in your sixth grade class. His thinning hair is always a shock.

You're about to turn back toward school when Ray and Tommy yell at Mr. Schoolman. *We* play here at recess; this is *our* diamond. Ray and Tommy, leaders of your loose pack, now stalled in shallow left field. Ray wears white Levi's, Tommy, black, Trimsters that make you shrink inside your Sears jeans.

Ray shouts a word he shouldn't. He waves a fist, his shoulders nearly ripping out of his Madras shirt. Mr. Schoolman tosses soft pitch, a younger kid swings. Tommy shouts a word he shouldn't. The loose pack reshuffles. Some guys move forward, others back. You hang back. Yells become a chorus. Mr. Schoolman is still pitching.

You are not angry. You got here late. Recess is almost over. You can't believe the direction the field is tilting. It's like a great funnel has formed, everyone tumbling down toward Mr. Schoolman, inside the precious diamond and on to the pitcher's mound. Yells now screams.

Spic, wop, polack.

Ray and Tommy edge closer to the infield, the loose pack breaking up. You hear a word you've never heard: mulatto.

Mr. Schoolman turns, finally, and stares. The screamers don't stop, not right away. Spic, wop, polack, mulatto. Some guys turn, and now everyone is walking back toward school. You're surprised by another new word, polattospicwop, a combination of the screamers' screams. Walking alone, you haven't said a word, but now you say that word. Out loud, not too loud; it's like you're testing a new language. Does anyone hear? You can't be sure.

Your teacher, Mr. Tyler, can silence the class with a look. His black hair glistens, even in dull classroom lights, and you barely hear him, he speaks so softly. This kind of behavior will not be tolerated. What did you hear, what did you say?

Some girls smile, and smirk. Barbara Schoolman's pretty face has red splotches. Mr. Tyler paces down and up each row. Sometimes you imagine his head exploding. This is one of those times.

Get out some paper. What did you hear, what did you say?

Ray gets up, walks quick but sure, drops a piece of paper into Mr. Tyler's chubby hand. The teacher unwraps and reads. His gaze sweeps all of you. His voice rises, rises, rises. I know, I know, I know there was more than one. Most screamers are still. Tommy gets up, hands Mr. Tyler a slip. Slinks. Desk.

You can't think. Oh, sure you can. You know what you said. You write: What I said. polattospicwop. You wonder, is anyone surprised to see you walk to Mr. Tyler? What is this, he says, looking at your paper. You shrug.

Most screamers are still still.

The three of you sit on a stoop in front of the convent. Sister John Mary sent you here. You tried to explain to her, you didn't scream at Mr. Schoolman. You tried to explain, well, it sounded lame. For a moment, you locked onto those small gray eyes swimming in her black and white habit. One thing I don't like about you, she said, is you hedge.

You squirm, moving from hip to knees to butt. Three hours sitting on a stone stoop. Your jeans feel like iron. Your shirt soaks through. Even Ray's white Levi's are smudged with mud.

Heading back to school the next Monday. You told your Mom and Dad on Friday night what happened. They seemed to understand you meant no harm. This morning, they erupted when you showed them the letter you are taking to school. What is this? We thought you didn't join in. Now you show us this?

You've written a letter to Mr. Schoolman, as Sister John Mary directed. Dear Mr. Schoolman, I'm sorry I called you a wop, a spic, a polack and a mulatto. It was wrong of me to do that. I hope you can forgive me. I will never do it again. Sincerely,

03ɛɔ൙ɛɔ

It doesn't seem to matter you never say a word like that again. Questions roll through your mind. Why did you say that? Why did you plead guilty? Did Mr. Schoolman keep your letter? Did Barbara read it? Why didn't you tell Ray and Tommy to shut up? Why weren't you stronger? The questions keep rolling until finally you think, enough already, time to move on.

Would you be stronger now?

LYN STEVENS

BUTTERFLY HOUSE

Amanda was in the living room feeding the caterpillars leaves soaked in sugar water when her phone rang. Late afternoon sunlight spilled through the open window throwing thin shadows from the five netted cages and lacy patterns of the monarch's wings on the wall. After the call she had to focus on simple tasks, zipping the butterfly cages, closing the blinds, putting her car keys in her bag, walking down the block, one foot in front of the other.

Her nail tore on the car door handle but didn't snap. Buckle your seatbelt, she said to herself. Put on some lipstick. Pale, not red. Your sixteen-year-old son and his friend have just been arrested for armed robbery. Find a peppermint in the glove compartment. Don't sit there like a zombie. Drive to Manhattan.

By the time she stepped through the glass doors of the sixth police precinct the news had spread inside her like venom. She charged up to the mammoth front desk. "I'm here about my son, Logan Hayes."

"Have a seat. Someone will be with you shortly," said the female officer, without making eye contact.

BB guns. An actual holdup. No more plastic deep-sea divers floating in *my* bathtub. Bedtime stories and homework help were also relics of the past.

"Please have a seat," the policewoman said, more sharply.

She turned to the row of dull blue plastic chairs. A petite woman in a floral-patterned headscarf sat stiffly in one of them—Adil's mother. Amanda couldn't remember her name. She walked over and sat down.

"What is this? What happened to my boy?" said Adil's mother.

"They didn't tell me. We should know pretty soon," Amanda said, nervously.

Policemen milled around, their belts heavy with guns and clubs. A beefy man in a turtleneck and badge approached her.

"You here for Hayes?"

Amanda jumped up. "I'm his mother. Is he OK? Can I see him?"

"I don't know yet, Mrs. Hayes. That's not up to me. Here are his things," said the officer handing her keys, a phone, a broken headset, MetroCard and student ID.

"Please, can I see him?" she asked.

"Detective Perez will be down shortly. He'll explain everything. Please sit down, ma'am."

Then he walked over to Adil's mother and she too leapt up. "Someone called me to come here. What is going on?" she said in a quivering voice.

Amanda looked down into her hands at Logan's treasures and immediately tucked the keys into her bag. One of the headset batteries was missing. She tried reattaching the back of the earpiece into place but it wouldn't snap shut. She reached back into her bag and slid the pocketknife and mini gold-plated can opener off his key ring, sickened by finding this arsenal of weapons in her own possessions.

When the detective had told Amanda about the fake guns on the phone, she'd acted shocked and outraged but the truth was she'd seen them several months before. Apparently, her ex-husband, Bobby had ordered the fake guns for Logan from a catalog along with a dartboard. Amanda told Logan she never wanted to see those guns again and stormed out of his room, too naive to realize her son had begun his descent into manhood.

She'd been worrying the torn nail for an hour when another policeman, Detective Perez, lumbered over. Amada bolted to a stand. "Please, have a seat," he said pulling up a chair and straddling it backwards. He was a short pear-shaped man. His scalp shined through his oily black hair. His bright white shirt pulled across his belly, the armpits stained yellow.

"Your son and his friend held a couple of kids up at gunpoint. The victims were smart enough to call 911."

"But the gun was a fake."

"If he had pulled that gun on me, I would have shot your boy."

She looked down at her hands and yanked off the nail.

Perez told Amanda that Logan had waived his rights and confessed to everything.

"Waived his rights?" she breathed. "He's a kid. He was scared. He probably didn't understand what waiving rights meant. He would have said anything. Without a lawyer being there I don't think you even have a case."

Perez leaned forward, looked her squarely in the eye and lowered his voice. "I understand this is hard. It happens with teenagers. They turn. I see it all the time. Look, I have kids of my own."

"I need to see him! Please."

"I'll give you a few minutes with your boy. You seem like a nice enough lady."

Pompous ass, thought Amanda. I am a *very* nice lady.

CB⧉CB⧉

Amanda was led up a musty back staircase to a small office with black file cabinets, a gray steel desk, papers strewn everywhere. Since the phone call, she'd been saving everything for this moment.

Logan straggled in through another door escorted by a uniformed cop. The shame, the rage, the fear, it all slid away. Amanda lunged and hugged him, stunned as always at the hardness of his sinewy muscles, his arms locked behind his back, hands in cuffs. It wasn't until they both carefully sat down opposite each other that she actually looked at Logan. He wore baggy sweatpants and a white T-shirt with pink and black lettering that said "Jessica's Bat Mitzvah, Mar. 5, 2017." The shirt hung to his knees. He had on his neon green Adidas.

"How are you? Are you OK?"

"I'm fine," he muttered with his chin on his chest.

"Look at me, Logan," said Amanda. How could you have held someone up? she thought. "I don't understand what happened." He raised his glassy brown eyes and stared right through her.

"Say something. Did they give you anything to eat or drink?"

"I'm OK," he mumbled.

Perez must have taken a seat behind the desk. Amanda couldn't see him and wouldn't look but she could feel him watching her.

"Do you have a bed? Did you eat?"

"They gave us bologna sandwiches and water. No bed. I'm fine, Mom."

"Did you do what they're saying?"

"I don't know," he mumbled again. It had been his default answer for the last several years.

"How could you not know? What were you doing with a gun? Were you on drugs?"

"No."

"Were you drinking? Is that it? Was this Adil's idea or did you two plan it together?"

"No. Noo." He was starting to whine.

It was all jumbled together, trying to understand what had happened, trying to interpret Logan's reaction to her questions and to the mess he'd made. "I don't understand it."

Logan shrugged. "How are the butterflies?"

"Is this what you're asking me? Now? Why on earth would you leave the house with a BB gun? Tell me Logan. Whatever it is, you can tell me."

"The guns were fakes." He cocked his head. "Anyway, I didn't even know I had it," he said coolly.

"What did you mean you didn't know you had it?"

"I didn't realize it was in my pocket." She didn't know if he was being stubborn, resigned, remorseful. She couldn't tell if he was being brave, or a wise ass. She couldn't understand what her own child's face was telling her.

Suddenly panic stricken, Amanda froze with the realization that she shouldn't be talking about it in front of the detective, not without a lawyer.

Logan shook his head from side to side.

"It's okay. Don't say anything."

His eyes started to fill. "They took my basketball jacket."

In the precinct lobby, Perez gave her a slip of paper with a phone number to call in the morning. He told her to go home. There was nothing more to do until the arraignment.

CB ED CR ED

Amanda switched on the side table lamp and sank onto the couch. Her whole body clenched in a ball, heart pumping so loudly against her chest she felt it pulsate on her thighs. Could he really be a bad person? Or was he just a clueless teenager? What if he got sucked into the system? What if they sentenced him? Held him by the roots of his hair, turned him around, and threw him against the bars?

In the semi-darkness a few butterflies fluttered between milkweed leaves. If she released them there'd be a chance some might make it to Mexico though others would die or be eaten. The flap on the smallest cage was still open. She forced herself to straighten up and zipped it up.

Stop thinking about it. Focus on something else. Something good.

Focus on the butterflies. She thought of the summer Bobby's brother Matt came down from Vermont and took care of them, even though Bobby had moved out of their house two months before. Matt was Logan's godfather, a soft-spoken science teacher whose hobby was painting the natural world. The best parts of Bobby. Logan liked him. They both did. They were both so needy.

One perfect summer day, ten years before, the three of them went for a walk along the shoulder of the highway. Amanda and Matt holding Logan's hands and swinging him in the air as they walked. They were near an off-ramp when Matt bent down to inspect some milkweed. "Hey, look," he'd said turning up the underside of the leaf to show them the eggs. "How would you like a house of butterflies?" he asked Logan. Logan smiled, blinking in the sunlight, unusually quiet and skeptical as only a young child could be. Amanda thought it would help him forget the screaming and fighting and pain of his family falling apart. And it did.

All that summer they collected Starbucks cups, cut big holes in the tops and attached netting. They watched caterpillars molt and eat and rest and molt again, took turns putting leaves in, taking frass out. In the evening Amanda and Matt sat together on the back patio in the glow of a citronella candle, drinking white wine and philosophizing about the meaning of life, while Logan sprawled on the sofa in the living room watching Nickelodeon. One night Matt confided in her that he was gay, something she'd already suspected. The family had no idea and he asked her to keep it secret in order not to destroy the tenuous relationship he had with his conservative family. If Logan stays as sensitive and instinctual as he is now, he'll figure it out on his own one day, he had said.

Her eyes drifted onto the clock on the TV. 2:12 am.

Bobby had been harsh with Logan, jealous of how she'd fawned over him, saw red anytime Logan disobeyed him. Backhanded him, more than a few times. But Bobby loved Logan too and Logan worshiped him, had a crying tantrum whenever Bobby went away overnight. Now Logan was convicted of armed robbery. *Bobby.* Shit. It was too late to call him.

Logan wasn't some poor boy desperate for some cash, and he wasn't a rich kid, seeking thrills. A B student, guard for his high school basketball team. The only white kid on the team. He was never bored going to museums with Matt and Amanda. He'd loved the dark passageway of the Cloisters, twirled in circles like a little dancer on a music box, spiraling down the

Guggenheim. Came home with his gym clothes soaked in sweat, stood at the sink washing aphids off milkweed. How could that same boy have pointed a gun at someone? When did he make the transition? Was he a deviant or just incredibly immature? Was he covering up for his buddy, Adil?

4:28 a.m. Amanda's thoughts still firing back and forth.

She thought of a different Adil and a different Logan. It had been Adil's eleventh birthday party, a bumper season for butterflies and they'd brought over the cages to release the butterflies in Adil's backyard to make the party special for the kids. Had Matt been there? God, she was so tired. On the drive over little Philippine girls dressed in white princess clothes were out in droves. Adil's mother greeted them at the door in a silky blue headscarf. His father smoked a fat cigar. Adil's family was Sudanese, not Filipino, as she'd thought. The dry brown grass, a Carvel cake shaped like a basketball. Logan unzipped the cages and thirty or forty butterflies soared into the sky. The kids went wild, jumping up and down, running around the yard, chasing the butterflies, tripping and falling and rolling around each other.

5:57 a.m. The day began a dark, dark gray. Out of the corner of her eye something twitched. Stiff-necked, she hauled herself off the couch, looked up and saw two butterflies clinging to the living room ceiling She shuffled to the window and using all her strength shoved it wide open. Rubbing her sore neck, she went to the kitchen to make a pot of coffee.

At 7 a.m., Amanda retrieved the slip of paper Perez had given her and called the NY County Court arraignment office. Around 11 a.m., when she finally reached a live person, they said it usually took twenty-four hours from the time of the arrest to the time of arraignment. Logan had been brought in at 6 p.m. the previous night. Amanda, Executive Assistant to the CEO of a software engineering firm, called in sick to work.

In the wet misty afternoon streetlights glared on the highway. Traffic snarled on the Queensboro Bridge. In the ten minutes it took to punch and re-punch Bobby's number to make the connection, she thought of how he'd wanted to move them all to Orlando, a better place to sell real estate, but she'd already guessed there was another woman. A fucking model. Still, her heart leapt with longing that there would be some camaraderie, some kind of deep understanding from Bobby. When he picked up, she choked back a sob, finally managing to get the words out and he told her to get a lawyer. "He's good kid. I'm sure it's just a mistake but I'll fly up in a day or two if you need me. Keep me posted."

"A day or two? Don't trouble yourself," she said and hung up.

As she drove, she counted money in her head. Her savings, two CDs, loans against her credit cards. Bobby's second cousin had married a federal judge. "He's a minor with no record. It could simply go away. I'll be available if you need me." From the lawyer at her firm. "Bail could be set anywhere from $10–50K. For such a serious crime they could deny it altogether."

Amanda found a parking spot on a desolate side street in lower Manhattan. Her $3 umbrella was a joke. She tilted it backward to see the street signs and was pummeled by rain.

The concrete pavement outside the courthouse was flooded. She ran on her tiptoes up the handicapped ramp on the side of the building. The puddle at the end of it was so huge she missed clearing it by a foot.

Inside Amanda pulled her phone from pocket and laid her shoulder bag on the security table. One of the guards took great pleasure in feeling her up with his metal detector, while the other poked through her bag.

She squeezed into line in the stuffy arraignment office. When she reached the scratched bubble filled plexiglass window she told the man she wanted to see her son.

"Arrest number?" he said without lifting his eyes.

She shuffled through the papers in the outer pocket of her bag. "7123785," she muttered, quickly shoving the scrap of paper back into her bag.

The man turned to look at his computer screen. He had droopy eyes, a face pitted with acne. Amanda imagined him sitting in someone's basement smoking pot, listening to Pink Floyd.

"What's that number again?" he said.

She sifted through the bag, found the scrap, stammered, read and re-read the number.

"Nope, not in the computer yet. Time of arrest?"

"6 p.m. last night," said Amanda timidly.

He looked up at her. Whether it was her pretty face or her nipples jutting through her blouse and open raincoat hardly mattered. His face glimmered and visibly softened. He cleared his throat. "It usually takes twenty-four hours ma'am."

"Is it ever less?" her voice pleading.

"Could be, but it's been a busy night. By the time we're done I bet we'll have processed three hundred arrests. Why don't you go home, get some rest. Come back later." He handed her a slip of paper with a list of xeroxed numbers. "Here, you can call us."

If he were to get assigned a docket number while she was back in Queens there was a chance she might miss his arraignment. Amanda wasn't going to let this goon see her cry. She looked down at the slip of paper. The telephone number had already been branded into her head.

Amanda's stomach growled. 3:42 p.m. She couldn't remember the last time she'd eaten. A block away from the courthouse wedged between bail bond shops was a Pho restaurant. The place had a cloying hot oil odor, shrill music, a sticky tile floor. She sat down at an empty table. At her feet, a dead fly lay on its back. The first and only swallow of soup stuck in her throat. Amanda felt hot and sick, despite being drenched from the rain. She couldn't blot out how crazed and alone she felt so she texted Matt, keeping it vague. Teenage trouble she wrote, asking if Matt could come down for a visit. Matt texted back to say he was busy preparing for show in a gallery in Burlington. Wow! How exciting! Amanda wrote back pretending that was okay.

At 4:30 p.m. she ran back to the courthouse in the downpour. Before entering the building she huddled beneath the shallow overhang and called Bobby's cousin, the federal judge. His wife answered and said he was in court.

"Why are you calling a judge? Sweetheart, a judge isn't a lawyer."

"I'm sorry. I need to find a good lawyer to represent my son. Please, can you help me?"

"I'll try to get a message to him."

Amanda wiped her face on her wet coat sleeve, combed her wet hair and traipsed into the courthouse to face the security guards and metal detectors again.

In the hallway, she scanned four sheets of paper taped to the wall with lists of names and docket numbers. By that time, she was an ice cube. She wandered the cavernous beige and brown marble hallways for an hour, sank with wobbly knees on a hard, brown bench. A woman strutted past her, hands and feet in cuffs, flanked by police officers on both sides. An inmate dressed in a leather skirt barely covering her ass, black fishnets, see-through, low-cut blouse, brassy blonde hair. The woman jerked her arm away from one of the cops, swiveled on her lace-up high-heeled boots, and Amanda saw her face, the thin red lips, fake eyelashes as thick as fur, tears falling down her sallow cheeks. She knew that every minute of that women's life was a crisis. She called Bobby's cousin, the federal judge and left a message. She called the lawyer at her job but got his voice mail too. She needed a lawyer. Now.

It was 9:30 p.m. At 10 p.m. the court broke for dinner. At 1 a.m. they would stop processing arrests only to resume again at 6 a.m. If Logan wasn't arraigned by midnight, he would spend his second night in jail and she'd have to wait until morning when it started all over again. Amanda laid her head on the bench and cried.

At midnight Logan's name appeared on the list. People were filing into one of two New York County Criminal Court arraignment rooms. And she had to go.

Amanda took a seat off to the side in the second row of benches. The stenographer was hugely pregnant, her skin, ashy. The court officer in the bright blue uniform slumped in his seat. Everywhere she looked someone had been beaten down by drudge work—legal aid lawyers sorting through stacks of information for clients they hadn't met, trying to bone up on the facts of a double homicide in minutes; uniformed guards escorting prisoners in and out of the holding cell, warning them not to turn around and face the room, while the judge, whose name plate said Edelstein, and looked as if she had presided over this courtroom for one hundred years, doled out bail decisions. When the third defendant took the stand, Amanda approached the wooden gate that separated the courtroom from the spectators to talk to one of the legal aid lawyers, a pudgy young lady with kinky hair in a dowdy pantsuit. Amanda bent down low.

"He's on the list. Logan. Logan Harris Hayes. He'll get seen tonight, won't he?" she whispered. The woman told Amanda there was no guarantee, but she would talk to the clerk to see if he would move Logan's papers to the top of the pile. "Asking for favors is tricky. It can backfire. If he feels like he's being taken advantage of he can just as easily move the papers to the bottom of the pile."

"Please do everything you can," said Amanda, tears swimming in her eyes. Her clothes were damp, her feet soaked, skin prickly with cold and sweat, the smell of the courtroom moldy, men's cologne, and disinfectant. Armed felons, rapists, and drug dealers rolled through the courtroom.

Logan didn't see her immediately. He looked into the room in glazed astonishment, an insect caught in a spider's web. They pointed him to a bench on a side wall, in the way back of the courtroom. He sat far away from Adil. He turned, eyes darting madly around the room. A guard snapped at him and his head whipped back around.

The lawyer took him into a glass booth on the side of the room. The two of them began talking. Logan nodded, drew the lawyer pictures in the air with his fingers. When he finally saw her, he kept glancing up, his eyes asking if she still loved him. Part of Amanda wanted to reassure him, another part wanted to see Logan cry.

Both of the boys stood with their shirts tucked into their sweatpants, their hands laced together behind their backs, their heads dipped forward. The Legal Aid lawyers took turns quietly speaking to the judge. The judge shuffled through papers. "What is this, some kind of aberration? Why are these boys in criminal court? Are the parents here?"

"They are your honor," said one of the lawyers.

"Released on their own recognizance. Parents, don't let your sons out of the house. Lock up your boys!" she declared and banged her gavel.

C3ЮCЗ80

Sunlight poured glorious and unheralded into their little house. The two butterflies were figurines on the ceiling. Come on, Amanda thought. Come out. Fly away. Escape. Now that the worry of jail time had vanished, a controlled anger filled the space. And guilt wrapped itself around Amanda's heart. Logan had shrugged off his old identity. Both of them had. Amanda was tougher, less hungry for his love. They passed each other like adept blind people, careful not to bump into each other for when they did, they smashed head-on.

On Logan's second day back Amanda came home from work and saw him slink out of the bathroom with a towel around his waist. His wet hair had grown past his ears. There was a dark blonde stubble on his cheeks and chin, like a spreading stain. His ribs stuck out. She promised herself she'd make him chicken parmigiana, his favorite, to love him wholly again, but the promise felt false.

She picked up the phone and called Matt. She needed an intermediary, for Matt to be a balm again.

"Bobby told me. Why did you keep it from me?" Matt said.

"I know I can't punish him forever, but I can't forgive him either. I don't know how," said Amanda.

"Patience," said Matt.

After the arraignment they had converged in the hallway. Logan's eyes were dark and sunken. Bruised skin beneath the bloodshot whites. He looked worse than the day before. Much worse. He hugged Amanda so fiercely it hurt. She sobbed loudly in front everyone, the Legal Aid lawyers, security guard, Adil and his parents. The lawyer told her that for a few weeks, he couldn't so much as spit on the street. "If Logan were nineteen he could be locked up for years but the fact that he's sixteen and has never been in trouble just might save him. I'm going for what's called a youthful offender. It'll help if we can get the DA on our side. Naturally, we have to get Logan's story straight. They'll be time for that after he's gotten a good night's sleep." She rambled on: grand jury indictment, discovery, hearings to suppress evidence. Amanda lost her at plea bargaining, sick of the damp and the soupy yellow light in the sinister hallway.

Amanda fought against the memory of it as she talked to Matt. "A butterfly is about to eclose," she told him. The chrysalis had spun a silk button and backflipped onto it. Its shell had turned from green to transparent, showing orange and black right through it. They spoke for a while about butterflies and Amanda sank back into the warm comfort of friendship with Matt.

Matt told Amanda his show was opening in two weeks. Bobby was flying up for it. "Come or just send Logan on his own, if you don't want to be here with Bobby and his new Victoria Secret."

"He can't go anywhere. Not now!" cried Amanda.

"It'll be over someday. Everything will be back to normal. You'll see," said Matt.

Normal for Matt meant living a secret life. She and Logan lived in a tricky, intricately coded new world. Amanda told herself she wasn't going to settle for that. She would reach out to Adil's mother. She would fight to get her boy back, to understand who he was.

Two weeks later Logan stayed home sick from school. Spent the day in and out of the bathroom. He missed fall basketball tryouts, so she knew he was really under the weather. He still hadn't written the essay for the DA. She took the day off to feed him rice and bananas.

As dusk fell, they sat together on the couch. He opened a butterfly cage and gently took out a caterpillar the size of his pinkie finger. It trailed up the rigid blue-green vein of his forearm. He took a finger and petted its fuzzy length.

Amanda laughed out loud, a strange caustic laugh.

"What's so funny?" said Logan.

"Remember you used to call it the poopie stage? Poopie instead of pupa." It was that innocence she wanted back but if that was where the love resided, then what?

"It was just supposed to be a game," said Logan. "I didn't mean for anyone to get hurt."

"But the game became real," said Amanda.

"I didn't know that," said Logan. "But now I do. I know."

Amanda fought back tears. She bent her head and covered her eyes with hands.

"Hey look!" Logan cried, straightening up. "In the cage." He nudged the caterpillar onto her lap and ran to get his phone to video the butterfly emerging.

Together they watched the chrysalis split out of its cuticle. The butterfly hung upside down on the netting, twisting back and forth, pumping blood from its abdomen into it wings to straighten them so they would dry out.

"It'll be ready to fly in a few hours. We need to release it," Logan said excitedly. "I'll go put on clothes." He pranced towards his room.

"Wait for me!" he shouted naturally, as if it meant nothing at all.

Learning Life Lessons
angst.
Wheels Within Wheels
feel the hurt
Moving Warily
Into the Future
A First Step Back
From the Brink
Who Puts It All on the Line
For Many, Being on the Bright Side Is

II
NATIONALITY/CULTURE

MARYAH CONVERSE

SID ISMAHAN'S BROTHERS AND DAUGHTERS

She was scrupulously cordial, never an angry line or unkind twitch on her round, walnut-brown face. Her Islam—the faith that she taught at school, but also lived and breathed—demanded radical hospitality and acceptance of the stranger, and could not countenance even the intention of unwelcome. It was equally clear, however, that *sid* Ismahan didn't think I should ever have been invited to teach in her school.

In the small village girls' school in northern Jordan where *sid* Ismahan and I taught, our colleagues were all credentialed, experienced teachers. *Sid* Ismahan, like most of the teachers, had a masters degree. By contrast, I was fresh off a bachelors in English literature and creative writing. The Peace Corps valued my youthful enthusiasm, my years of study abroad, and my experience as a cultural coach to exchange students, but I had just a semester of daily substitute teaching under my belt, and no experience being wholly responsible for my own class. I had the added disadvantage of being the only non-Muslim for miles, not being related to my students by blood or by tribe, and speaking Arabic like a semi-literate but inarticulate three-year-old. Not yet two weeks into my two years in our little community, and I already felt each one of these truths keenly.

Almost two weeks at her school, and I had already seen that students sought *sid* Ismahan out, at morning assembly and between classes, for counsel or approval, but without mobbing her, shoving and grabbing, as they did me. The girls sat with perfect respectful stillness when she was in their classrooms, and although she was a strict taskmaster, she never had to raise her voice.

Perhaps they obeyed because she was quick to remind her girls of the wrath of God, and they believed with visceral fear in the threat of hellfire, but that wasn't why students respected her. They loved her because she loved them, each of her students individually and sincerely. Corporal punishment was a cultural norm in the community, despite being illegal, and *sid* Ismahan carried an eighteen-inch length of scrap wood that she rapped against the doorframe or teacher's desk to get a class's attention. It was exceedingly rare, though, that she needed more to bring a student into line than her patient look of maternal disappointment, more painful than any big stick.

ℭℬℭℭℬ

It was Sunday, May 2, 2004, the start of my third week as a Peace Corps English teacher in the school, just over a year since the overthrow of Saddam Hussein, and the Iraqi Interim Government had not yet been established. The Marine Corps was patrolling the increasingly violent and lawless streets and provinces of Iraq, while the Peace Corps had just returned to neighboring Jordan after a brief hiatus, myself among them.

As the teachers did most mornings, we were gathering in the headmistress *sid* Muna's office. She had a dark, wide desk at the far end, dwarfing her assistant's and secretary's desks to the right. Behind *sid* Muna's desk rose a tall, wide window, with ornate iron bars outside and blue sateen curtains patterned with paisley, pulled closed, leaving the room quite gloomy. Along the left wall was a blackboard with a neatly chalked grid detailing the names, qualifications and subject areas of all the school's teachers. As the teachers trickled into the headmistress's office by threes and fours as usual that Sunday morning, we sat beneath it, squeezing as many women as possible onto a long, chocolate-colored leather sectional.

I hadn't been learning Arabic long and couldn't follow their conversation well, aside from the preliminaries. Just like every morning, each teacher entered saying, "*As-salaamu 'alaikum wa-raHmat allahi wa-barakatoh*"— Peace be upon you, and the grace of God and His blessings—and shaking the hand of each woman in the room. This morning, though, there was a deeper solemnity to the often-hurried greeting. They invoked God's peace as if they needed the blessing more than usual.

It was *sid* Ismahan, the older of the two religion teachers, who opened up the leading national *Al-Ghad* newspaper to an unusual two-page spread of full-color photos and held it out to me. "You have to see these, *sid* Maryah," she said.

I shook my head. "I saw them yesterday on the internet." It had been the first of a two-year-long tradition of Saturday mornings in a particular internet café in the city, reading emails and a roundup of news. That Saturday, the news had been grim.

The photos had been splashed across newspapers around the world that week, harsh souvenirs from Baghdad's Abu Ghraib Prison of the torture and sexual humiliation of Iraqi prisoners by their American army jailors. The day before, alone in a cubicle in a dim internet cafe, I had forced myself to look at each grainy image, one after another in the blood-red frame of a CNN slideshow.

"I don't need to see them again," I told *sid* Ismahan.

Sid Ismahan would not be dismissed. "Look again." She had a combative light in her eyes that I was already coming to know well.

"I know what they are," I protested. "They're awful and I don't need to see them again."

Thrusting the paper in my face anyway, she insisted, "You have to look again. Really look at them. These are our brothers, and you have to see them." She might have meant they were her Muslim brothers, or her Arab brothers, or that her tribe straddled the borders with Iraq and Syria. It didn't matter.

I took the whole broad sheet of newsprint between my outspread hands and looked again. Blurred genitalia and barking dogs, that unforgettable man in the black blanket poncho and burlap hood, arms outstretched, balanced on a car battery. And a young woman leaning in from the right, with an impossibly bright smile and two thumbs up.

I wanted to flinch, to grimace, to close my eyes. I forced myself to remain as gravely impassive as I could manage. I had expressed my disgust, and now seriousness felt more appropriate. Everyone's eyes were on me, *sid* Ismahan's most of all, and the words she hadn't said hung heavily in the air anyway: "These are our brothers" . . . *and those are yours.*"

There was a thick lump in my throat, somewhere between disgust and anger. How could my fellow Americans, my brothers do such terrible things to another human being? And that woman, grinning, two thumbs up, her desert camo fatigues tight against hips as wide as mine. She could easily be my sister, with the same long, straight, dark brown hair, my same rounded, corn-fed jaw. Who was she? How could she?

I looked, carefully but not too long. Finally, I closed the paper and pushed it away, shaking my head, mumbling about the shamefulness of it all. I sat with my elbows pressed tight against my waist and was intensely relieved when it was time for us to get up and file out onto the playground, where the girls were lining up for morning assembly.

I had barely begun to work with these women. I didn't know them at all, and I was still a stranger to them. All we had between us that morning was the thorny imbalance of power between my people and theirs. *Sid* Ismahan never mentioned it again, but her disapproval lingered.

෨෨෬෬

Private First Class Lynndie England was a year younger than me, a twenty-two-year-old from rural West Virginia. With her broad smile and two thumbs up, she quickly became the reviled media scapegoat of the Abu Ghraib abuses. We were the same age, and she had my hair. I looked at her face and saw kids I grew up with.

There are many military families in the dairy country that blankets much of central Pennsylvania's rolling hills. On almost every flagpole below the Stars and Stripes flew a white silhouette on black, the POW/MIA flag. I understood, by the time my fourth-grade class was writing "Dear soldier" letters and filling care packages to the troops of the first Gulf War, that every family in my elementary school catchment had been touched by the Korean and Vietnam Wars.

In high school, I remember classmates saying they were joining up so they could afford college. They went in with their eyes wide open, but it was a different time than when their parents had gone to war. The most dangerous thing my classmates thought they would be asked to do was rescue farm kids like themselves when the Mississippi River flooded, or joint military exercises with the South Koreans.

As a child, I had found little respect and few friends in Pennsylvania. Not unlike my Jordanian community, southern York County was clannish and insular. The same few families—Kilgore, Pomeraning, Keller, Good— had dominated my end of the school district for generations. My parents, Boston born and bred, and by extension my siblings and I, were unrelated, unknown, suspicious.

Worse, we hadn't been born again, were unapologetic atheists, not even Catholic or Jewish. We didn't go to church on Sundays, or Bible study on Wednesdays, or youth group on Fridays, or summer Creation Camp, or prayer group in the choir room before school each morning. My sister's class was the cruelest. One September day, they brought their Bibles to Honors Biology, quoting chapter and verse of why she was going to hell for believing in evolution. The first-year teacher was either helpless to intervene, or didn't believe in evolution, either. He never taught again, but my sister transferred to private school anyway.

By the second half of high school, though, I had something my sister never had: a posse of defenders, drawn together by a shared intellectual hunger. I had Catholic Sarah, now an astrophysicist; Methodist preacher's kid Rebekah, now a child psychologist; and Nate, who was dating one of my Girl Scout friends at the time and married a fellow Navy man after the repeal of Don't Ask, Don't Tell. We liked to debate various topics of religion versus science during our trigonometry class.

Once, the choir director's nephew Bryan, one of the leaders of the morning prayer group, asked me about my religion. When I said my family had recently become Unitarian Universalists, he sneered, "Oh. One of those universalists." It would take me decades to really understand how the heresy of universalism, the idea that whatever happens after this life happens to all of us in the same way, was a threat to his whole theology of exceptionalism.

"Oh, just leave her alone!" exclaimed Rebekah, also a leader of the morning prayer group, and possibly understanding quite well why he would sneer. "She's a good person. She'll figure it out eventually." I thought that last was awfully optimistic and a little naïve of her to believe of a stubborn rationalist like me, but I appreciated the gesture of support however it came.

Many other times, my friends stepped in for me, a defensive perimeter that made high school bearable. By the time I left Pennsylvania, I had even come to understand that many of my classmates said even the most deeply wounding things out of well-meaning love and compassion, and honest fear for the state of my soul. They might have all sounded like the same broken record, but they weren't just parroting their preachers' words at me. They were certain of the existence of hell and as frightened of their souls and mine residing there for all eternity, just as certain and frightened as *sid* Ismahan's students.

I might not have agreed when they tried to "save me" or bullied my sister, but those kids I grew up with were passionate Christians with strong moral convictions. Any one of them could have found themselves in the place of those soldiers at Abu Ghraib, and I couldn't bring myself to imagine them blindly following orders without consideration for the moral implications of their actions. Neither did I want to think of them as participating willingly and clear-sightedly in the abject humiliation of prisoners of war.

ঙ৪৪০ঙ৪৪০

And so, that Jordanian spring, I spent hours trying to reconcile for myself how someone like Lynndie England, who could have been Nate or half a dozen other classmates, even Bryan, who could have been me or Sarah or Rebekah under different economic circumstances . . . How could she have done those horrible things, and taken such pictures with such grins?

I tried to explain these things in the teachers' room at that rural girls' school in northern Jordan, to women who had those close family ties to Iraq and its people. For most of these women, I was the only American they had ever met, might ever meet. I needed them to understand that I condemned what had happened in that prison, that it didn't represent the values on which I believed our country to be built. At the same time, I felt compelled to defend the sons and daughters of rural America who, for me, were the faces of the American military.

ঙ৪৪০ঙ৪৪০

I knew what it was to be the Token American. A few years earlier, on an unassuming September afternoon, I was on my way home from a tour of the Opera House in Dresden when my sister's friend texted me from the other side of Germany. "Do you see what's happening in America?"

Rolling my eyes, I texted back, "What did Bush do now?" But then I returned to my host family's empty house just in time to see the second plane auger into the Twin Towers.

I stood there, alone, dumbfounded, thinking of the pleated blue burqas of Afghanistan. Hadn't those women suffered enough? My mother's family had hosted an Afghan exchange student in the 1970s, a woman who returned to her country to become an ER doctor in Kabul, then a refugee, and eventually a doctor in Virginia and, with her Afghan doctor husband, owner of a health care clinic for the uninsured. I wondered what they were thinking at that moment, how their daughters were experiencing that September morning at college.

The next day, I began slowly crossing the continent. I was on a sleek, well-appointed InterCity Express train when the entire German rail system halted on its tracks for three minutes of silence for the victims in New York. Everyone who heard me speak English sucked in a breath, was silent a beat, and said, "I'm so sorry." Three days later, I arrived in Norwich, England, for my university junior year abroad. There were regular candlelight vigils on campus as soon as the British students began to arrive. I felt embraced, buoyed along in a current of fellowship.

It didn't last.

By October, sympathy was fast evaporating, and anger had taken hold. "With us or against us"? "Freedom fries"? How dare we? How could we let our government behave like that? Britons demanded to know, holding me accountable for the representatives I had elected. I agreed wholeheartedly, harboring an equally strong need and struggle to understand. I returned to college in Baltimore a year later with the same questions. How had my country become such a self-righteous bully in the world? Had we always been that way?

I joined the Peace Corps after volunteers had been evacuated from Jordan, for fear of what backlash might come when the Coalition invaded Iraq. When backlash didn't arise, I eagerly joined the first cohort when Peace Corps returned to Jordan.

Ostensibly, I went to *sid* Ismahan's community to teach English and help Jordanians become better English teachers, but she wasn't wrong about my lack of qualifications. I knew it, and I knew that I was there to do more than teach. I had come to learn—Arabic, Islam, culture, politics—and to atone. I needed to give something, be it ever so paltry, to make up for what my American brothers and sisters had done. I had come to win hearts and minds, and then to go home with the authority to say, "Arabs are good, generous people who love their children and their grandmothers, too."

C3 80 C3 80

My Arabic was limited, just two weeks out of training, so I depended on translation from colleagues, and after a few days, everyone lost interest in the painstaking conversation. Everyone except *sid* Deena, a computer science teacher with perfect English.

We would sit across the big pine table in the center of the large, brightly sunlit teachers' room and gesture earnestly at each other. I still felt compelled to defend "our boys," yet I was torn, empathizing with the Iraqis suffering for the abuses of a president they never elected, and with the American soldiers who hadn't signed up for war.

Sid Deena was sympathetic. In Jordan, many poor rural sons go into the military for practical economic reasons, too. They don't expect to fight for their country, either. At most, they expect to be "blue helmets," as United Nations troops in conflict zones and humanitarian crises around the world. I had the impression that it united the Jordanian armed forces around a sense of purpose in the wider world, and in return the United Nations forgives the dues that resource-poor Jordan can't afford to pay.

What *sid* Deena couldn't comprehend was how our soldiers in Iraq could think it was okay to demean another human being in such ways. "This was wrong. How could they not see that?" And how could I justify or even explain it?

"You have to understand," I said, "how young they are!" I was only a year older than Lynndie, and some of the soldiers in Iraq were as much as four years younger still.

"Just because they're young doesn't mean they don't know right from wrong," *sid* Deena insisted.

I knew she was right, but it made my gut clench on the defensive. "Most of them had never traveled a hundred miles from home before they joined the military. We dropped them in the middle of the desert, told them that Americans are the good guys and Iraqis are the bad guys. They brainwashed them. That's what militaries do, what they have to do, and they're good at it."

That explanation left an equally sour taste in my mouth. I didn't want to think of my Pennsylvania classmates as weak-minded, even if I thought their faith was irrational. "They have to think of the other side as bad guys," I babbled on with increasing desperation. "You can't shoot at a man to defend your brother when you think about the other side in shades of gray. It has to be black and white."

"No one's shooting at them behind the walls of Abu Ghraib," *sid* Deena countered.

"They still had to take orders. Three thousand miles from everything they know, and their commanding officers gave them orders. They're just kids!"

As young as I. Would I have had the fortitude and moral rectitude to refuse the orders Lynndie had been given?

All the time that I was wrestling over all this with *sid* Deena the computer teacher, I was also always aware of whether *sid* Ismahan the Islam teacher was in the room. I wondered whether she understood enough English to follow our conversations, and if she did, what she might be thinking about my answers. While I accepted that she might never like me, I wanted her to respect me.

ഇഇ

A short, thickset woman, *sid* Ismahan wore no makeup, a simple dark hijab, and a black *jelbaab*—the ankle-length, duster-like coat common among Muslim women. In rural Jordan, *jelbaab* are very expensive on a public schoolteacher's salary. While many of the more affluent young teachers wore their *jelbaab* closely tailored, it was common for a married woman like *sid* Ismahan to wear a *jelbaab* loose enough that it would still fit her throughout nine months of pregnancy.

One day, I realized I hadn't seen *sid* Ismahan for several days. I asked *sid* Deena.

Smiling broadly, she said, "You didn't hear? She's gone on *'umra*, praise God. Not Hajj—it's the wrong month for that—but *'umra*, the little Hajj. *'Umra* won't wipe away all your sins like the greater Hajj, but it brings *barakah*—blessings from *ar-Rahman*—the Merciful."

Sid Deena leaned closer, lowering her voice. "She wants a baby. Many times she's been pregnant, and then—" *Sid* Deena looked down, flicked the edge of her hand across the pine tabletop in front of us. "It goes away." After a moment of respectful silence she said, "*Sid* Ismahan is hoping that if she goes to Mecca and Medina, if she drinks from the spring of Zamzam that God made for Hagar in the desert, then God will give her a baby."

Suddenly, I had a new sense of why *sid* Ismahan was such a passionate, devoted teacher. Students loved her because she made them feel seen, and now I realized that was because she loved each one in place of the children she couldn't have.

ഇഇ

Later, *sid* Ismahan announced that she was pregnant, and she celebrated with her closest friends in the headmistress's office, but only for a few brief days. Too much pride or celebration might draw the attention of the fire spirits the Qur'aan calls *djinn*, or might cause God to deem her more proud than grateful, and result in counterbalancing bad fortune.

Not many weeks after, *sid* Ismahan disappeared again. *Sid* Deena murmured in my ear, "She lost the baby." This time when *sid* Ismahan returned, she spent all her free class periods in the windowless cabinet of the school's kitchen with two or three teachers she was closest to. Each time she emerged, her eyes were red and weary.

🕉🕉🕉🕉🕉

Months later, we were playing a game in the teacher's room that I call, *Say this!* They would insist that I repeat after them and erupt in laughter when I did. Sometimes the words were funny because they sounded so comical or incomprehensible coming out of my mouth. The difference between *sayf*—sword, and *Sayf*—summer, or between *Hammaam*—bathroom, and *Hamaam*—pigeon would take me a year to master. Long before Jordan, though, while studying abroad in Europe as a teen and undergraduate, I had learned to never repeat a word unless I was absolutely certain of its meaning, because sometimes the name of the game is to get you to say something impolite.

Sid Abeer, the plump, matronly second grade teacher, said with a grin, "Okay, Maryah, say this: *La illaha . . .*"

Even if I had not recognized the phrase, it would have been enough that the teachers sat up a little straighter with a certain perceptive glitter in their eyes. "No." I shook my head, still smiling but no longer laughing.

Sid Abeer frowned, confused at my sudden refusal to play. "*Yalla,* Maryah!" She tilted her head, turning big, innocent eyes on me. "Just say it. It's easy. It doesn't mean anything. *La illaha . . .*"

I shook my head. "It's not nothing," I said. "I know what it means. It's the beginning of the *shahada*—the statement of faith. And if I say it in front of you—" I pointed to the half circle of expectant teachers as I counted, "One, two, three, four, five—if I say the *shahada* in front of you seven good Muslim women, that makes me a Muslim."

From the back corner of the teachers' room, the stern voice of *sid* Ismahan demanded, "And what would be wrong with that, *sid* Maryah?"

"*W-allahi*—I swear, not a thing," I declared loudly and clearly. "There is absolutely nothing wrong with becoming a Muslim if I believe from—" I gestured, scooping from the pit of my stomach towards my heart, and turned to *sid* Deena for translation. "There's nothing wrong with becoming a Muslim if I truly believe from the bottom of my heart that Islam is the true religion. What's wrong is if I become a Muslim because you women tricked me into it."

"That's right," *sid* Ismahan said definitively. She waved her finger at them all. "*Haraam 'alaikum!* Shame on you all!"

⋈⋈⋈⋈

After that day, I worried less and less about *sid* Ismahan frowning at me. I no longer felt that she was listening in on my conversations with disapproval. Over time, students seemed to see that I had earned a small degree of her respect, which in turn helped them to respect me better.

Sid Ismahan and I had not resolved our differences. There was no indication that she believed I belonged in her school, or that I had valuable skills to transfer to her colleagues. Nevertheless, I had established that I was not a threat to their way of life or belief. There was a tacit acknowledgment that we could coexist in mutual dignity.

Occasionally, I would overhear *sid* Ismahan say to a cluster of students, "Miss Maryah is a teacher who came a long way to be here for you. Be respectful." Even more occasionally, one or another pair of high achieving girls would seek my help or knowledge on an extra credit assignment, saying, "*Sid* Ismahan said we should ask you."

We would never be friends, but it would be enough.

⋈⋈⋈⋈

It would be enough that, three years and three thousand miles later, on a cold Indiana winter night, on the phone with my ex-boyfriend from Peace Corps days, when he said that I should start a blog, I thought first of *sid* Ismahan. There were a lot of people I knew better in Faiha', whom I lived closer to, whom I talked with well into the wee hours of the night to the flickering light of a Steven Segal fistfight on national television. In many ways, I trusted those people more. But *sid* Ismahan haunted me.

"These are our brothers." And those are yours.

On a gut-deep level, I knew that, although I had gone to Jordan largely for myself, to learn Arabic and immerse myself in a culture that I could observe and weigh and dissect, I returned to my country for *sid* Ismahan. I don't mean because she didn't want me in her community. I owed it to her to honor her community with the stories I told on my return.

Peace Corps calls it the Third Goal, because President Kennedy didn't just want Americans to transfer skills and spread the gospel of democracy in the unaligned Third World. He and Robert Sargent Shriver, Jr., also charged their volunteers with a third responsibility, still integral to the mission today, to share upon our return what we learned about the world and ourselves while abroad. Maybe Kennedy's Third Goal, too, had a cynical political motive, to counter the stories that our boys in uniform were bringing home from the quagmire in Vietnam in hopes of softening political opposition to the war. Lynndie England in Baghdad's Abu Ghraib, and me in a village school in Jordan . . . maybe we were both pawns in that same struggle.

Whatever the political reasons, this was my personal reason for going to Jordan—to build my empathy for these Arab Muslim students, colleagues, and neighbors; to find humility about my place in the world; and just maybe, to teach some of that empathy and humility to Americans back home.

So, the first post of my first blog was also the first time I put down in black and white the hardest lesson that *sid* Ismahan had taught me, at the very beginning of my service:

"These are our brothers." *And those are yours.*

And I made a promise to continue to work for *sid* Ismahan's respect. More than a decade later, that promise is still with me every day.

NANAKO WATER

BE WORTHY OF YOUR HERITAGE

1987 Ghana

If ye love wealth greater than liberty, the tranquility of servitude greater than the animating contest for freedom, go home from us in peace. We seek not your counsel, nor your arms. Crouch down and lick the hand that feeds you; may your chains set lightly upon you, and may posterity forget that ye were our countrymen.
—Samuel Adams, founder of Lane's prep school

As the flight approached the stopover in Lagos, Nao overheard her neighbor, the missionary, ask the flight attendant, "Excuse me, Miss. Have they got the situation in Lagos under control?" The woman nodded yes and continued down the aisle.

Nao tapped the missionary's shoulder, "What situation?"

The missionary (she learned his profession shortly after takeoff from the stopover in Schiphol) said, "Oh, for awhile there, every time we touched down in Lagos, men leapt out of the bush brandishing machetes and threatening to slash the tires until we handed over our money. That's all."

Nao leaned back into her seat and sighed. *There's nothing like unequal wealth to bring out the violence.* She remembered the rich Nigerians she met back in Boulder, at CU. *Oil money made those guys millions.* Although this was her first trip to Africa, she knew more than she realized.

Her final destination was Accra, Ghana where her husband, Lane, would meet her. In fact, Nao and Lane were quite cosmopolitan by any standard. They met eight years earlier in the School of International Affairs at Columbia University and the two of them were now living in two different countries. Two different worlds. She worked in Tokyo, Japan, and he was doing dissertation research in a village somewhere outside Ouagadougou in Burkina Faso.

Nao scanned her flight magazine to cram on Ghana. Flight Lieutenant

Jerry Rawlings, a half-Scottish man of the people, was the leader. He seemed vaguely American in his handsomeness and lack of pretension. Nao also read about Liberia, a former American colony to the west. *Why have I never heard of this country?* She read, "Liberia began as an American settlement before the American Civil War, as a place for free slaves to live and prosper. Almost twenty thousand freed slaves, free-born blacks and Afro-Caribbean relocated to Liberia." *What does relocated mean? I'll bet Liberia was the brainchild of an abolitionist.*

Years earlier at Columbia, Nao heard stories about Africa. Lane's fellow Africanists were seasoned Peace Corps types, who wanted to get their master's degree to work for the UN or some other development agency. The Africanists loved to tell tales of violence, disease and sex. Shock the folks back home in Michigan. On the other hand, Nao's fellow Japanologists were trying to answer Americans' questions about Japan Inc. *How do the Japanese do it? They're not like us, but they've succeeded.*

Nao was surprised when Lane said, "It's a good thing we're in different fields." As if they were competing in two different Olympic events.

At Stanford, Lane did coursework for three years in African history while Nao worked in the International Center, advising foreign students. When Lane submitted his dissertation proposal, he was disappointed when the Foreign Language and Area Studies people offered him no fellowship. Nao secretly hoped Lane would then shift towards a more practical goal instead of history. But Lane's father, Dr. Hart, immediately offered to foot the bill for Lane to go to Ghana. She shouldn't have been surprised. Dr. Hart had already paid for Lane's Stanford tuition, married student housing and even a small car. Nao's father-in-law's generosity was beginning to grate on her nerves. But Nao's anxiety was put to rest when the Japan Fulbright Commission offered her a plum job in Tokyo. *That must be a special sign*, she thought.

೦೩೫୭ ୧୫୭

When the flight finally arrived in Accra, the missionary said, "Well, my dear, I'll keep you and your husband in my prayers." Nao walked out into the sultry, thick evening air. The lack of night lighting was a shock. But she immediately spotted Lane who almost glowed white against the crowd of dark Africans. Thinner than ever, Lane looked like a dehydrated bamboo stalk in the midst of a lush forest. His blond hair was greasy, sweat stains appeared in the armpits of his dirty T-shirt, and his khaki pants sagged under his cinched leather belt. The darkness, heat and dust excited Nao. Only twenty-four hours earlier she had been walking through the gleaming corridors of Narita Airport.

She was happy to see her husband. The next two weeks would be completely out of her hands. *I'll let whatever happens, happen.* Lane had rented one room of a modest un-airconditioned family house, from a local Ghanaian family. He introduced her to their host, a stocky woman, her head wrapped in a colorful *kente* cloth, and three children who sat wide-eyed, silently regarding this strange Asian woman in their home. *There was not going to be much privacy with only a thin door between them and us. No chance for Lane and I to really thrash it out.*

The Ghanaian woman spoke little English and Lane spoke haltingly in Akan, one of the eighty languages Nao learned were used in Ghana. The woman silently took Nao's dirty clothes away to wash. With the heat and dust, Nao would have to have her clothes washed every day.

It had been many months since Nao last saw Lane. He departed east from Stanford, and she went west. Lane's weekly aerograms to Tokyo were filled with "I miss you. I love you" and details about his primitive living conditions. But he offered little insight into his dissertation work. Meanwhile in her letters to Lane, Nao described her busy life in Tokyo. Japanese students pouring into her office, eager for cultural and educational experiences in America. Nao felt her empathy for Lane drying up like an earthworm in the Colorado sun. She worried, *What was Lane doing? What was their future together?*

Lane laid out the huge paper map on the double bed and outlined his plan for the next two weeks. He said, "We'll explore Accra, via public transport, of course. Nao, you're going to see the real Africa, not the sanitized version. Then we'll go out to the Cape Coast where the slave forts are."

Nao's hopes rose, like a faint wisp of smoke from a barely burning hearth. *Is Lane was going to come through*, she thought. Even if he failed to notice his wife's discomfort, and failed to talk about their future together, Nao was willing to hang onto this marriage if she could get another sign. Something to tell her to believe in her husband.

Lane took her on a city bus, a dilapidated vehicle so well used, there were holes worn through the floorboard. As the line of people got on, the seated men and women promptly took the children of the newcomers and placed them on their laps. Everyone made the best of the situation and took no notice of the white man and the Asian woman. As the bus wove to and fro to avoid potholes, Nao noticed some women dressed in beautiful cotton *kente* fabric wrapped around their bodies but others wore blouses, dark skirts, but of course, no nylons in this weather.

Lane scoffed, "It's a shame these women wear Western clothing."

Nao was shocked but said nothing. *Who was he to say what African women should wear? It was only a generation ago that Japanese women started wearing Western clothing.*

As they walked around the campus of University of Accra, a tall young man waved at them. He was standing by one of the white colonial style buildings which dotted the campus along with Old Man Palm trees. Lane waved back and the young man approached, smiling. Seeing the joy on Lane's face, Nao first thought, *Does Lane know this man?* The young man was dressed in worn but clean clothes.

The tall young man said in good English, "Hello, my friend. Are you enjoying the day?"

Lane said, " Yes, thank you. My wife is visiting and I'm showing her the sights." Nao noticed her husband beam with pride. *See? I have friends here.*

The young man laughed showing his beautiful white teeth as he shook Lane's hand. "Very good. Very good. I am so happy you like our country." He nodded to Nao who smiled back.

He said, "Please tell me, sir, from where do you come?"

Lane said, "I'm from California."

The young man clapped his hands and said, "Oh! California! Hollywood! Rambo! I love Rambo."

Nao wondered if Lane knew who Rambo was. They never watched action films.

Lane said, "I was just showing my wife your wonderful campus."

Was this man someone Lane knew? Maybe he could tell Nao something about this place. She had just noticed a curious stone monument carved in Japanese. A monument with the name Noguchi and the year 1928. *Who was this Japanese man, and what was he doing in Ghana in 1928?* It would be many years before Nao understood the significance of this Noguchi. Eisei Noguchi was a bacteriologist who inspired other Japanese, including her father, to immigrate to America.

Puzzlement flashed across the young man's face at Lane's words. But his white teeth flashed back on. "Please tell me, sir, do you do development work?"

Lane smiled. "Why yes—in a manner of speaking."

The young man grew serious. "Please tell me, sir. Will you help me?"

Nao saw Lane tense. The young man said, "Please, sir. I need you to sponsor me so I can go to America."

Nao saw right away—disappointment wash across Lane's face. Lane wanted something this African wouldn't or couldn't give him. *Friendship? Forgiveness?*

When the young African saw Lane's closed face, he turned away and didn't seem to even notice Nao. The young man must have thought she wasn't American. He turned away and walked back to the building where he picked up a broom and began sweeping the sidewalk.

After getting off of the bus to the Cape Coast, Lane took Nao through a dusty road lined with shacks. The landscape was unfamiliar but Nao was surprised to see wide baskets full of dried fish. *They preserved fish in the same way the Japanese did. Hoshizakana.* And the fufu looked so similar and was prepared just like one of Nao's favorite foods—*omochi.*

It began raining and they stopped under the eaves of one shack to wait for the storm to pass. A thin man bent with age (or hard work?) approached Nao and Lane and motioned for them to come inside. He spoke little English, but it was clear he wanted to get them out of the rain. Inside the dirt-floored single room, Nao and Lane were instructed to sit on the only chairs, while he and his family sat on the floor. The man was a gracious host, entertaining Nao in his broken English until the rain let up.

Listening to her Ghanaian host, Nao was reminded of George Meegan, an Englishman she met on her last Outreach Program outside Tokyo. When Meegan realized Nao was American, he eagerly told her about his Guinness World Record adventure. He had spent seven years walking along the back roads from the southern tip of South America, all the way through North America to the northernmost part of Alaska. Almost twenty thousand miles on foot. The Englishman relied on the hospitality of poor people like this man all along the way.

Meegan said, "The only time I felt I was in danger was when I walked through the American South."

Nao felt ashamed. She could imagine the cold hospitality that greeted this foreigner on foot.

❦

The highlight of Nao's trip to Ghana was the three-hundred-year-old slave forts. There were few visitors. Huge whitewashed stone buildings were built close enough to the ocean so the human cargo could be easily loaded onto wooden ships bound for America. Nao walked through a passageway where countless men, women, and children must have walked. The stone passageway grew more and more narrow. Until only one person at a time could have passed through the opening onto the slave ship. There was no turning back. *Did these people wonder where they would be taken? If they would ever see their homeland again?*

Walking through the slave fort, Nao remembered Lane telling her of his family secret. Lane had told her the story when they first met, but its significance failed to register in the excitement of her moving from Colorado to NYC. Nao grew up as the eldest daughter of Japanese immigrants in Colorado while Lane grew up as the only son of New England Brahmin. Lane's family was littered with medical doctors, graduates of Princeton and expensive boarding schools. Lane, his father, uncle and grandfather had all attended the same prep school and often mentioned their prep school motto —Be Worthy of Your Heritage.

❦

Lane told her, this happened when he was a teenager, back home from boarding school for the holidays. He was looking through his parents' attic for signs of that heritage, and was delighted to find an old ship captain's log. Then young Lane's heart sank when he realized how his worthy ancestor made his fortune—transporting slaves.

Nao remembered vague references to Lane's nervous breakdown. At a local restaurant near Lane's home, Dr. Hart pointed out to her, a substantial man seated across the room, "Oh, there's Dr. Brown. Lane's psychiatrist."

At the slave fort, an epiphany crept into Nao's brain. She had previously thought Dr. Lane and his wife were just exuberant. So different from her own parents, *but in a good way.* Mom and Dad never praised Nao or offered encouragement. At least directly. When Nao asked her mother why they were so different from her friends' parents, Mom said, "*Demo sonna koto shinai.* But we (Japanese) don't do that sort of thing."

At the beginning, Nao was charmed by Dr. Hart's excitement over anything Lane showed interest in. Reggae music. African studies. African art. But the charm began to wear away over the next seven years. Dr. Hart's avid interest in his son. *All in the effort to prevent another nervous breakdown?* She began to see her parents-in-law's warmth as a sort of desperation.

She remembered the night Lane proposed. Only five months after she and Lane met, Dr. and Mrs. Hart invited them to a concert at Carnegie Hall and then a sumptuous dinner at the Russian Tea Room. At the end of the decadent dessert, Lane suddenly got down on one knee, produced a Tiffany box, and everyone stopped talking. A tear glimmered in the corner of Dr. Hart's eye as he held his wife's hand. Nao could only hear her Japanese parents saying, *Never. Never make a scene.* She mumbled, "Yes" but she wanted to say, "No. No, I'm not ready."

⌓₭⌒⌔

The blazing African sun was relentless. After they walked through the slave fort and all of its exhibits, Lane took Nao to a shabby outdoor beachside bar where a lone elderly waiter silently greeted them. They ordered the only thing on the menu—Guinness beers. Served room temperature. The Atlantic ocean glinting with the late afternoon sun was so bright, Nao had to shade her eyes. In the distance she saw the bare-chested fishermen standing in their simple boat, throwing nets into the azure sea. Powerful arms and bodies. Wet, black skin glistened as the muscles rippled beneath the skin. *She* had never seen such vigorous, dynamic physiques.

It was easy to imagine these fishermen three hundred years ago. Back then, in the New World, the colonials dreamed of getting rich off of the virgin land. When indentured laborers started dying in the fields, they tried using Native Americans. But Native Americans succumbed to the diseases from the Old World and did no better. That must have been when these traders noticed Africans. These black people withstood the heat, malaria, yellow fever, as well as survived the brutal voyage across the Atlantic. The white traders were clever, figuring out how to harness and make money off of these sturdy Africans. *But they must have been terrified, too. Lying awake nights.*

After Lane and Nao sat on the terrace for some time, sipping their bottles of warm Guinness, trying to catch a cooling sea breeze, the old waiter came back and pointed to the fishermen. He said, *Best you leave before the fishermen come back.* Nao saw Lane tense. He was afraid.

Before leaving Ghana, Nao noticed her supply of underwear had dwindled. The lady of the house must have taken them when she did the laundry. Nao smiled, imagining a thriving black market in sensible underwear somewhere in Accra. *No problem.* When the plane stopped over in Schiphol, she could pick up what she needed in the airport. But despite a good hour, looking through all the airport shops, Nao could only find what she imagined businessmen picked up for their mistresses back home. A set of expensive lacy panties and a bra, in scarlet red.

ଓଃଫ୍ଠାଓଃଫ୍ଠ

1989 Tokyo

Lane agreed to handle all the paperwork for the divorce once he got back to the States. Nao didn't want anything. She didn't want to hire a lawyer. But knowing Lane, she guessed that he would probably get his father to do the dirty work. She imagined Dr. Hart picking up the phone. Maybe he called an old prep school classmate, one who would be discrete and not ask too many questions.

"Hey, Bud. I need a favor."

"My son needs to get out of a marriage that didn't work out."

"Yes, that Japanese girl he met at Columbia."

"No. No. She's the one who wants the divorce. But Lane's agreed to it and asked me to help."

"Let's see. They married in '81. So that's seven years."

"No, there are no children."

"No, I don't understand it, but his wife doesn't want anything. Nothing."

ଓଃଫ୍ଠାଓଃଫ୍ଠ

1990 Tokyo

When Lane called Nao with the news that Dr. Hart was dead, she immediately thought, *Oh my God, I've killed him. As if I stabbed him with one of his own scalpels.*

Lane told her his father was found in his car outside New Jersey Memorial where he had just finished his shift as head thoracic surgeon. He had had a heart attack. Across the Atlantic, across the African continent, across India and China, Nao imagined the doctor's heart breaking when his only son told him, "Sorry Dad, you can't fix this."

In retrospect, Nao wondered if maybe Lane had been right all along. History was what needed to be studied. But not history based on facts and figures. Or artifacts and fossils. No, this had to be a history of spirit, emotion and thought. Where would one find this history? In brain cells and nerve endings? Or would there be faint imprints left in the earth, like invisible footprints? No, this history lay in the collective soul of mankind. An inaccessible memory locked in the genetic code of the very first man and his awareness of a human credo.

KAREN LOEB

WHAT IS DISCARDED

Everything had to go. That was the plan. Isabelle had price tags on all the furniture, which she was selling for half of what she'd paid for it two years before in 1968. She ran her hand over her teak roll-top desk, remembering how she had coveted it when she first spied it in the Crate and Barrel. It was an unusual item for that store, and she was sure it was one of a kind and would be gone in a flash. She had to act fast, but it was a monetary dilemma for her—could she afford to pay out $350 in cash? She wrestled with her quandary all afternoon as she examined her checkbook and bank account. She went for a walk in nearby Lincoln Park to help her decide, past flowerbeds filled with asters and hollyhocks.

The park betrayed none of the turmoil of just a few weeks before during the Democratic Convention, when Chicago police were doing military drills during the day so they'd be prepared at night for the riots. Many people, including her, wondered just who had rioted—the protesters or the police. She sided with those who thought it was the police. She always regretted that she hadn't been among the action, that she was part of the whole world watching it on TV. And what did she do after that? She went out and bought all this fancy furniture, replacing thrift store tables and chairs and an especially ugly painted desk. She convinced her friend Ralph to help her take it all back to the White Elephant on Fullerton. For the shop it was a bargain—they got to sell it again.

She never had money before. It wasn't much money—she was a fifth grade teacher, after all. But it was a salary, and it was more money than she had ever had. She had a studio apartment with stained glass inserts in some of the windows and a fireplace that really worked. No one could believe that she had found it for only a hundred dollars a month in such a posh neighborhood on Lincoln Park West. And she had this wonderful teak roll-top. From the start, she decided she wouldn't grade papers on it. It was only for letter-writing and for poems, which she wrote frequently.

Two weeks after the convention, even before the Chicago 7 trial, she had bought the desk with its modern Scandinavian lines. Other teak furniture had followed because she wanted things to match. Now, two years later, she couldn't wait to sell everything. Her clothes were in white Samsonite suitcases. Admittedly, they were jammed, but they snapped shut. By nightfall, she was leaving the apartment forever. Ralph said she could sleep on his couch for the two days before her plane took her south. Books and other small possessions she was storing in her parents' attic. They were already safely there, sitting among dusty trunks, and a stuffed falcon that they had been keeping for another relative.

There were two entrances to her ground floor apartment. One had a Dutch door, and she had the top opened. She was having a private sale. That is, she didn't advertise in the paper. Instead, she told friends and asked them to tell others. Whatever didn't sell, she and Ralph would haul to his station wagon and take to the thrift shop.

೮೮೩೧೮೩೮

She knew she was playing follow the leader. Her friend Dot had quit her job as a first grade teacher a few months back and was now in the Peace Corps in Nepal. At first, Isabelle couldn't wrap her mind around this. She leaned over a huge atlas at the library trying to find Dot's tiny village. She couldn't imagine how her friend was surviving. Dot, who wore make-up and refused to do anything before she had a morning shower and bagels from the Ashkenaz bakery department because no other bagel in the entire city was acceptable. Dot, who wasn't even Jewish. Dot, who once a month trekked to Rogers Park to stock up on the bread that Isabelle thought of as varnished wooden doughnuts and put them in the freezer to make them even harder. She had heard Dot declare, "I can't function unless I have one of those bagels." Isabelle was fairly certain that they didn't have them in a tiny mountain village in Nepal.

When Dot told her what was up—that she'd sent for Peace Corps information, filled out an application and gone to a meeting already, Isabelle was incredulous. "You are not serious," she said.

Dot pursed her lips. Recently she had cut off her long, thick mane, settling for a short curly style that she said she didn't have to do anything with after she washed it. She ruffled her hair. "Why do you think I cut my hair? They don't have showers where they're sending me."

Isabelle stared at her. "You're really going? This isn't some kind of joke? You'd even go with the war still going on?"

"I quit my job," Dot said. "I am done, finished and otherwise completed with the Chicago Public Schools. And the last time I looked at a map, Nepal was nowhere near Vietnam."

When Isabelle frowned, Dot said, "Do you really want to spend the rest of your adult life teaching long division to fifth graders?"

"We're still working on the times tables. I'll be lucky if we get to long division by the end of the year."

"See what I mean?"

Isabelle didn't see, at least not then. She believed that it was important for her students to learn their multiplication tables, and that she was the magician to help them do this. No one else seemed to have cared if they learned the tables, she reasoned, which is why she had fifth graders who didn't know them.

Postcards began arriving with exotic-looking stamps. Stamps from the U.S. had men with wigs on them. Stamps from overseas were brightly colored and depicted festivals and artifacts of the country. The stamps pulled her into a reverie, and she purchased her own atlas so she could flip through it at night trying to imagine actually being in a foreign place. *I helped dig a well*, Dot wrote to her. Isabelle was amazed. Her friend had gone there to teach English, and she was digging a well. *Today I learned to make vegetable curry. We eat lentils every day. If you don't serve lentils to a guest, he's insulted.* Isabelle tried to think of the last time she had eaten lentils. It might have been ten years ago when she was fourteen.

When she told her parents of her plans to quit her job and teach English in Bolivia, she brought Ralph with her. Not because she was afraid, though she was a little, but because she already had her books and other paraphernalia in his car. He was tall and skinny with brown hair that stood up like a broom, and he had a perpetual look of a little kid who has been knocked down by a bully near the merry-go-round in the playground and doesn't know what to do about it. Somehow, with this demeanor, he survived a one-year tour in Vietnam as a medic. He followed Isabelle inside her parents' north side bungalow. They had never met Ralph, though she had known him since college. Her father was wearing his after dinner garb—his pajamas and a ratty robe. He squinted at Ralph, maybe trying to remember if he had seen him before. Her mother was a little more formally dressed—she had on an apron over her bathrobe. "I'm going to Bolivia," Isabelle announced through all the frowns.

"And my name is Mickey Mouse," her father said. He glared openly at Ralph. "Where's Antonio?" he asked, referring to a boyfriend in the dim past she had introduced to them.

"Isabelle Sutter, what the devil are you talking about?" Her mother managed to smile at her and frown at Ralph simultaneously.

"I quit my job," Isabelle said, ignoring the Antonio query. "I'm going with an American Friend's group to Bolivia for a year."

"You're going *where*, young lady?" her father yelled.

"You won't last five minutes," her mother intoned.

Isabelle suggested to Ralph that he go to the car and begin bringing things to the front porch while she talked more with her parents. "Good idea," he said.

"First, let's get one thing straight—you are not quitting your job," her father announced, wagging a finger at her. "You have a good job, a secure job, and there's no way you're quitting it. Who quits a job? No one, that's who."

"I already gave my notice," Isabelle said.

"Honey, are you feeling okay?" Her mother lifted her arm as if she were aiming toward Isabelle's forehead to test its temperature.

Isabelle looked down at the shag carpet. "I didn't outright quit," she mumbled. "I asked for a leave of absence."

"What's that?" her father said. "Speak up."

Isabelle glanced to the porch where Ralph was piling boxes of books. She shut the door. "I took a leave of absence."

"Well, that's a little more sensible. But why are you ashamed of it—you think your friend out there will look at you in a worse way because you're a smarty pants?" Her father shook his head.

She cringed inside when he used expressions like *smarty pants*. *Miss-know-it-all* and *see the big picture* were probably stationed on his tongue ready to spring out.

When Ralph came back in she introduced him. "So are you quitting your job too and going to Bolivia or wherever it is?" Mr. Sutter asked.

"No sir," he said. "I would never quit my job."

"That's more like it. Where do you work, son?"

"At the post office. I sort mail and I'm a delivery sub. Someday I hope to have my own route."

"I'm a P.O. man myself," Mr. Sutter said. He held out his hand to shake Ralph's. I've been working at the Rogers Park P.O. for thirty years."

"Groov-y," Ralph said. "I knew—Izzy has filled me in."

"So how'd you even get a job at the P.O. It's harder than one of my wife's cupcakes to get in with them."

"They give preference to vets—you know, returning from the war."

Mr. Sutter nodded in appreciation. "I was in Europe when we marched into Berlin. Don't you think twice about how the idiots in this country are treating your group. Why I could . . . " He was about to go on when his wife came in with snacks. "I don't like that Isabelle is going overseas." She set down windmill cookies arranged in a circle on a plate.

"It's not across an ocean," Ralph pointed out. He blinked hard, seeming surprised that he had come to her defense.

"It's just due south of here, Mom. I think it's the same time zone, or close to it." Isabelle nabbed a cookie. "We brought some of my things to store upstairs, so we'll start carrying them in. If that's okay, I mean."

Her mother looked bewildered. "I guess so, honey."

"How can that be?" her father asked. "With the time zones, something so far away."

Ralph smiled at Isabelle. "Well, sir—it has to do with longitudes and all. If you're on the same longitude, you're pretty much in the same time zone."

ଓଃ஭ଊ௸ஐ

Some of the teachers from her school arrived first. They were from her floor, and she ate lunch with them every day. They each bought small items: trivets, a frying pan, ice trays that made cubes in the shape of strawberries. For a while it went like that, and Isabelle began to worry that her big-ticket items weren't going to sell. Then a man who was a friend of one of the teachers sauntered in and immediately said, "I like that bookcase." It was a teak shelf unit that matched the roll-top desk.

"How about the other bookcase over here?" Isabelle asked.

"Oh, yeah, that too." But she couldn't convince him to buy the desk.

By the time Ralph arrived, she was more encouraged. "Things are looking pretty empty around here," he said. "Who took the couch?"

She had tried on numerous occasions to educate him with the correct term: hide-a-bed, but he insisted it was a couch. "Some guy who knows my neighbor bought it. He brought a friend and they hauled it out."

"I'm glad I missed that one," Ralph said. "That couch weighed as much as two tombstones."

"Now I know how you really feel," Isabelle said.

"I would have helped," he said. "You know that. But I'm glad I didn't have to."

There was a knock on the bottom part of the Dutch door. "C'mon in," Isabelle called.

It was a woman with hair in a flip, sprayed into place. It was so mid-1960s, Isabelle couldn't help smiling. She herself had styled her hair that way in high school. Recently, she had worn one braid down her back. Now, following Dot's example, she had cut it short, only her hair wasn't curly. Instead it sprouted in several directions because of long-forgotten cowlicks.

"I'm Julia Myers," the woman said. "It doesn't look like there's a whole lot left. This is my fourth or fifth sale I've been to today. I have absolutely no furniture, so obviously I need some." She was wearing a colorful silk jacket that she unbuttoned and tossed on a folding chair in the corner, a parachute descending.

"How come you don't have any furniture?" Isabelle asked.

"Grad school." She allowed a long pause before she continued. "I've landed a job with the Historical Society, so I can finally afford nice furniture. I have some things that are pretending to be furniture, like a davenport with one leg missing that I prop up on bricks." She laughed as she began walking around the apartment.

Ralph had been standing near the kitchen. He pulled Isabelle over. "What the hell is a davenport?" he asked in a low voice.

She mouthed the word *sofa.*

Then he asked this Julia person, "How'd you hear about the sale?"

"Excuse me?" She looked at Ralph from head to toe, as if she were examining some quaint life form found on Planet X. "I assumed you'd recognize my name. I'm the person moving in here, that is, after they clean and paint it." She sniffed, and ran a finger over the fireplace mantel, checking for what? Breadcrumbs? Ash residue? Isabelle and Ralph exchanged looks as Julia wandered from item to item—the stereo, the footstool matching a chair that had already been purchased, a large rubber plant, piles of towels. "Really,

I don't see much here."

"Most of the stuff has been sold," Isabelle explained. "The sale started at nine this morning." She didn't like picturing this person inhabiting her space. The apartment had been a find, *a real steal* was how one friend put it. This woman was as annoying as being woken by a mosquito at 3 a.m. She didn't deserve a steal of a place

"Wait a minute, what's this?" Julia buzzed over to the desk, rubbing her hand along the curved roll-top. She carefully lifted it up and down a couple of times. "This is quite lovely—if I buy it, bonus! I won't even have to move it. What are you asking?"

"There should be a tag on the side."

Julia looked all around it. "There isn't."

Isabelle walked over. The tag had come off. She guessed it was that blue square lying over near the fireplace. She had half-priced what she'd paid for things that were fairly new, so the desk was going for $175.

"Well?" Julia asked.

"It was an expensive piece," Isabelle began.

"Don't you think I know that? It certainly stands out next to those shabby towels and that odd footstool. Who has just a footstool?"

"Three hundred," Isabelle blurted out, glancing, she hoped furtively, at Ralph, who produced a half-smile.

"What?" Julia asked.

"Not a penny less."

"I'm not arguing," Julia said. "I know a bargain when I see one."

"Okay," Isabelle said. "You've got yourself a deal."

"Is a check okay?" Julia was already rummaging in her basket purse.

"Why not?"

Julia used the mantel to write on. As she was starting the check, she noticed a stack of record albums. She went over to them, bending to flip through them. "These are for sale, I take it?" The five or so she picked out she removed from their jackets one by one, examining them for scratches.

She added the new purchases to the $300 price, and finished the check. Isabelle put a sold sign on the desk with a note that said *Do not remove—property of new renter.* Then Julia picked up the records she bought, saying she'd take them with her—she wanted to listen to them. "I'm so psyched about living here—I can't wait." She hugged the records close to herself with *The Freewheelin' Bob Dylan* facing out, eyed Ralph again, and marched out of the apartment, calling back through the Dutch door, "I'm going to tell the rental office that my desk is here, so don't try any funny stuff, like selling it to someone else."

Isabelle took a deep breath. Some of the breath included a flowery scent that had been attached to Julia's skin. "I'm glad she's gone. Can you believe her? That hair-do was something else. It was cast in stone."

"Well, I'd call it a classic style. I guess you really didn't like her." Ralph smiled, walking over to the large plant.

"That's right, take her side." Isabelle flounced around the apartment, gathering up stray items.

"Believe me, she didn't score any points. Let's get this stuff together and haul it to the White Elephant."

"You're too good for me, as usual," Isabelle said.

"Don't say that." Ralph stopped with the rubber plant in mid-air. "I don't ever want to be too good for you."

"Whatever that means."

"Take it how you want to," he said. "I think I'm going to keep this plant—I don't think thrift stores take living entities, especially ones that are five feet. And guess what, I'm not paying you for it."

"Considering you gave it to me when it was just a little shaver, that's okay," Isabelle said, immediately regretting tapping an expression her father would use.

She went along each wall of the room, gathering a few stray things. Then she noticed it: the silk jacket lying in a jumble on the chair. She touched it—yes, it was silk, definitely, not polyester, and it was lovely. Isabelle didn't like to admit it, but it was something she would buy—a patchwork of colors with little designs like paisley, diamonds and flower shapes with tiny mirrors embedded like a necklace all around the jewel-neck collar. *Made in India*, the tag said, confirming her impression. She held it up to herself. The sleeves were the right length, and the material felt like whispers against her skin.

"What are you doing?" Ralph asked.

"Nothing," she said, sensing her face flush. "What did you think?"

"You can't keep it."

"I wasn't planning to. Okay? I'm sure she'll be back for it."

"You can put it in a desk drawer—that way she'll get it when she moves in."

"One of the painters might take it. I can contact the rental agency." She put it in a tote bag, and they started loading Ralph's station wagon.

"This is a two-trip deal right here," he said, assessing the items for the White Elephant shop.

"You have the cutest ways of saying things." She smiled. She couldn't get the thought of that jacket out of her head. It felt so soft, so perfect. She resented Julia for leaving it.

At Ralph's on Dayton St. later that evening, with the rubber plant looming over them, they sat on his living room floor looking over her Bolivia material. She was going to be teaching math and English to elementary kids. Upon arrival in La Paz, she'd be in a six-week Spanish immersion class first, offered for new people in the program. She didn't know yet if she'd be in the city or a small village. "This is impressive, what you're doing," Ralph said. He ruffled his fingers through her new short hair. "I like the crop you're growing." He cleared his throat. "I can make up a bed for you"

"Okay."

"Or—"

"Or what?" she asked.

"You could bunk in with me. It's been a while."

"A long while, mister. I thought we were over and done with that phase."

"We don't have to be," he said. "We could start it up again, for two nights."

For her answer, she leaned against him, smelling his clean fresh aroma, like sunlight and air, even after a long day. "You're a good friend," she said.

"Ouch, damn it, don't call me a friend." Ralph shook her arm a little. It makes me seem like a puppy dog."

"I get the side near the window," Isabelle called, jumping up and running for the hallway.

After a shower, and in bed finally, she wound herself around Ralph. For a moment he trembled in her arms. She felt his heat. "It's been too long, Izzy." Then he kissed her deep and slow, their teeth tapping.

The next day she did things like paying bills, closing accounts, saying goodbye to her parents in person. There was the matter of the silk jacket that threaded through her memory as she did all the errands. She finally called the rental company in the late afternoon. "Did Julia Myers call about anything—did she leave me any kind of message?" The office manager, a woman with a nasal voice, said that Julia had called. Isabelle felt her heart rate drum against her chest. "She mentioned that she had bought a desk from you, and she wanted to make sure the painters covered it."

"Did she say anything else?" Isabelle asked.

"No—that was it."

"Well, if she has any questions or anything, I'll give you my parents' number. She could leave a message with them."

"I'll take it, but I'm sure there won't be any problems."

That evening Ralph noticed a patchwork sleeve poking out from the tote bag. "What about that thing?" he asked.

"I called the rental company." Isabelle's voice was edgy. It hadn't really been an outright lie.

"Good. What'd they say?"

"I gave them my parents' number. I guess I'll take the jacket there, and she can contact them."

"That's progress. You know, I bet she doesn't remember where she left it—she said she'd been to several apartment sales."

"Let's order a pizza," she suggested. "We can eat it in bed and watch a movie on TV."

"Or not watch a movie." Ralph was already dialing Uno's.

The next day, when Ralph went to work, she got dressed and then did something she'd been wanting to do for two days. She tried on the jacket. It fit her perfectly, and her spirits were buoyed up by it. The glittering mirrors around the neck were cleverly inset. It felt so good, the silk, the kind that floated as she walked. To test the material, she paraded in front of the closet mirror, waving her arms, watching the silk drift in the breeze she created. But it felt dangerous too. She didn't know clothes could feel dangerous. She was determined that she would wear this jacket one time outside. Then she'd make an extra trip to her parents' house, leaving it with them for Julia to claim. She promised herself that she would. And if she didn't have time to go across town to do that, she could always mail it to them. She could mail it from La Paz if she had to. There were all sorts of ways she could get it to them. But first she'd wear it. Just this once.

THE NE NORMAL
America Is
In Terrible Dang
This Is
America
INFECTIOUS
IDEOLOGIES
IT CAN'T CHANGE OVERNIGHT
BUT WE GOTTA START SOMEWHERE...

FREDERICK G. YEAGER

MR. GORBACHEV, TEAR DOWN THIS WALL

With five trash bags in my right hand and whistling, I walked toward the wall my dad built on our lawn. Every Saturday for the last two years, I filled five bags, sometimes more and sometimes less, with burned-out candles, dead flowers, stuffed animals, beer cans, and broken beer bottles people have left at the base of the memorial or thrown at it and spray-painted over the bright-red letters, Fight'em With Us, and the flyers somebody pasted on the wall.

CR ☙ CR ☙

The wall is six feet high, ten feet long. Dad used concrete blocks and slathered concrete over them to give the memorial wall a uniform appearance. There is a chunk of the Berlin Wall in the middle of his wall that can be seen from either side. Our house is on a corner lot, and so he set the wall at an angle so people coming down either street can see it. It's not really a wall that keeps anybody off our lawn. It's kinda like the Vietnam Veterans Memorial Wall. It looks like a wall, but it's a memorial.

It's a mystery to me why some people leave things, and some people throw beer cans and beer bottles at the wall, and some people spray-paint graffiti and paste flyers. Who knows? All I know is that every Saturday, I cram everything into trash bags and paint over the graffiti and flyers.

Horst, the trash ain't gonna pick itself up, I said to myself. The sooner started, the sooner finished. I hitched up my pants and opened the first trash bag. I had filled three of them when I realized Mr. Handerly from across the street was standing beside me.

"It's an eyesore. I told your dad that wall'd be a trash collector."

"Hey! It's not that bad. With all that paint in different colors, it looks like modern art. I bet I could hang it in the Dallas Art Museum," I said.

Handerly looked at me like I was crazy and walked back across the street.

I was picking up the last of the trash and thinking about my dad when I realized Handerly was back. "You again. You were just here. Your wife kick you out of the house?"

Handerly did not answer, but stood there, looking at the wall. After about two minutes, he said, "It's an eyesore. Whatda you think it'd cost to take it down?"

"That wall's *not* coming down. My dad built it. It stays." Handerly did not say anything, just turned around and walked back to his house.

❧❦❧

I was three, and we were living in East Berlin when my parents and four of their friends decided to tunnel under the Berlin Wall. The night before they escaped to West Berlin, the other four told my parents they could not bring me. I would cry and alert the guards, they said. My mom told them she was not coming if she could not bring me. She bundled me in five or six blankets for the crossing. As she likes to say, not even my nose was sticking out. The six of them, my dad carrying me, crossed to freedom without a problem.

Two years later, we immigrated to Texas and settled in Arlington, just outside Dallas. Three years later, the wall came down. When my dad heard that the Berliners were tearing down the wall, he flew to Berlin, joined in knocking it down, and brought back with him a chunk of the Berlin Wall that he put in the middle of his wall.

I was sixteen when Dad decided to build his memorial wall to freedom, liberty, and democracy. He thought including the piece of the Berlin Wall in his wall made it a memorial. I could not understand how that made his wall a memorial. To me, it was just a wall with a chunk of the Berlin Wall in it.

Whenever he had a few too many shots of Schnapps, Dad would stand at the window, look at his wall, lift his glass of Schnapps, and shout, "Mr. Gorbachev, tear down this wall."* One day, he said to me, "Horst, you can build a wall to keep people in or keep people out. In or out, it keeps people from following their dreams, from finding the life they want."

❧❦❧

After Handerly left, I stood there, looking at the wall with its flyers and graffiti. I said to myself, it has to be that nut bunch that calls itself Fight'em

With Us that paints the graffiti and pastes the flyers. Maybe it's that guy who was three years ahead of me in school who did it. He was your typical bully: fat, without many friends. He was a real slob: dirty shirt half unbuttoned, pants cuffs dragging the ground. He called me a Nazi whenever he saw me alone. One day, I told him I'd kick his ass if he called me that again. Two months ago, I passed a guy on the street who was skinny, shaved head, and wearing khakis and a nice shirt, buttoned. I am pretty sure it was him and that he's part of that Fight'em With Us nut bunch.

One time, I passed two guys on the street I'm sure were from that nut bunch. I heard one of them ask, "Where'd he come from?"

"What's it matter?" said the other. "They're all foreigners."

"My wife says he's not married. Lives with his mom."

"Betcha he's gay. They're everywhere nowadays. You can't walk down the street, they're not eyeballin' you and hopin'."

There were two of them, so I didn't say anything.

Ψ⁝ʒ⁝

My friend Mihail drove up just as I finished picking up the trash and shouted, "Hey, Horst. Whatcha doing? Wanna go for a beer?" Mihail's Russian. His parents moved here the same year my parents did.

"Where we goin?" I asked as we drove off.

"Harry's OK?"

"It's good for me," I said.

Harry's is the only bar in town that has an eighty-five-inch television. When we walked in, twenty-five or thirty guys were watching the Texas Rangers and the Houston Astros.

Mihail and I are Rangers fans. What else would we be? We live in Arlington, where the Rangers play their home games. We took our beers to a table in the back and watched the game. In the fourth inning, a Ranger hit a home run with bases loaded and brought the score to five-zero. As the Rangers continued to score, three or four of the Astros fans started giving Mihail and me the finger and shouting, "Here's to you and them fucking Rangers." Mihail began to give it back to them when the Astros scored. Harry stepped in and said, "Cool it or leave." Two of the Astros fans got up and headed to the door. On their way out, one of them said loud enough for Mihail and me to hear, "Fucking Russkies. They're everywhere." Mihail started for him, but

I held him back.

CЄ⁊ഠC⁊ഔ

The next day, I was mowing the lawn and picking up the trash when Mrs. Sammerson, a friend of my mom's, walked by on her way to church. She stopped as she always does and said, "You always keep your lawn and your dad's wall looking so nice." She always says that if I am in the yard when she walks past.

"Mr. Handerly doesn't think so," I said. "He calls it a junk collector."

"Don't you pay him no mind. He's such a grouch. I don't know how his wife puts up with him."

As soon as she left, Handerly came over. "What'd that old gossip say? Anything happening I should know about?"

"She's a nice lady. Why don't you like her?"

"I'd like her a lot better if she minded her own business."

"Hiding something, are you?" I asked. He stood there a few minutes, looking at the latest flyers.

"Any idea who stuck those flyers there?" I asked.

He shook his head and said, "Ask your friend. She knows everything that's goin on."

CЄ⁊ഠC⁊ഔ

Saturday again. I was picking up the trash when Handerly wandered over. "A lot of beer cans and broken beer bottles. Who do you think throws all that trash here and pastes those flyers?" he asked.

"I'll bet you a hundred dollars it's that Fight'em With Us nut bunch."

He stood there, looking at me and did not say a word. I pointed at a flyer and said, "Look at that. Immigrants are murderers and rapists. Pretty nasty stuff. Who'd write something like that?"

He did not say anything, just stood there and watched me pick up the trash. I wondered why he was still there when I heard horns honking, motorcycles, and people shouting and laughing. When they got to where Handerly and I were, the cars and motorcycles stopped. People piled out of the cars, including a skinny guy with a shaved head, carrying a bullhorn. I was trying to decide if he was the bully from school when he raised the bullhorn and said, "It's time to take America back from the crooks, rapists, and murderers. They don't belong here. It's time for them to go back to where they came from."

I could not believe what I heard. I walked up to him and said, "Stop that. This is my property. You can't say stuff like that on my property." He ignored me and kept shouting into the bullhorn. I dropped the trash bag I was holding, grabbed my cell, and dialed 9-1-1. "There's a demonstration going on at my house. Send the police."

Sirens screaming, the police arrived in less than five minutes. Two police officers got out of the car. The short, fat one walked up to the skinny guy shouting into the bullhorn and said something to him. He ignored the police officer and kept shouting into the bullhorn. The police officer reached up and knocked it out of his hand. Six of the biggest, toughest-looking guys I've ever seen came from out of nowhere and gathered around the guy. When the tall police officer saw the six mean-looking giants, she pulled her gun and fired into the air. Shouting and shaking their fists, the crowd, the guy with the shaved head, and the six giants backed up. The fat police officer picked up the bullhorn and said, "All right, folks, break it up. Time to go home. Leave, or we'll arrest you." Everyone except Handerly left. The fat police officer looked at me. I gave him the thumbs-up sign, and he and his partner left.

Before long, everyone was gone. Except for Handerly. He just stood there, looking at me and smiling. Then he said, "Why'd you call the cops? They were just exercising their constitutional right to free speech. I thought that wall was supposed to be a monument to freedom. Some monument to freedom." He turned and walked away before I could punch out his lights.

Mihail drove up as I turned to go to the house to check on my mom. He jumped out of his car and yelled, "Horst, I heard shots. You all right? What's going on?"

"I need to check on my mom," I said. With Mihail behind me, we ran to my house. Entering, I shouted, "Mom, where are you?"

"Upstairs. I'll be right down."

When she came down, I said, "Didn't you hear all that noise? Why didn't you lock the door? What were you doing up there?"

Ignoring me, she said, "Hallo, Mihail. Wie geht es deiner Mutter?"

Mihail smiled and said, "My mother is fine. Thank you for asking, Mrs. Wolff."

"Möchtest du einen Kaffee?"

"Mom. I keep telling you, 'Speak English.'"

Ignoring me, she said in German-accented English, "I've got some apple strudel I took out of the oven an hour ago."

Mihail smiled at me, turned to my mother, and said, "I would enjoy a cup of coffee and a piece of your excellent strudel, Mrs. Wolff."

ଔଌଌଔଔ

The next morning, I checked the wall. There was trash everywhere. Not just beer cans and broken beer bottles, but banana peels, condoms, pizza boxes, and everything else imaginable. I called the police. In about ten minutes, a police officer with whom Mihail and I hunt pheasants drove up.

"Hey, Horst. What's the problem?" he said, getting out of the car.

"Hi, Ray. Someone trashed the place last night," I said, pointing to the garbage covering the yard.

"Any idea who?"

"I'd bet it was that Fight'em With Us. They don't like immigrants or anybody who wasn't born in America, or who's the wrong color, or talks with an accent."

Ray said, "If you wantta file charges, you'll have to come down to the station." When I did not say anything, he said, "It might not be a good idea. It'll only encourage them."

"I guess you're right."

"I'll talk to Sarge and see if we can have a patrol car drive by a couple of times a night."

"Thanks, Ray."

I was cleaning up the garbage when Handerly walked over. "Quite a ruckus yesterday," he said. "Why do you think they were protesting here?"

I looked at him and said, "I've no idea, but I bet you do."

"Why would I know?"

"Because it was that Fight'em With Us nut bunch you're a part of."

"You don't know what the hell you're talking about." His face turned beet red, and shaking his finger at me, he said, "Let me tell you something, *buddy*. I'm sick of seeing all this trash every time I look out my window. And that god-damned wall. It's an eyesore. You do something about it, and you do it now, or I'm going to Town Hall." He turned around and went back across the street. I heard the door slam when he went into his house. I'm surprised he didn't break it, he slammed it so hard.

CRISCRISO

On Wednesday night, Mihail and I went for a beer. Instead of Harry's, we went to the Night Out Bar down the street. Over a beer, we discussed Fight'em With Us. "Why do you think they hate us?" asked Mihail. "We haven't done anything to anybody. We didn't shoot or rape anybody. Our parents are good citizens. We pay our taxes just like everybody else."

"Doesn't matter," I said. "Some people always have to have something to complain about. With that nut bunch, it's us immigrants."

We had another beer, and I said, "Drink up. I've got a tough day at work tomorrow."

CRISCRISO

Saturday, whistling and with five trash bags, I walked to the wall. There were no candles, no flowers, no soggy stuffed animals. No beer cans or beer bottles. No garbage. Nothing. Handerly was standing in his yard, watching me. I shouted, "Hey, Handerly. Look, no beer cans." He turned around and went into his house.

Mihail pulled up, and we were debating whether to go the Night Out or drink the beer I had in the fridge when we heard horns honking, motorcycles racing their engines, and people shouting and laughing. "They're back," I shouted and ran to the house. Mihail was right behind me. Mom came running from the kitchen. "What's happening?"

"They're back," I said, jerking open the closet door. My shotgun wasn't there. "Where's my gun?" I shouted.

"No!" said my mom. "No gun."

I looked at her and said, "Where's my shotgun?"

"Horst, no gun. Someone'll get hurt."

"Where's my god-damned gun?" I shouted. She started crying. That was the first time I had ever yelled at her. "Mom, I'm sorry, but there's a mob out there. Who knows what they'll do. Give me my gun."

"No!" She turned to Mihail and said, "Mihail tell him. No gun."

Mihail said, "Maybe she's right, Horst."

I ran out of the house. A guy, about six-foot-six and weighing at least two hundred seventy-five pounds, was helping the skinny guy with the shaved head set up a loudspeaker. Mihail and I ran towards them. I pulled out my cell, dialed 9-1-1, and shouted into the phone, "2711 Avenue C. Send the police—I'm being attacked."

The giant helping the skinny guy knocked the cell phone out of my hand and punched me in the face. Mihail hit the skinny guy with a stick he found in the yard, knocking him to his knees.

All hell broke loose. Two guys were punching Mihail. The six-foot-six guy was punching me. The other guys and the women who came with them were screaming, "Get that SOB! Hit'im again."

I heard sirens, and a few moments later, a police van screeched to a stop. Six police officers in riot gear marched into the middle of the melee, nightsticks swinging. Somebody threw a tear gas bomb—it must've been the police. Some of the guys ran down the street. The women followed them. Then the rest of the guys got into the cars and on motorcycles and drove off, stopping to pick up the guys and women on the street.

I turned and with blood running from my nose and tears running down my face stumbled to my house. At the door, I tripped, slammed into it, forcing it open, and fell on the floor. Mom came running, crying, "Horst, are you all right?" I stood up. She helped me into the kitchen and handed me a wet cloth.

"Mihail! I've got to help him," I said.

"Stay here," she said. "I'll get him."

"You can't go out there," I shouted. She didn't hear me. She'd gone for Mihail. In a few minutes, she led him into the kitchen, handed him a wet cloth, and pointed to the sink. "Splash water on your eyes," she said. And to me, "You too." Outside, it was quiet. The police and everyone else had gone. In about twenty minutes, Mihail left.

CLESOCRED

It was late when I rolled out of bed the next morning. Mom cut me a piece of strudel and poured me a cup of coffee. She sat there, saying nothing, while I ate the strudel and drank my coffee. After I finished, I said to her, "What're you thinking, Mom?"

"I think it's the wall that brought those people here."

I said, "You mean Dad's wall?"

She looked at me, her voice showing hesitation and uncertainty, and said, "I think your dad should not have built it." After a few seconds, she said,

"Walls are funny things. Like your dad said, they keep some people in and other people out. They divide communities and sometimes families. More often than not, they create bad feelings. And sometimes, the wall is only in a person's mind. Locking him in and not letting him see what's happening around him." Amazed, I looked at her. "Sometimes, what's happening is not so good, but even so, you have to deal with it. If you don't, the problem only gets bigger. But people don't see that because they're hiding behind that wall in their mind. If something good's happening or something's changing, they don't see that either." She looked at me and said, "Horst, I think it's time to take the wall down."

I was stunned. I could not believe what I'd heard. "You mean Dad's memorial wall? Why would we wantta take it down?"

In a clear voice with no hesitation, she said, "Mr. Handerly's right. It's an eyesore. I never said anything to your dad because he was so proud of his wall. It's concrete, not nice stone or marble like most memorials. It's not a nice-looking memorial, or wall, for that matter."

I looked at her, trying to decide if she was serious. Puzzled, I said, "But it's Dad's memorial wall. He built it."

After a few minutes during which neither of us said anything, she said, "Maybe we can give the piece of the Berlin Wall to a museum." After a minute, she said, "With a nice plaque with something like: In memory of those who died searching for freedom, liberty, and democracy. This piece of the Berlin Wall donated by the Wolff Family, Hans, Anna, and Horst."

After a few seconds, during which I considered her suggestion, I smiled at her and said, "Mr. Gorbachev, tear down this wall."

She smiled and said, "I don't think I ever told you why your dad was always saying that. We were listening to President Reagan's speech. The minute President Reagan said, 'Mr. Gorbachev, tear down this wall,' your dad jumped to his feet. He started jumping up and down and shouting, 'Ja! Ja! Reisse diese Mauer ein. Reisse diese Mauer ein.' I am sure the neighbors heard him shouting, 'Tear down this wall.' He was jumping up and down so hard, I thought he'd go right through the floor."

෩෫෨ඎ෨

That night as we ate dinner, Mom said, "I think we should apologize to the Handerlys."

"Apologize to the Handerlys? He told that bunch of thugs to come here."

"You don't know that."

"No, but I'd bet he's a member of that Fight'em With Us."

She said again, "You don't know that." Then she laid it on me. "Didn't you hear what I said about people building walls in their minds and letting troubles grow because they can't see over the wall in their minds? Get rid of that wall in your mind! If Mr. Handerly is a part of Fight'em With Us, that's his wall. He has to look over it and do what's right. You and I, we're going to be friends with our neighbors. As soon as we finish dinner, we're going to apologize to the Handerlys for not tearing down that wall before now."

After dinner, I reluctantly followed Mom to the Handerlys. Mom pointed to the door, and I knocked. Mrs. Handerly opened the door. "Hello, Anna, Horst," she said

"We'd like to talk to you and Mr. Handerly," said Mom.

"Come in," said Mrs. Handerly and led us to the family room where Handerly was watching TV. "Horst and Anna would like to talk to us," said Mrs. Handerly, turning off the TV.

"We've decided to take down the wall. We're sorry we didn't take it down earlier," said my mom.

"Yeah. We're sorry we didn't take it down sooner," I muttered not too loud, but loud enough for Handerly to hear me.

Mr. Handerly and I discussed how to tear down the wall and agreed I could probably knock it down with a sledgehammer. Mrs. Handerly, smiling at her husband, said, "Honey, why don't you help Horst take down the wall."

His face showed he was not happy with her suggestion, but he said, "When do you wantta take it down?"

"How about tomorrow after I get off work," I said.

*From a speech by President Ronald Reagan on June 12, 1987, at the Brandenburg Gate, West Berlin, Germany.

Hidden Scars
others hope it
return sense of calm
A MOMENT OF GUILT ...A SENSE THAT SOMEHOW WE WERE ALL RESPONSIBLE
THE BAD THINGS
NG TO US.
What's really going
Everywhere
Resistanc
the thought that should count
UNDERPREPARED

III
CLASS/COMMUNITY
ଔଷ୍ଠାଇଷ୍ଠୀଷ୍ଠାଇଷ୍ଠୀଷ୍ଠାଇଷ୍ଠୀଷ୍ଠ

LINDA A. VANDLAC SMITH

AMERICAN DREAM POEM

Like my immigrant
great-grandmother,
grandmother, mother,
I have sunk my hands
in suds and bleach
pulling low-thread-count
white cotton sheets
through hot water until
the dinginess is gone.

Outside they've hung
on a line unfurled
like a banner, family
crest stripped bare,
on a dirt farm
along a low-rent highway
now in the suburbs
on sunnier days.

You might never know
how easily vomit,
those guttural accents
are spot-cleaned
in a single generation
until beyond scrutiny
not an acid lilt remains

How semen and blood
mix and multiply
scrape together whatever
it takes to get by
another harvest
another wash day
however long the soak
to lift the stain

How the sweat rings
of an hourly wage scrub
away beneath hope's bristles
in that uncertain walk
down the foreign hallways
of high school.

Even a century's passing
and college degrees
provide little escape,
calluses and the agitator
of a digital washer both
fighting for percale corners
in an unbalanced load
shit leaching out
into wash water
then filtering back
through the weave
sun waiting in the backyard
to sanitize them again.

JAKOB KONGER

A BRIEF REFLECTION ON APARTMENT CLOTHESLINES

Once my mother caught a man stealing clothing from us. This was a very long time ago, when my mother still washed our clothes by hand and hung them to dry outside the bedroom window. Anyone who passed could see our clothes then. Anyone who could reach could pluck them off.

One day, as often happened, one of my dresses fell from the clothesline, a thick light blue dress my mother had had to save up for and which, because it had cost a full week's rent, I was only allowed to wear on special occasions, such as my grandmother's funeral. Usually my mother waited to retrieve clothes that fell till she'd finished hanging the whole wash, worried as she was about ruining clothes from too much soaking, but this dress had too much value to let it lay out in the street. She left the clothes in the sink and went down after it.

We lived three floors up from the street and, perhaps from some conviction the dress was too precious for her to ball up under her arm, my mother carried a heavy metal serving tray down the stairs with her, one large enough to lay the dress out flat on. Because of this, it took her some time to get down to the street, long enough that a man she had not seen from the bedroom window had been able to wander into the alley. When she got there he was crouched over the dress.

My mother hit her tray on the wall of our building to get the man's attention. He was a tiny man in a thick black canvas jacket—obviously a drifter by the smell of him which, along with the pinch of sweat, was reminiscent of damp earth after a rainstorm. His hair was matted so flat against his head it looked like a ragged cap. He hadn't the sense to drop the dress at my mother's warning, but instead pressed it against his mud-stained shirt. He kept his eyes trained on my mother's face, as though if he watched her long enough she'd let him be.

My mother hit her tray against the wall again. This time she clearly meant it as a threat. The alley was deep and narrow, and the sound reverberated to its end. I heard the sound through the open window to the bedroom, where I'd been sleeping while my mother did the wash. Because I had heard it twice now, I sat up to look out.

The man continued staring at my mother. To my knowledge, he didn't even blink. He was, despite his impoverishment, an attractive man. He had the long, high cheekbones of a man in a clothing catalog—likely the result of malnutrition—and the deep shadows that formed in the creases of his face were the kind that made you want to lean in close, to see what facial features they obscured. He held my dress before him like a shield and approached my mother.

"Ma'am, please," the man said. "I have nothing."

He didn't seem like the kind of man to have a family. If anything, I could imagine him abandoning one. He was unmistakably a drifter. He probably had plans to sell the dress.

"I have nothing either," my mother said. "I'm sorry."

My mother hit the man on the head with her tray. She hit the side of his face, near his left ear. Once the sound of the tray stopped resonating, I heard him cry. He sniffled quietly but didn't sob.

My mother held the tray out to him to indicate he should set the dress on it. I was leaning out the window now. The man wiped his nose with the sleeve of his jacket, rubbing some dirt over his face, but he didn't set the dress down. There was a flat red square across his forehead now. He only kept staring at my mother.

After a moment, she hit the man again, this time on the top of his head. His knees gave out at once. He fell head first onto the muddy pavement, using the dress as a cushion for his face. My mother waited a moment to see if he would get up again, and when she saw he'd do nothing more than shiver she pried the dress out of his hands, letting his head fall onto the pavement. She balanced the tray on one arm and tried to lay the dress out flat on it, but when this proved too difficult she set the tray on the man's back. With both hands she shook the dress out and pressed it flat against the tray. She lifted it up and went back into our building. I watched the man lie in place till I heard my mother at the door, then I lay back in bed as though I hadn't noticed anything. When I was able to look again, the man was gone.

Upstairs, my mother put the dress back in the sink and washed it again. When she came into the bedroom to rehang it, she saw I was up and asked me to help carry clothes out. I refused. I didn't speak but simply lay in bed.

Once the dress was clean and dry, I hid it. We only had one closet, so I couldn't put it there. Instead I snuck into the basement at night and balled it up behind one of the boilers. My mother had no reason to ask about it again for years, as I'm sure she believed it was in the bottom of the dresser still, and even though I grew, we had neither the money nor the time required to resize it. It was able to stay holed away somewhere beneath us, gathering heat and dust. When, years later, my grandfather died and we organized a funeral, my mother searched the entire apartment for it. She went through every cupboard and under all the pieces of furniture we had, murmuring over and over *the proper dress*, but she kept to our apartment, not the basement. In the end I was not allowed at the funeral at all.

Before she left for the church, before she gave up looking for it, my mother sat me down at the kitchen table and asked if I had the dress. She stooped her shoulders down so that her face was at my level. She looked straight at me, refusing to blink.

"It's your responsibility to keep track of it," she said. "When did you wear it last?"

"I don't know," I said. "I never wear it."

She kept on staring at me, not saying anything. Eventually I had to look back at her, or else she'd have known for sure that I was lying. There was a desperation in her look, one she expressed by moving her eyes across my face as though searching for some crack through which she could catch a glimpse of the truth I was hiding. I was scared she was preparing herself to slap me, just as she'd hit the drifter years before, but still I just stared back.

After a moment, my mother looked away.

"Well, I guess it's gone for good," she said, and for all intents and purposes this was true. I never went to the basement again, and for all I know the dress could be there now.

MARK PAWLAK

FAMILY LAUNDRY

"I was [lower class] before I came up in the world, true, but lower-middle class, not working-class. Very important distinction. My old dad got wild if you said he was working-class. Worse than calling him a Jew."
— Kingsley Amis, *"Stanley and the Women "*

I would paint childhoods of brick walls and
mother's flowered red apron,
red brick the houses;
brick community
in which courtyards of paved-over grasses
it is evening
and the children are playing, among garbage cans,
hide-n-seek
from the shadows of squalor;
and where the moon in a rage
is roaming the neighborhood
for a single tree to break against.

Let them hang that in their museums!
—from *The Buffalo Sequence*

This untitled poem is one in a sequence about my childhood that appeared as a small press chapbook in 1974. It was my first book publication. I was thrilled to have a collection of my poems in print to share with friends and fellow poets, even if just a slender volume. Three years later, an expanded edition appeared in a finely crafted version from a nationally prominent literary press. Having a full collection published with the potential for reaching an audience beyond Cambridge and Boston was confirmation that

I was a real poet. It boasted an introduction by a renowned American poet, who championed my work, and it garnered positive reviews in a few places ranging from the *American Poetry Review* to the *Buffalo Evening News* to the *Polish-American Journal*. I was proud of my accomplishment and thought my family would be, too. It never occurred to me that my parents would be anything but pleased I had "immortalized" my blue-collar Buffalo childhood. Wrong! I'd sadly miscalculated: a failure of imagination on my part. The book caused a furor back home.

My father, a man of few words, was too angry to speak, but my mother, ever the spokesperson for the two of them, didn't hesitate to inform me that what I had done in publishing these poems was the equivalent of airing the family's dirty laundry. I'd told the world that we had once lived in a housing project; worse, I had described those childhood years when my family struggled to make ends meet with fondness. Mom made it clear I had embarrassed her and Dad by suggesting that we were once lower class.

Mom's second line of defense—or attack—was to argue that the Langfield projects of my youth were nothing like what they had since become, nothing like the projects where my current Cambridge high school students resided either, for that matter. Mom claimed that our neighbors back in the 1950s were all hard-working folks; whereas today, she continued, in 1970s Buffalo as also in Cambridge, the project tenants were families on the public dole, single mothers on welfare with lots of kids instead of two-parent households—not the kind of self-respecting working people we had known. She also noted that housing project tenants were now mostly African American. The brick courtyards I so fondly evoked in my poems, she added, had become dangerous drug and crime infested habitations.

I had to grant that there was some truth to Mom's argument, even if she'd overstated. My memory of my brick and asphalt childhood neighborhood *was* colored by my adult observations of my then current students' housing project lives; things had run downhill considerably since the 1950s. Nevertheless, what is important here in recalling Mom's response to my poems, was her investment in covering over that difficult period in our family's life, a time of economic hardship she and Dad had successfully navigated by means of grit, determination, and just hard work. It was a period my parents had put behind them and had conveniently forgotten once their fortunes improved, instead of something to be proud of having overcome, as I thought.

෩෨෦෩෭

Erasure

"For a long time after World War II the middle-class American family . . . seemed to be moving on a steady upward economic course," wrote Nicholas Lehmann (*New York Review of Books*, 1994). "But in the early 1970s, at about the time of the OPEC embargo, family income leveled off. . . . Perhaps," he added, "what makes the middle class seem so imperiled today is that the buoyant years between the end of World War II and the 1970s are being used as a point of comparison . . . ."

Those post-World War II boom years were exactly coincident with my childhood, adolescence, and early adulthood—my formative years. It was a phenomenon never experienced in our country before and not one that is likely to come again. Lehmann, quoting Katherine S. Newman's study *Declining Fortunes: The Withering of the American Dream*, described my parents to a T as belonging to "the generation that entered adulthood in the affluent years following World War II," to whom "opportunity seemed limitless." People who held blue-collar jobs and whose values were thoroughly working class, like my parents, were nevertheless able to afford the trappings of a middle-class existence because of the boom. By the time I was in high school, ever increasing salaries and the high value of the dollar had enabled them to afford such luxuries as a split-level home in a new suburban housing development, a new car every five years (instead of yet another used one), and a college education for their three children: brother Chuck at Northwestern, brother Greg at SUNY Albany, and me at MIT.

But, up until my brothers and I left home, Dad would still make us sit, one after the other, in a chair in the middle of the kitchen, where he'd drape us in a sheet, and give us haircuts. He used the same barber kit he had acquired as a cost-saving measure back when we lived in the projects. Mom, for her part, still hemmed our pant cuffs, and "took-in" or "let-out" waistlines. And together Mom and Dad still preserved peaches, tomatoes, and waxed beans, buying them cheap in bulk, or visiting pick-your-own orchards in season. My brothers and I joked about the basement shelves lined with Mason jars: "Enough to last us through a nuclear winter."

It's not surprising then that my parents and I viewed things differently. They had chosen willful amnesia until my poems had inconveniently reminded them of early hardships. They wanted to focus instead on their then current social status, believing the illusion that, for them and their children, things had always been the way they were now.

ႄၷႄၷ

Joads

I was heartened when I chanced upon *Coming of Age in California,* one of several books by Gerald Haslam, a writer whose background echoes my own, and who experienced, albeit indirectly, a hometown literary reception analogous to mine. Haslam's collections of stories, memoirs, essays, and critical studies chronicle the lives of people in California's Great Central Valley small towns and cities: Modesto, Merced, Visalia, Delano, and Bakersfield. I feel I know him like a brother, we have that much in common: We both grew up in blue-collar families; we were both first generation college students; and we have each made careers of teaching in universities and writing and publishing books about the people and places that nurtured us.

Haslam was born in Bakersfield, and grew up in nearby Oildale, the son of an oil worker and a mother of Mexican descent. He and Merle Haggard were high school classmates. (Haslam is eleven years older than me.) After graduating, he worked as a farm fieldhand, a store clerk, and an oil field roustabout and roughneck. After serving two years in the Army, he attended Bakersfield Junior College, then San Francisco State University, eventually earning a PhD from The Union Graduate School. "Class consciousness," he wrote in *The Other California,* "has been an inescapable aspect of growing up in this place where some friends summered at the country club while others toiled in packing sheds."

What I found especially resonant, in reading Haslam's accounts, was his description of his community's attitude toward *The Grapes of Wrath.* As a high school student, he had attempted to borrow a copy from his public library, but it wasn't kept on the shelves with other titles. As he tells it, the book was locked in a drawer in the librarian's desk. Community standards at the time held that it wasn't appropriate reading for impressionable minds.

Steinbeck's great novel was essentially banned in much of the Central Valley because it offended the powerful farm-owning class, and because—and this really struck a chord with me—it reminded the Okies of the poverty they had come from. "No one I asked had anything good to say about the novel or its author," Haslam wrote, "but no one ever mentioned agricultural economics or unions or sedition, either. . . . No, everyone I queried in 1952 alluded to foul language, nasty scenes, too demeaning characterizations. . . . I seemed to have read a different novel. The characters in *The Grapes of Wrath* talked just like Buford Roy Daniels, like Mr. Clay and Mrs. Pruett, like the Bundys, the Haggards, the Purvises and the Hillises with whom we lived and socialized."

Reflecting on that time, Gerry Haslam could see, as I could not yet when I sent a copy of my poems home, was that, "Steinbeck's Joads were an economic notch below those good people, in part because our Oildale and Arvin friends had already begun to make it in the Golden State by the time I knew them: they were working, they were buying houses, their kids were attending school." The descendants of Dustbowl Okies came of age, married, had children during the postwar economic boom, much as my own parents did, when the rising economic tide lifted all ships. They were able over a span of years to pull themselves up out of hard-scrabble existence to a modicum of comparative luxury, lower-middle class if not middle class. "Earlier hardships remained unrevealed," Haslam noted, in a statement that tailor-fit my own parents, "because they did not seek pity."

My mother would argue, and the people Haslam writes about would likely concur, that you are defined as much by your dreams and aspirations as by your economic reality. This is America after all, where you are what you make yourself to be unless circumstance—job-loss, illness, alcoholism, drug addiction, institutional racism, or any number of other things—conspire to undermine your strivings at every turn. But barring setbacks, and if you are lucky enough to live through a period of good economic times, then why not believe you always were what you aspired to become like the humble caterpillar that progresses through multiple instars then pupates to finally emerge, metamorphosed, as a butterfly with resplendent wings?

CQ🔊CRBO

Class Dismissed

In a certain way, my mother's disagreement with me about social status, our mutual confusion about the murky boundary between working class and middle class, is just a version of the unresolved arguments among the Cambridge high school kids I was teaching when I wrote my "Buffalo Sequence" poems. The ones who lived in the projects—some, but not all, from single parent (female) households; some, but not all, on welfare—spoke of themselves as working class. Their classmates who lived on adjacent streets in apartments in wood-frame three-deckers, in that mixed Irish and French Canadian blue-collar neighborhood, were in their view middle class (they weren't into discriminating between lower-middle and middle class). Conversely, the three-decker apartment dwellers, spoke of *themselves* as working class and considered the projects dwellers lower class, i.e., poor.

For me it's not an either/or question but rather both. I'm both the kid who grew up working class and the adult who lives a professional middle class life simultaneously. Like the wiggle cards of the 1950s, viewed from a certain angle one aspect appears, but tilt the card and the other comes to the fore.

"Many members of the middle class became middle class only a generation or two ago, thanks precisely to the post-World War II boom . . . ." [Nicholas Lehmann again] "The newness of the status only makes the possibility of slipping back to the socio-economic status of one's immigrant grandparents seem greater and more frightening." The fear of sliding back down that ladder is what propelled my parents to vote for Ronald Reagan in 1980, believing that he would fulfill his campaign promise to "Make America Great Again." Today, having dusted off Reagan's slogan, Donald Trump would have no doubt persuaded my parents to join his camp, too, were they still alive.

Our national paper of record recently printed an Op-Ed that tried to make sense of why many blue-collar workers who lack college educations supported Donald Trump for President, seemingly against their class self-interests. It cited Jonathan Rothwell who conducted a recent Gallup Poll: "People often compare their standard of living with the standard they experienced while growing up. The most dissatisfied individuals," noted Rothwell, "tend to be the ones who don't think they have matched or exceeded their parents' economic standing." He concluded that "they have merely bought into the American idea of progress—which implies that every generation should have a better life than the previous one—and found their own situation wanting."

The post-war boom, along with the 1950s McCarthy inspired Communist scare, conspired to banish "working class" from our lexicon. Until the surprise election of Donald Trump, the term had largely gone the way of steel mills, auto plants, and labor unions in rust-belt cities like Allentown, Buffalo, Columbus, and Detroit. Post-election, its usage has been revived by the liberal media to explain why white voters of marginal means believed a billionaire real estate mogul offered their best chance to realize the "American Dream."

Poverty, meanwhile, hasn't gone away. The poor are, if anything, worse off than they were ten or twenty years ago. Such categorical terms as "poor," "middle class," and "upper class" are still in common usage, but the "service" worker has replaced the "blue-collar" laborer, and "the one percent" is used to designate those we once called "filthy rich." The slipperiness of class definitions, which my parents and I argued over, was nicely captured by Bronx-born Nuyorican poet Edwin Torres in remarks he made during a forum on writing and class held at The Poetry Project at St. Mark's Church in the Bowery (circa 1996):

> I work in my home—*working class*
> It's on computer—*middle class*
> I sometimes have a latte while working—*upper class*
> It's in a paper cup—*working class*
> I sometimes write about art openings and yachts—*upper class*
> It's always sarcastic—*middle class*
> Writing doesn't support me—*working class*
> If I get a grant, it helps—*lucky ass*
> My glasses look like designer frames—*upper class*
> They cost five dollars—*working class*
> I have the appearance of a beatnik—*poetry class*
> Aquí Se Habla Español—*Spanish class*
> I've been asked to speak on this panel—*working class*
> I could go on and on—*class dismissed.*

C.W. SPOONER

SHOE DOG

It was a few minutes past closing time as I unlocked the door and let the last customers out into the cold Minnesota night. We wished each other Merry Christmas several times as they headed for the parking lot. I held the door open for a minute, letting the icy blast of air flow around me. The temperature would dip below freezing again, typical for Minneapolis that time of year. It hadn't stormed for a few days and mounds of dirty snow had been pushed to the edges of the lot. The covered walkway along the open-air mall was equipped with speakers playing songs of the season. I paused to listen to Frank Sinatra sing "Have Yourself a Merry Little Christmas."

The holiday season of 1964 had been a good one at Grove Shoe Southtown. We'd sold a lot of merchandise, mostly fur-lined slippers, knowing they'd likely be returned right after Christmas. But hey, that was the shoe business. I relocked the door and waved to Paul at the back of the store. He hit the switch to douse the lights, except for those in the back room and the strings of colored bulbs lining our display windows. I walked to the rear of the store to join the rest of the staff. Our manager, Dan Harden, kept a refrigerator in the back stocked with Coke in those classic little bottles, and my favorite beer—Grain Belt Premium. Our tradition at the end of a hard day was to sit for a few minutes and enjoy a cold one before heading home. But this night was different. Dan had called a staff meeting.

We pulled together folding chairs, boxes—anything that constituted a seat—and waited for Dan to join us. There was Paul, a high school student, smart, cocky, full of fun; Norm, in his mid-thirties, Dan's best friend and classmate from their school years; Aileen, Dan's wife, a pretty blonde, sharp-tongued and witty, who came in on weekends to help out at the front desk; and of course, me, in my second Christmas season as a part-timer, logging as many hours as I could, trying to make ends meet for my family.

Dan walked into our circle and turned slowly, looking at each of us in turn. "Okay, listen up. We have a problem." He paused, cranking the drama meter all the way to the right. "We've been coming up short in the register. It's been going on for a while. Twenty here, twenty there. It has happened too often to be a simple mistake, making incorrect change or something." He stopped again and looked around. "The owners know about it and they are all over me. My job is on the line. This cannot go on. It has to stop now." Another pause. "Does anybody have anything say?"

I looked at Norm and Paul in shock. It couldn't be one of us. We were too close, like a family, too loyal to Dan to ever dip into the till. My mind went to two other employees, newcomers to the team, guys who generally worked the early hours. I didn't know them that well. Maybe it was one of them?

Norm spoke up. "Jesus, Dan. That's heavy. But I know Chet and I know Paulie, and it's not one of us. And it sure as hell isn't Aileen."

We laughed and looked at Aileen, but she wasn't smiling. Dan glared at us, but he had nothing more to say. He reminded us to check the work schedule for the coming week, then said the meeting was over. We bundled up—coats, scarves, gloves, hats, galoshes—and headed for home. I was still in shock as I merged onto the freeway, thinking about the guys I worked with.

I couldn't picture Paul taking money from the register. The image just wouldn't come into focus. Dan was Paulie's role model, his idol. He even imitated Dan's snappy dialog with customers. And he was just a good, hard-working kid. There was no way Paul was stealing from the store.

As for Norm, he and I had really hit it off. He was a great guy and we had a lot of interests in common, like sports, politics, jazz music. We even drove the same model car, a 1963 Corvair Monza. Mine was bronze, his was silver. The Corvair was probably the worst car General Motors ever rolled out, the subject of Ralph Nader's indictment of the U.S. car industry in his book, *Unsafe at Any Speed*. But the Monza was a sexy little beast, a sporty model with bucket seats, and we loved our certified lemons no matter what Ralph Nader said. Norm was easy going, funny, well-read, and it was easy to see why he and Dan were best friends.

No, it couldn't be Paul or Norm. It had to be one of the early shift guys. Didn't it?

℘℘℘℘

Work smarter, not harder. That's great advice to live by, but I could never make it happen. My solution to the problem of keeping a roof over my family's head and food on the table was to add hours, or an additional job, or both. In other words, *work harder.*

Sarah and I married in 1961 at the age of nineteen, and by the time we were twenty-one, our beautiful daughter Kaitlin was born. I worked for Northwest Airlines in the reservations office at the Twin Cities airport, which meant answering incoming calls from prospective passengers and booking flights throughout Northwest's system, plus connections with other carriers. Good, honest work that didn't pay worth a damn. Three hundred and thirty-three dollars a month to be exact. Oh, you got passes for free travel, more than you could use, but that didn't pay the rent. We weighed the cost of childcare and discovered it didn't pay for Sarah to continue working in the accounting department at Sears. Instead, she would stay home and take care of Kaitlin and we would take on the duties of managing our twenty-unit apartment building. That involved showing vacant apartments, taking rental applications, vacuuming the halls and stairs, managing the trash incinerator, and logging tenant complaints to be passed on to the mother ship for action. The benefit was a deep discount on the two-bedroom manager's apartment located on the basement level of the building.

It wasn't enough. Expenses continued to outweigh income.

That's what led me to Southtown Shopping Center in the fall of 1963, looking for a part-time job. I filled out applications at Sears Roebuck and Montgomery Ward, then strolled down the open-air mall looking for other possibilities. I stopped in front of a store—Grove Shoe—and pretended to inspect the merchandise displayed in the window. My older brother had worked in a shoe store while attending college and I tried to recall the stories he'd told me. It had been a positive experience for him, being a union job in the city where we lived at the time. He'd made out well, given base pay plus commission. Grove Shoe started to look pretty good. I gathered my courage and went inside.

A young man with sandy blonde hair, wearing dark slacks, a short-sleeved white shirt and tie, greeted me with a smile. "Hi! What can I help you with today?" I was impressed by his casual, confident manner.

"Hi. I'd like to speak to the manager." I tried to return his smile.

"Sure. He's in the back. Have a seat over here and I'll get him." He motioned toward a row of chairs in the men's section.

I'd put on my best suit—the one I'd been married in—and polished my shoes to a high gloss for this job-hunting excursion. I took a seat, looked around and saw a display of Florsheim shoes. Impressive! I couldn't afford Florsheims.

"Hi, there. Paulie tells me you'd like to see the manager. That would be me." The voice came from a tall, lean, dark-haired man, maybe mid-thirties, wearing what appeared to be the uniform of the day—dark slacks, short-sleeved white shirt, the collar opened, tie loosened. "My name is Dan Harden." He thrust out his hand. I stood and shook it firmly.

"Mr. Harden, nice to meet you. I'm Chet Stark."

"What can do for you, Chet?" He smiled and gave me the once-over. "And call me Dan. Mr. Harden is my dad's name." He chuckled, shoulders shaking, and his smile widened.

"Dan, I'm looking for a part-time job. I was wondering if you have any openings?"

"Could be, could be. Have a seat and let's talk. Tell me about yourself, Chet."

My heart was racing as I sat down. Maybe I was about to get lucky. I explained my job at Northwest and the fact that it didn't cover the bills. I needed to supplement my income and could work evenings and weekends, including Sundays if the store was open.

"What do you know about the shoe business, Chet? Any experience?"

Tough question. All I knew was my brother's anecdotes. I remembered him talking about "running stock," though I had no idea what that meant. I decided to pad my resume' with my brother's experience. "Well, I've never *sold* shoes, but I worked in a store during high school running stock."

That did it. I could tell Dan Harden was impressed. He offered me a job—minimum wage, no commission—and we discussed the hours I'd work. And that was it. I'd start that coming Saturday, a full day, ten to six.

Now all I had to do was call my brother and ask for help.

Cℰℬℭℰℬℭ

"So, you're going to be a *shoe dog*? Ha! Good luck with that." My brother Rich was amused by my career move. "How did that happen?"

I described the path that took me to Grove Shoe Southtown, including my assertion that I knew how to run stock. "Rich, you gotta give me a quick primer. What does 'running stock' mean?"

"It's the worst job in the business, little brother. But it's not rocket science. All the shoes in your stockroom will be arranged on the shelves vertically by style, and within style by size. When you get an incoming shipment, you just have to move boxes around to make room for the new stuff while keeping everything in order. Did you take a look in the back room? How tall are the shelves?"

"Pretty tall. I saw a couple of rolling ladders back there to reach the top."

"Yeah, that makes it harder when you have to shift stuff around. Like I said, not rocket science, but a hell of a lot of work. Oh, and by the way, if your coworkers send you out to borrow a 'shelf stretcher', don't go." Rich laughed out loud.

"What's a shelf stretcher?"

"It's the shoe biz equivalent of a snipe hunt, Chet. Don't fall for it."

Brother Rich was right: running stock was the worst job in the business, especially since the air conditioning didn't function very well in the back of the store. Moving boxes around in the summer was a real bear. Other than that, it was a good gig and Dan was a great guy to work for.

Grove Shoe was a small chain that originated in Cottage Grove, about ten miles south of the Twin Cities. Dan had been hired as a salesman, quickly rose to manager, and turned that outlet into a winner. The owners were so impressed, they moved him to Southtown Shopping Center, their first foray into the Twin Cities market. Dan did not disappoint. In his first year at Southtown, he doubled the volume of sales. He did it through sheer hard work and the force of his personality. And he loved taking chances, buying discontinued styles for pennies on the dollar, then selling them at deep discounts. The margins were slim, but Dan believed in volume, volume, volume. He was a tiger.

Dan was full of mischief, always laughing, cracking jokes. One of his favorite stunts was to call me out from the back room where I'd been moving stock around and introduce me as his resident expert.

"Mr. Stark, can you come here a minute?" I'd emerge from the back to find a young mother seeking the right shoe and perfect fit for her child. "Ma'am, Mr. Stark here is our children's shoe expert. He's completed certification programs specializing in children's corrective shoes. Mr. Stark, I'd like you to check the shoe I have here for little Johnny and tell me if the fit is right."

"Sure, Mr. Harden, glad to. Hello, Ma'am. Hi, Johnny. Okay, let me see what we have here." I'd go through the complete process, measuring Johnny's foot with the Brannock device, slipping the shoe on his little foot, checking the fit in the heel and toe, checking the width. All of this was very impressive to the young mom. Of course, my verdict would be that Mr. Harden had done a fine job and this shoe was a perfect fit for Johnny.

"Thank you, Mr. Stark."

"You're welcome, Mr. Harden. Nice to meet you, Ma'am, Johnny."

With that I'd retire to the stockroom. There were similar routines for men's and women's shoes, and it was amazing how many certifications I had earned. We peddled a lot of product, and had fun doing it.

Dan and Aileen were a great couple, obviously devoted to each other, but they had their differences and didn't try to hide them. They were sniping back and forth one day, really going at it, and she told him, "Yeah, well you're no prize package." Dan cracked up and immediately turned it into an ongoing joke. When anything went sideways around the store, we'd break out that tag line: "Yeah, well you're no prize package." Dan was a smoker and he'd punctuate the line by holding his Marlboro between his teeth while grinning from ear to ear.

What a guy! What a couple!

And now, a week before Christmas, we had a thief in our midst.

ᔥᔥᔥᔥ

Dan didn't say another word about the situation, and I assumed his impromptu staff meeting had solved the problem. I put it out of my mind. Christmas passed and we geared up for the *Season of Returns*, when most of those fuzzy slippers we sold would come flooding back into the store. The returns this particular year would also include what we referred to as Beatle Boots. The Beatles phenomenon had sparked a shoe fad that involved endless iterations of pointy toed boots with elevated heels, without question the ugliest footwear ever made. They were a hot item before Christmas. Now they were all coming back. Return season was a busy time and we were running shorthanded. Norm had been conspicuous by his absence.

I was at the register, finishing a sale, when Dan joined me. "Hey, boss, where is Norm? We really need some help."

Dan waited until the customer was out of earshot. "Norm won't be back."

"What? Why not? We really need him, Dan."

Dan was quiet for the moment. "Chet, I'm gonna share this with you. But I want you to keep it to yourself. Okay?"

"Yeah, sure."

"It was Norm who was taking money from the till."

"What? You're shitting me. No way in hell!"

"It was him. I caught him doing it, slipping twenties out of the drawer and into his pocket."

"You saw him do it?" I couldn't believe what Dan was telling me.

"Look up, Chet." He pointed toward the ceiling. "See that hole right there, in the corner of the tile?"

The store had a false ceiling, acoustic tile and lighting fixtures suspended from heavy wire. I looked up and saw the hole, about two inches in diameter, in the tile directly above the cash register.

Dan continued, "I crawled up there and watched for hours, watched you guys taking payments, making change, the whole thing. I saw Norm take about sixty bucks. I confronted him and he confessed."

I was dumbfounded. It was a minute before I could speak. "How the hell did you get up there?"

"Wasn't easy, believe me. But I had to do something. The damn owners were coming down on me hard. Told me if I couldn't fix it, they'd find somebody who could."

"But why, Dan? How could this happen? Norm's such a great guy."

"I know, I know. It killed me, Chet. You know how long we've been friends?" His eyes welled. "We were running buddies in high school, for God's sake. But Norm's going through a divorce. Child support, alimony, the guy was drowning, literally going under."

I felt a knot in my gut, unable to process this story. I shook my head, thinking about Norm and the desperation he must have felt.

"You know," Dan said, "I really thought it was you, Chet. I mean you told me how tough it is, supporting your family, making ends meet. I just figured—"

I practically snapped my neck turning toward him. He thought I was the thief.

The knot in my stomach tightened and I felt heat rise on my neck, anger washing over me. I remembered my father telling me again and again, "In the end, all you really own is your integrity, Chet. Never forget that." I hadn't always lived up to my dad's standards, but I'd never stolen anything.

Dan's comment weighed on me all day. I couldn't put it out of my mind. The more I thought about it, the angrier I became. I stayed until closing time and when we gathered in the back of the store for a cold drink, I removed the plastic name tag that read, "Chet Stark / Grove Shoe Southtown," and handed it to Dan.

"Goodbye, Dan. I won't be coming back. You can mail my final check."

I put on my winter gear and walked out the back door to where my Monza sat leaking oil on the pavement.

℡℠℞℠

About a week later, I was in the baby's room changing Kaitlin's diaper while she smiled and made cute baby noises. I dropped the wet diaper in the pail, recoiled at the odor as the lid closed, and made a mental note to look for a larger container. Sarah had recently informed me our second child was on the way. A flutter of panic stirred in my chest. How was I going to cover the doctor and hospital bills, not to mention everything else? Did I dare let the car insurance lapse and take my chances on the icy streets? No, that would be stupid, especially with babies in the car. I was going to have to hit the bricks and find a new part-time job—or go hat-in-hand to Dan Harden and ask him to take me back.

Sarah and I had pored over our situation, searching for a solution. She wasn't very happy with me. Oh, it was great that I stood up for my honor and all. But how much honor could we afford? And hadn't I lied about my experience in order to get the job?

The reminder stung like hell.

I was about to pin Kaitlin's diaper when the doorbell rang. Sarah answered it, and I heard a brief conversation involving a male voice. I assumed it was someone looking for an apartment. She came into the room and smiled at me. "There's someone here to see you." She took over the diaper duties while Kaitlin twisted and turned on the changing table.

I walked quickly to the front door. There stood Dan, a six pack of beer under his arm.

"Mr. Stark, I'm glad you're here." He flashed his patented grin. "I need my children's shoe expert."

I stared at him and my emotions flew all over map. I was annoyed, still a little angry, but mostly relieved. At least he'd come to me and I didn't have to go begging. And right there it hit me. Dan, Norm, and I had one sure thing in common: we were scared shitless, hanging on by our fingernails, trying to hold our lives together.

I nodded toward the beer tucked under his arm. "Is that Grain Belt?"

"You bet."

"Premium?"

"I know it's your favorite."

"Is it for me?" I was doing my best not to smile.

"Only if you accept my apology, for saying stupid things without thinking, 'cause Lord knows, I'm no prize package."

Now what can you say to that? I said, "Get your ass in here."

And just like that, I was a shoe dog again.

ALLISON WHITTENBERG

THE CIRCUMSTANCES

The man whipping my double latte
Has a deep knife scar
Across his throat
Whoever got him got him good
I wonder . . .
Was he victim or victimizer?
There's a stereotype for each scenario

Was it one of those mismatched fights—fist to switchblade?
Did he welch on a deal?
Does he have a bad-ass girlfriend?
Could it be from a jealous ex?
Accidental. was it?
Had he done time?

Is earning six-fifty an hour
Making four dollar
Cups of coffee
Getting on the right track?

KATE PASHBY

ANYTOWN, USA

I read enough Young Adult fantasy
to know that immortality is a curse

as you watch all your loved ones die
why, then, does mere survival feel the same?

entire Rust Belt kindergarten classes
wiped off the board by fentanyl

not enough alumni at the class reunion
for the mourner's kaddish

families devastated by opiates
for three generations

supposedly the clean and sober are the lucky ones
until we aren't

a single relapse with a single needle
is all it takes to die

but many relapse more than that
many others don't even make it that far

white people didn't care about the crack epidemic
until it reached their doorsteps

just as straight people didn't care about AIDS
until they started dying of it

immortality is always someone else's problem
until it's yours

PATRICIA BARONE

ROBERT AND MIKE, A LOVE STORY

If you have to call it "Indepedent Living,"
you live on the edge of loss, so Robert said "pad."
They'd brought their king-size bed, the Waterford,
a leather bar and books. A TV so Mike could feed
his political needs with the News Hour, but Robert
turned it off when Mike got mad and tossed
his wine at the morons on screen.

With common walls thin, the prim married couple
other side, complained to the director: "*Why* do
Christian people have to stand—no decent way
to put it—homosexuals? The slender one's okay, but
the fat guy howls. Their bed sounds begin at night fall!"

Robert knew for months that Mike just wasn't right.
Then, offhand, the doctor said, "Dementia. Memory Care
is just a floor away." All Rob heard was Locked Ward,
too far away for them to be: "Together forty years!"
Younger at only sixty-eight, Rob fretted that Mike,
alone in a fearful rage—strapped down?—would die.

Then Schatzie Oster, a licensed practical nurse
with eyes as blue as truth and muscular legs—
a former farm wife—happened to evaluate
Mike at Happy Hour, so Robert offered
beer and wine. She asked if he had mints.
He did, so it was safe to sip one ounce of Bud.

Mike, seventy-six, napped, so Robert whispered
their story, and her eyes were soft and steady.
"Together you'll move to Assisted Living," she said.
"I'll make sure you don't have righteous neighbors."

Assisted alright, as long as Schatzie did it, but one p.m.
a registered nurse lost her cool when Mike spit his pill
and mooned her. Rob removed him to the bedroom.
Livid, the R.N. sputtered, "Alzheimer's—he should be
locked in. After another eval—this time by me!"

"Not her," said the Charge Nurse, Schatzie's friend.
"Common sense doesn't come with a degree.
Michael's meds take time. They stay."

One calmer afternoon, Mike, who didn't recall
checkers, played dominos with Robert, and watched
Your Cheating Heart. By chance, Mike switched
to news, and Rob returned from the john to find
Mike glassy-eyed before the president he hated.

"Who's that?" Mike asked. How Robert missed
his lover's curses; he wept in the stiffest whiskey
and gave Mike watered wine, against the rules.
Then Schatzie came and offered her shoulder.

MELVIN AND MARY, ANOTHER LOVE STORY

Melvin

In Assisted Living, I asked Schatzie,
our favorite nurse, to wheel my Mary
up from another floor, Skilled Care,
to lie with me each afternoon.

She lifted Mary into bed with me,
then closed the door. Never, with a wink
or look, did she remind us that we were old.
She didn't tell a soul, but then I broke my leg.

I exist in the room next to Mary's, farther
away from her than ever—we're never alone.
The doctor said, "You must adjust to aging
and loss of privacy."—"Easy for you to say,"
I said, "You're not sleeping in a single bed."

Shatzie

You'd think there was a law against love
for people over seventy! "A younger couple
has a double bed," I said to the director, who
replied that Melvin and Mary weren't married.

"So what," I said, "about their long life together?"
Our lawyer agreed, so the boss released the key
to the guest room (also used for death vigils).
Unbelievable—she gave them a leaflet on safe sex!

All eight children felt ashamed but the youngest.
"Let's not act like bastards. Common law's good
as church." The eldest said our chapel was better
and invited her parents to a wedding, their own.

Mary said they wouldn't—"Not until Robert,
our neighbor, can marry Mike." I say, Amen.

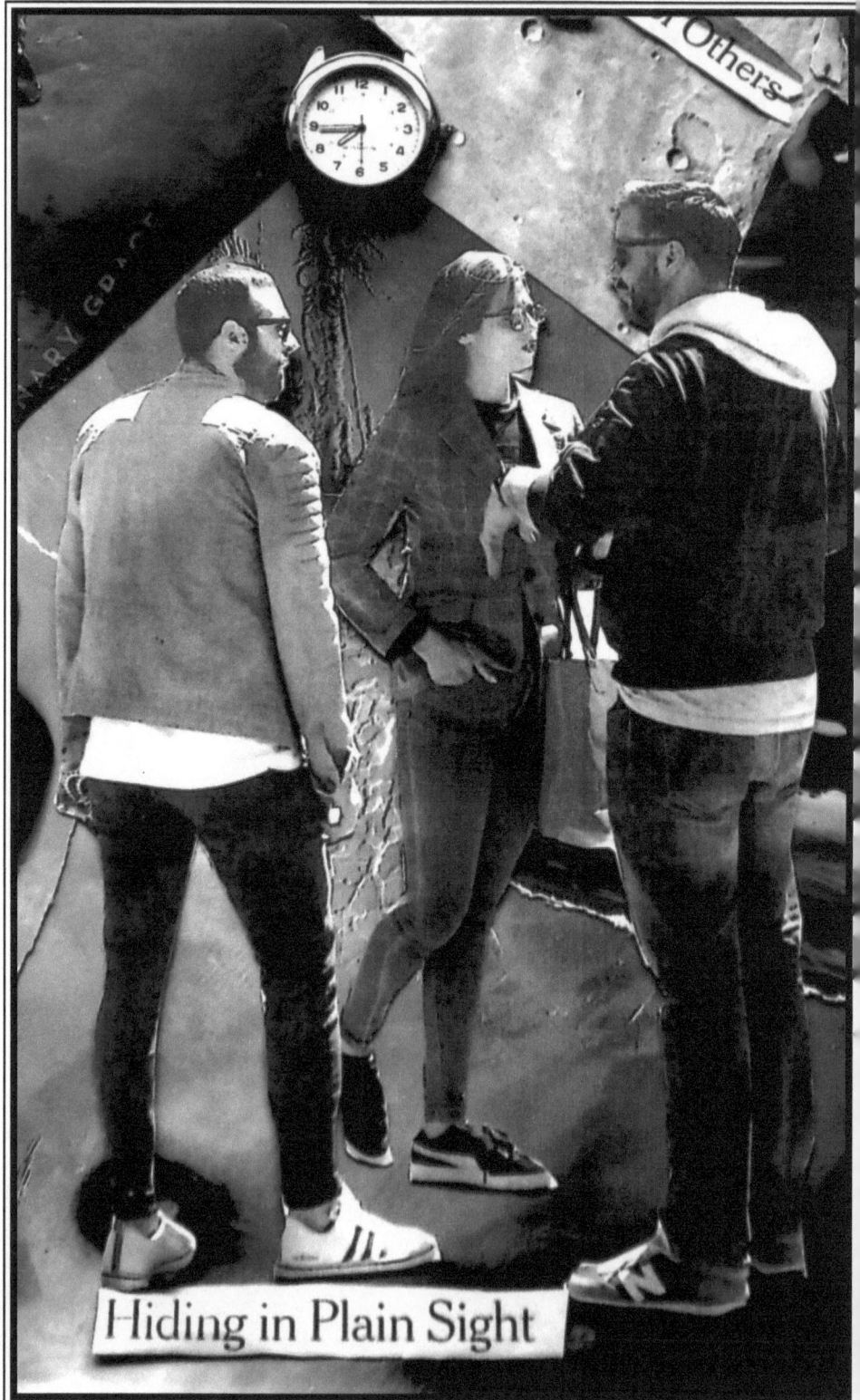

TERRY SANVILLE

DRIVING WITHOUT LIGHTS

All lies. But as a high school kid in 1965, lying seemed so easy while telling the truth much harder. My best friend Ray and I told our parents we were driving south, to Pacific Ocean Park for a day of barfing our guts out on the amusement rides. Our *real* destination? Ray's girlfriend's house in Bakersfield, two hundred miles to the east. Ray had met Marsha, a hot little redhead, at some intrastate scholastic event. They were both geniuses. But it definitely wasn't Marsha's brains Ray traveled halfway across California to fondle.

We left Santa Barbara early Saturday morning and took the coast route south to Ventura. My beat-up '59 Renault Dauphine strained to keep up with freeway traffic.

"Yeah, ya know, she asked me if, ya know, I wanted to go all the way," Ray confided.

"She did? Really? So what did you tell her?"

"What do ya think?" Ray said, grinning. "But her parents are always around, and if we got caught . . ."

"So what do you want *me* to do about it?"

"When we get to her place, lend me your car so we can drive somewhere."

"Are you kidding? You want to do it in this matchbox?" I had a quick vision of Ray's six-foot-three gangly body banging around in the Renault's tiny back seat, legs sticking out windows, elbows in eye sockets.

"No, stupid," Ray said. "I told Marsha to bring a blanket. We'll find someplace, ya know, where we can . . . "

"And what am I supposed to do while you're out there committing mortal sins?"

While Ray and I had been brought up Catholic, the promise of first time sex easily overpowered any religious scruples. Besides, there was always *confession*, although I didn't envy the prospect of telling some gray-haired

Irish priest about screwing some nubile babe and feigning sorrow for my sins. I felt mostly sorry I wasn't in on the action. Maybe Marsha had a girlfriend?

"We'll drop you somewhere and pick you up later," Ray said.

"Great, simply great," I muttered. "Why don't ya just ditch me at the next off-ramp and I'll hitchhike home."

"Nah, too dangerous. Besides, I'd probably crash this toy car of yours on the highway."

"At least I *got* a car."

At Ventura we turned inland, passed through groves of orange trees and the sleepy town of Santa Paula, then struggled over the Grapevine Grade, rowing the car uphill in its lower gears. By early afternoon we putt-putted down a shaded residential street on the south side of Bakersfield and turned into a driveway. The Renault's engine crackled and stank of burning electrical wires. We barely got out of the car when Marsha ran from the house and threw herself into Ray's arms, standing on her tiptoes and stretching her slender body to reach his mouth. She wore pink Capris and a pullover sweater that did little to hide her large breasts. They stood French kissing in the driveway. Marsha's shoulder-length blaze of hair hid Ray's face. I nervously eyed the front door, expecting her parents to come popping out at any moment. Finally, the lovebirds came up for air.

"How ya doin,' Toad?" Marsha asked and smiled.

"Great. Always wanted to see Bakersfield."

"Oh come on, it's not that bad." She gave me a quick kiss on the cheek.

I'd been called Toad ever since second grade when Jimmy Donovan said I looked like the main character in his illustrated edition of *Wind in the Willows*. So yeah, I got a big bump in the middle of my nose, moles everywhere, and hardly any chin. But that's enough to deal with without being called a stupid nickname. Actually, I didn't care what the girls called me so long as they were friendly.

"Come in and meet my parents," Marsha said, "then we can go to the park."

I raised an eyebrow. Ray shrugged. Her parents seemed nice enough, your basic *Ozzie and Harriet* couple. Ray fed them a story about how we had come back from a school trip to Sacramento and decided to drop in for a quick visit. They bought it without asking questions. In a few minutes we escaped to the car and cruised through town. Marsha brought along a blanket. Looked like she took it right off her bed. Damn that Ray, it had to be his height that attracted the babes, surely not his wavy grease-coated hair or that stupid grin.

Marsha pointed and I slid the car to a stop along the curb bordering a city park, complete with a central lake. Couples in canoes enjoyed the spring sunshine.

"Come on guys, I'll get us a boat," Marsha said and took off toward the rental stand.

"So what's this about?" I asked Ray.

"Beats me. Maybe she just wants to warm things up before, ya know . . ."

"Hey, you're the Casanova. I'm counting on you for pointers."

Ray grinned and ran to catch up with his girlfriend. We paddled around the lake for a couple of hours, with me doing the paddling and Ray and Marsha making out in the bow, trying to remove each other's tonsils with their tongues. There was also a fair amount of copping of feels, but I tried not to stare. Finally, Marsha broke free and stood up, her face beet red. The canoe rolled and the three of us tumbled into the warm muddy water, its surface overlaid with sycamore leaves splattered with goose poop.

Laughing, Marsha swam to shore, leaving Ray and I to retrieve the paddles and practice our Boy Scout method of clambering back into a canoe. Afterwards, we lay on the hot grass and stared up at the robin's-egg blue sky. Marsha's hair became a frizzy red ball as it dried. She looked even better without lipstick and makeup. I dropped off to sleep, my clothes steaming in the afternoon sun.

I awoke alone, the park mostly deserted. My Renault sat patiently at the curb, waiting for its master to coax it home. In the distance, Ray and Marsha stepped from a grove of trees. He had the blanket thrown over his shoulder and held her hand. Neither looked at the other. Jesus, they had done it and I had slept right through the grand event! Probably for the best. But Ray had better fill me in on the details or it would be a long ride home.

Nobody talked as we drove Marsha back to her place. On our way out of town I stopped at a Chevron station and asked the attendant to fill her up. It took three bucks of regular. While a real gutless wonder, the Renault only sipped gas. Even on my box-boy wages I could afford to drive just about anywhere. Ray stayed quiet the whole time.

We headed west on Highway 99 into the sun. "All right, so you want to talk about it, or what?" I asked.

"Nah, not really."

"Well, what was it like? This is a big deal, ya know."

"Hard to describe. Marsha is really somethin', I tell ya. She's way ahead of me."

"What da ya mean?"

"Ah, nothing. But if *I* had a car I'd be over here every weekend." Ray grinned and punched me in the arm.

"Hey, don't damage the goods, creep."

"Yeah, well I'm a creep with a bitchin' girlfriend. What da *you* got?"

"The car that's taking you home, so be nice or I'll ditch you in a broccoli field."

"Sorry. It's just hard to explain, the sex I mean."

"You could try."

"Nah, it's too personal."

"Okay, okay. So . . . how about them Dodgers?"

Ray cracked up and we settled back for the slow drive over the Grapevine toward Castaic Junction, the car's radio cranked up with us singing along with Herman's Hermits to *I'm Into Something Good.* We made it to the top and coasted down the back side.

Ray sniffed. "You smell that?"

"Yeah, it's just water overflowing from the radiator."

"No, it smells different, like rubber. You'd better pull over."

I jammed on the brakes and turned off the highway into the parking lot of some kind of truck repair shop. A line of semis with their hoods flopped open awaited service. We got out and walked to the back of the Renault. Smoke poured from the slotted vents above the engine cover. I carefully reached for the latch but it proved blistering hot. I grabbed a rag from inside the car and managed to get it open. Billows of gray smoke wafted skyward. A guy dressed in greasy coveralls ran toward us with a fire extinguisher. I watched the spark plug leads melt and fall away.

"Stand back, guys," the mechanic ordered and sprayed a fine white powder over the engine. The smoke stopped but the motor continued to crackle.

"What do you think would cause that?" I asked the mechanic.

"Hard ta tell. But ya definitely cooked that dang toy motor. My guess is ya ran it without water."

"No way. I had it checked in Bakersfield and it was full up."

"Then it could be a stuck thermostat. But that sucker's fried, one way or another."

"Can you fix it? I have money to pay."

"Don't know. We might be able to get to it tomorrow, maybe on Monday."

The color drained from Ray's face. I'm sure mine looked the same. "Why will it take so long?"

"These pipsqueak French engines aren't worth shit. When ya heat 'em up, the head warps and they leak from the seals. Gotta plane the head flat, do a valve job, all new gaskets and sparkplug leads. It's a lot of work, and we got a full schedule."

"But we've got to be back to Santa Barbara tonight," Ray whined.

The mechanic grinned. "Sorry boys. You're outta luck. Maybe by the end of tomorrow, but no sooner."

"All right, all right, just do it, okay?" I followed the mechanic into the office to fill out the paperwork and leave a ten-dollar deposit. Afterwards, Ray and I stood at the edge of Route 99 and watched traffic roar past.

"So now what do we do?" Ray asked.

"Better call my Pop and have him come get us."

"Are you crazy?" Ray said. "We'll be grounded for life. Maybe we could hitchhike home."

"Yeah, maybe. But how am I gonna explain the car?"

"That's a problem. But we got a lot of time to figure it out. Let's get going. At least your Pop won't have to drive down here to pick us up."

"Yeah, maybe he'll only ground me for half a life."

We pasted grins on our faces and stuck out our thumbs. But motorists roaring down the Grapevine were definitely not predisposed to stop for two nerdy kids wearing short-sleeved Madras shirts and black Converse. The sun went down and the repair shop closed, leaving us in the dark. A cold wind raised goose flesh on our bare arms.

"Did Marsha take the blanket back with her?" I asked. A shiver racked my body.

"Yeah. Sorry. We didn't even use it."

"What da ya mean?"

"The ground was too wet from the sprinklers so we couldn't, ya know, lie down."

"So how did ya . . . "

"You figure it out. Do I need to draw ya a picture?"

"No, I get it, I get it." I slapped my arms and did jumping jacks in place to keep warm. But the minute I stopped, the night wind sucked away my body heat. I thought about Marsha's naked body in various poses. But after a while even those visions of carnal ecstasy couldn't distract me.

"Maybe we should start walking," Ray said. "At least it will make us warmer."

"Ye . . . ye . . . yeah. Okay."

We shuffled along the highway's black shoulder, holding our arms and extended thumbs out as we went. It began to rain. When our shirts got soaked, the dye ran down our arms, creating dark tattooed rivers. I stuffed my hands in my pockets and listened to Ray mutter to himself, "What an idiot, fuckin' idiot. Can't even drive somewhere without everything screwin' up. You think my folks will ever let me take a trip again? Hell no . . . this is fuckin' stupid . . . damn."

It was past eight o'clock when a '54 Mercury pulled over and its vault-like front door swung open.

"*Hola hombres. Cómo están?*" the driver said. He was a round Mexican with a thin mustache. His wife of equal girth occupied the front seat with two pint-sized children in back.

"*Lo siento. No hablo Españole,*" I said and tried to remember my sophomore Spanish.

"Ride you want?" he asked.

"*Si*, thank you, ah, *muchas gracias.*"

"Where you go?" he asked.

"Santa Barbara," Ray said.

"Only go Santa Paula. Take you there."

"*Gracias, gracias,*" I said.

The woman stepped out into the rain and we climbed in back with the kids. The door clicked shut. Our driver eased out the clutch and the heavy Mercury accelerated. He shifted into second, and kept accelerating, the engine screaming. But right about the point where he should have shifted into third, he pushed in the clutch and let the car roll free until it slowed down.

"*Lo siento*, no got gear threes," he explained.

"*No es probleme,*" I said and he laughed.

For the next couple of hours we relaxed in the stuffy car as it charged

ahead then slowed, repeating its motorized wind sprints over and over. The
couple's shy kids wouldn't talk with us. In the front seat, the man and his wife
kept up a running argument in Spanish. I couldn't make heads or tails of it
but every once in a while they'd mutter the word *gringos*. So I felt happy when
we rolled into Santa Paula and got out near a corner Shell station. It was after
ten and only the nearby bars showed any signs of life. Some tough-looking
pachucos in muddy khakis and work boots stood smoking outside a saloon.
They stared our way. One of them pointed.

"Ah crap, get ready to run," Ray muttered.

"Run where?" I asked.

"Maybe we could hole up in the gas station and ask customers for rides."

"Yeah, that might work."

A half-dozen saloon patrons moved toward us. We trotted to the gas
station's office. But the high school kid inside waved us off and locked the
door. We turned to face the advancing gang, our backs pressed against the
cold plate glass. The lead pachuco threw down his cigarette, shoved a hand in
a front pocket and grinned.

A battered early-fifties Plymouth rolled across the hose in front of us
and the service bell rang. Two yahoos in leather jackets with greased-back
hair occupied its front seat. The pachucos stopped in their tracks and stared.

I moved to the driver's open window. "Say, you gentlemen wouldn't
want to give us a ride?" He was a big dude with mutton chop sideburns.

"Where you boys goin'?" He grinned, showing off gold teeth.

"Santa Barbara," Ray said.

"We might take you there, if ya buy us gas," the yahoo riding shotgun
said.

"Yeah, sure," I said. The bar gang retreated to the corner and talked
amongst themselves, glancing our way.

The station attendant came outside. "So what'll it be?"

"Fill 'er up," I said.

"Holy shit, this heap's never been filled since I owned it," the driver said
and laughed. "Get in, we'll take ya wherever ya wanna go."

Ray and I hastily climbed in back. The bar gang shambled back to their
posts outside the saloon.

"Yeah, we broke down just north of Castaic on the Grapevine," I said.
"Been trying to get back home since sundown."

"Figured you boys were pretty much shit outta luck," the driver said.

"We got nothin' better ta do. Haven't been to Santa Barbara in years," his shotgun partner said.

"So ya want a little somethin' to take the chill off?" the driver asked.

"Nah, it's plenty warm in here already," Ray said.

"No dummy, he means booze," I said. "If you got a bottle, pass it back."

The driver retrieved a pint of *Old Granddad* from the glove compartment, took a pull and passed it to me. I tilted the bottle and felt the liquid fire cauterize my throat. Ray grabbed it from my shaking hands and took a pull. His eyes got as big as ping-pong balls, but he managed to swallow the brew, gasping and sputtering afterward.

Neither of us had eaten anything since downing our sack lunches hours before. My stomach immediately absorbed the liquor into ye ole bloodstream, just like we'd been taught in biology class. I felt a great benevolence toward our current benefactors and for Ray.

"You guys are the best. I mean, jeez, we'd be screwed if it wasn't for you . . . ya know, sharin' your booze . . . and this being the day my friend Ray here lost his cherry."

"TOAD, shuddup, ya idiot," Ray complained, slurring his words.

"Toad, that's your name?" the driver said and laughed, ignoring Ray's lost virginity. "That's, like, really bitchin', 'cause ya sorta look like a toad."

"Thanks for the compliment."

"Yeah, Toad's waiting to be kissed and turn into a handsome prince," Ray said. He still held the bottle and took small nips in between giggling fits.

"All right, Romeo and Toad, settle down back there," the driver said. "Ya got to tell us where you live in Santa Barbara before y'all pass out."

"We live on the west side near Valerio Street. I'll show ya when we get there," Ray said and yawned.

We rolled out of town into the dark countryside west of Santa Paula. The car's radio broadcast XERB with Wolfman Jack from Chula Vista. With the car's heater cranked up, I faded in and out of consciousness. Ray passed out. But our benefactors took it slow. That old car could barely reach 45 before it started shaking itself apart.

Along a moonlit stretch of Highway 101 that bordered the Pacific, the Plymouth's lights blinked out. We continued forward into blackness. The shotgun yahoo fumbled with the wiring under the dashboard. The right side of the car dipped down as we drove onto the shoulder. The driver jerked the wheel and we shot toward oncoming traffic. A semi leaned on its horn and narrowly missed us. Its passing air blast pushed us to the right. Seconds ticked by but the driver held his speed, as if daring the night to throw something at us we couldn't handle. I held my breath. That darkened passage felt like the real deal, the kind of adventure I wouldn't soon forget. In a few moments the lights flickered back on. Ray cut loose with a loud snore.

At the south end of Santa Barbara, I opened the window and let the salt air wash over me. I had a killer headache and my stomach felt like it brewed battery acid. Ray looked greenish, but at least he could sleep through it. I guided the driver through the quiet city. Way past midnight, we motored down Hillside Avenue.

"Could you pull over here?" I asked them about a block from Ray's house. I didn't want to roll up in that heap and have to explain everything to his mom and dad.

I poked at Ray. "Come on, we're here. Time for beddie bye."

"Huh? What? Where the hell are we? Who punched me in the head?"

I hauled him out of the car into the black morning and handed the driver two dollars. "Buy yourself a six pack on us. You guys were great."

"Hey, if ya ever come through Santa Paula again, I could use another fill-up," he replied. The Plymouth drove off into the night, blue smoke puffing from its tailpipe.

We stumbled down the sidewalk. I shoved Ray toward his porch and watched him fumble for keys and press through the front door of his parents' house. I had a mile-long walk up Valerio Street hill to my home on Calle Poniente, giving me time to finish crafting the story I'd tell my parents. The day's events tumbled through my teenage brain, seeking some sense of order and meaning. I remembered the way Marsha smiled at me when she called me Toad, braving the gang of pachucos in that strange dark town, climbing into cars with strangers, and downing god-awful booze like an experienced wino.

From Valerio Street I turned up Calle Poniente. The German shepherd in the corner house woofed a few times but settled down. The lights blazed in my house, the front window curtains pulled back, my mother searching the street, waiting for my Renault's headlights to appear. I sucked in a deep breath, knowing a wave of relief then scorn would soon come crashing down. But after driving without lights, I knew I could take it.

This Is N
Way
hange?
ocusing attention
offer ho
isten
DEPEN
ove's Languag
IT TAKES HARD WORK TO BEHAVE LIKE AN
DISCIPLINE. YOU WANT IT TO BE SIMPLE, AND IT RARELY IS.
Home Truths

IV
FAMILY
ଓଞ୍ଜନଲ୍ଲ

GROW UP.
should count
HERE'S THE ANSWER:
BEHAVE RESPONSIBLY.
Nailing the Jelly of Reality to the
'New normal'
I'm not insane;
my mother had me tested.
the opposite of poetry in motion
What It
All Meant
Advocacy Is Love's Language
Try Talking to Strangers

AMBIGUITY
ଗୋଳମାଳ

ELLARAINE LOCKIE

AIRING DIRTY LAUNDRY

"What is it about hanging wash that disturbs people so?"
—*Galloping Bungalow*, diorama by David A. Thornburg,
Los Angeles Museum of Jurassic Technology

We hang from a cotton cord
dripping intimate details
that won't wash out
Labels sale-scissor slashed
broadcasting bra cup capacities
Brands that bare income brackets
and sizes sacred to fitting rooms

Dark secrets defenseless
in the scrutiny of daylight
Like elastic stretched and slack
Unmatched socks with holes
And stains betraying bodily functions
or housewifely inabilities

All open to invasion by omniscient eyes
that see us uninhabited
and envision unclad bodies
Conjured up as writhing shapes beneath sheets
blowing provocative in a breeze
Or as peeping Toms
prompted by public panties

Perhaps the source of anxiety
is simple inhibition
A throwback to puritanical oppression
Or the more discomposing possibility
that we are ghosts animating empty garments

Departed spirits that gesture death
as we float on gossamer dread
Our fingers crooking fears so diabolic
that we are often deferred drip free
to indoor dryers

LINDA MAXWELL

UNSULLIED

"Do I have a clean uniform to wear to the hospital tomorrow?"
My mother would ask around homework time.
The response always required a trip through the den,
Out to the garage and into the chilly washroom.

Sometimes it meant spraying
Or soaking
Or scrubbing
Or sending the white polyester through the wash again
With extra soap and care.

So it is with homework
And housework
And heart-work
and life-work.

We just start over—
Cleansing one shrouded stain at a time,
Trusting the season and the imperfect cycle
However late in the gloaming,
However early in the wearing.
However harmful sin professes to be,
We believe our souls can be

Spotless.

J. J. STEINFELD

THE IMPOSSIBILITY OF THE
ESCAPED FATHER'S LAUGH

No amount of time can diminish the memory of my father's laugh. He had an extraordinary laugh that came from deep inside his being, and it was as if he were trying to surround life and say that nothing could vanquish him. I heard that laugh all through my early years, and I occasionally joked with my brother and sister that I had heard it clear as a bell when our mother was pregnant with me. I picked up the expression "clear as a bell" from my father, and got in the habit of saying "clear as a bell, ding-dong, ding-dong . . ." My father never said the "ding-dong" part. Once, as a foolish Saturday-morning prank, my brother tied me to a chair, and my sister pulled a shiny silver bell from her coat pocket and started to ring it, first in one of my ears, then in the other, back and forth, louder and louder, asking me if I could hear our father's laugh. "We have decided that 'clear as a bell' is an evil incantation and you must stop repeating it," both my sister and brother said to me in voices they tried to make sound adult and spooky. They were teenagers then, me a bratty, big-mouthed ten-year-old, and it had been about a year since we last saw our father. The prank wasn't funny to me after a while, but my sister wouldn't stop ringing her bell until my crying became louder than the bell ringing. I have tried to imitate my father's laugh, but my efforts are always inadequate, even if I've had a few too many drinks and believe that my powers of reviving the past are stronger than they actually are.

The last time I saw my father, I thought he was going to cry, but all of a sudden he laughed, pushing away the gloom and scariness that was thick all around me and my sister and brother. We were in my parents' bedroom, and it had just started to snow, a particularly early snowfall. My mother had brought the three kids into the room before breakfast, and left us with our father. "Your father will explain and he will apologize," our mother said as she walked away from us. At the door, without turning around to look at anyone in the room, she yelled at the top of her voice, "I know he can explain to his children . . ." I could hear her running down the hall and then down the stairs and for a second I felt like following her, but then I heard my father's laugh. That long-ago laugh is encased in my memory, as is the less than half hour we were in the bedroom talking to our father. I remember my brother sitting on the edge of the bed, looking at our father, and my sister standing by the window, looking out, counting snowflakes she said a few days later, when we were at the dinner table and our mother was trying to convince us that the unhappiness in our family would not last forever. After the laugh, our father handed my brother an envelope, and gave my sister a large notebook that he took out of a dresser drawer. Later I learned it was a diary my father had kept for a long time, but my sister never let me read it. My brother opened the envelope in front of me, and a stock certificate was inside. Even at twelve years old, he had started to develop an interest in the stock market. I received a wallet with a check for twenty-five dollars in it, and twenty-five dollars in those days . . . It was a leather wallet that I kept with me for years, slept with under my pillow occasionally, only if I was really scared about something, thinking in my little kid way that the wallet had protective, magical properties, until some school bully grabbed it out of my pocket, and shoved it between the grates of a sewer. That was the closest I ever came to wanting to kill someone, but that bully was just too big and strong for me. It was more accident than any fighting skill, but I managed to knock out one of his teeth.

I was only nine years old at the time, but I remember everything that happened in that room exactly, in detail, and I remember it as a child and I remember it as an adult returned in time, observing, yearning to participate, not to alter events, but to savor them. I am no artist, having the most meager artistic abilities, yet I have drawn and painted and dreamed that scene so often that I can close my eyes and watch the four of us in the bedroom, hear my father's extraordinary laugh. He hugged me the longest and the hardest, whispered in my ear, "I didn't talk to God honestly . . ." We never saw my father again. As the police were taking him to jail, he escaped. There are many versions of the story and I don't see the point in repeating any of them, because I believe none of them is true. He escaped, and that was that. For months, every time the phone rang, I thought it was him. Sometimes, even today, when the phone rings, I think it might be my father, calling me to say where he is hiding. That is how I think of my father, hiding, or with a new identity. When I was younger, I imagined that he hid in a cave nearby and only came out to get food. When I got older, I thought he lived in a foreign country. Explorer, inventor, secret agent, daredevil pilot . . . there was no shortage of occupations I imagined for him. In dreams, I gave him assumed names, disguises, all the documentation he required to travel anywhere in the world. Yet he chose never to return home, and I could not will his return, even in my dreams.

After my father escaped, my mother became depressed, but she struggled along, saying that adversity and misfortune could be teachers, and she managed to learn from her hardships. She even returned to school and fulfilled a lifelong dream of becoming a nurse. Both my sister and brother moved away before each of them became twenty, my brother going to university but dropping out during his first year, and getting his own apartment. Not completing university certainly didn't stop my brother from becoming successful in business and having a lovely family. I've always admired how he can balance family and work. In my own life I have not been as successful, not in monetary terms, at least, but comparing myself to my brother has never been a satisfactory exercise for me. Over the years, when I was having financial difficulty with a business I was trying to run, he would lend me money, and never worried if I paid him back, never rubbed my face in it. Except once, about three years ago. We were celebrating Christmas at his house and I got annoyed with the way he kissed my daughter. She said it was no big deal, pointing to some mistletoe that was completely on the other side of the living room, but I told him the kiss shouldn't have been on the lips and shouldn't have been so long. An uncle's affection, he said, and I got more annoyed. She's only fifteen, and has enough adolescent turmoil to cope with, without having a horny uncle pawing all over her. I hadn't meant to call him a horny uncle, but it slipped out. He shouted at me for everyone in the house to hear, "I've lent you over seventy thousand dollars, my dear improvident brother, and you have paid me back eighteen thousand, five hundred. Not one cent of interest have I charged you . . ." He called me up on New Year's Day and apologized for *his* outburst, but he never apologized for kissing my daughter.

My brother has lent me money since then, and I do intend to pay him completely back. My brainy, successful brother. It was only recently that he told me he had been expelled from university for an evening of carousing that became too disorderly. I had always thought he quit. Cheap wine, he said, offering an excuse thirty-four years after the fact, then shook his head and said he wasn't even a drinker back then, like me.

My sister, at nineteen, did move back home for a brief period. I was fourteen and missing my father as much as ever, while my brother was seventeen and going through a period of real anger at him, and we were squabbling frequently over why my father had to escape. My sister, who had a crazy theory that our father had run off with another woman, was pregnant at the time and told everyone that things hadn't worked out. It was my brother who asked who had made her pregnant. Even my mother was irritated by the question. "A younger man," my sister answered, and laughed, but it was a laugh nothing like our father's. I doubt if there is a gene for that extraordinary laugh. A few weeks after the baby girl was born, my sister moved away, but after a couple years of having little to do with anyone in the family, she became the one who makes the effort to stay in touch, and I can remember only the odd time she did not visit for Christmas. I am almost fifty now, my brother fifty-three and my sister fifty-five. That little baby girl, my oldest niece, became a singer, and my mother to this day refuses to listen to anything she has recorded.

One time—I think it was during a birthday party my brother and I were throwing for her—I saw my mother pound a radio broken with her fists when her granddaughter's first big hit was being played, the song already a decade old by then. I always made a point to get her music, and have traveled a fair distance to see her in concert, but I understand what upset my mother. She described our family in some harsh lyrics, even though she never had any closeness with us. I've suspected for fifteen years now that my sister had given her daughter our father's diary. I told my mother that her granddaughter's first big hit was my sister's story, that my sister perceived the family and what happened to our father through a confused teenager's eyes, and my mother accused me of taking her side. I think only five, perhaps six, of my niece's songs are about our family, but that is more than enough for my mother not to forgive her. Strange, in the video for one of the songs, a mournful ballad about a frightened, tormented man who abandons his family, there's an actor who even looks somewhat like my father did. When he was in his early forties.

I never lied about my father to the woman I married, from our first date on, but the truth she received had been shaped and reshaped by years of my emotions dealing with his escape, and it was the adult who told her the story. When our only child was old enough, I told her as much as I could remember about my father. I wanted to open my hands and show her, cupped in the palms, the truth, as far as I knew the truth about my father, her grandfather, who could escape from any confinement.

When she was eight years old, my daughter had an experience that she still remembers. There was a man who watched her in the schoolyard. Her description was of a shabbily dressed man, maybe in his seventies, wearing a toque and a scarf on a warm afternoon. He had a loud laugh. She told her teacher, and her teacher called me. The laughing white-haired old man never showed up at the schoolyard again. The laugh she described was nothing like my father's. I was concerned with that episode, and in the back of my mind wondered if my mother hadn't told my daughter a few stories that might have influenced how she reacted to what was probably a lonely, disoriented old man wandering around a neighborhood school.

My daughter, when she was fourteen, got into trouble for the first time. That is, trouble with the police. It was a package of pencils she took from the store. The second time, she pushed over a display rack of magazines. Rotten pornography, she told the police. Another time it was a store window. She broke a liquor-store window. She never drank, though. For all her problems, she would have nothing to do with alcohol. And whatever problems I had with booze were under control before she was a teenager. Her other grandfather is a retired police detective, and took it upon himself to help her. Before it was too late, he said often at family get-togethers. Sometimes, when I was attempting to talk to my daughter, or to deal with her unruliness, I tried to imagine my father handling the situation, and using his laugh to remedy things, but when I laughed for my daughter, I saw on her face how ludicrous she considered my flawed attempts.

That last time with my father, when he was talking to me and my sister and brother, before he whispered to me that he didn't talk to God honestly, he told us that he was a wrongdoer, and he would be sorry for his wrongdoing for the rest of his life. *Wrongdoer* and *wrongdoing* were the words he used, as he was giving us our gifts. My daughter is not a wrongdoer at all, even though she has broken the law. She has a spirit that requires, at times, a desperate language.

I had a bad patch a little while back, my marriage in shreds, but I was determined to hold it together. My wife said I should see a professional and I agreed. I wasn't thrilled about the idea of seeing a therapist, but my marriage was important to me. My wife arranged everything. The therapist I was seeing asked during the first session—we hadn't been talking for more than ten minutes—what my father's crime had been. I sat there silent for I don't know how long, and she asked me again. "My brother has the newspaper clippings, my sister the diary. My niece's songs about the family were never specific—'. . . the crime that broke a mother's heart / the crime that made her kids liars at school . . .' Lyrics like that," I said, and I spent the rest of the first session talking about the time I got to hang out with my niece and her band.

During a vacation from sixteen-hour days trying to make a go of my then current business, I went to see my niece perform. I was able to go backstage, had a little pass her manager clipped to my shirt. After the concert we were in her dressing room, I'm sitting there with musicians in their twenties and thirties, a joint being passed around, and she offered it to me. I had already had some drinks before going to the concert, nothing serious, but I didn't want to get my head any more clouded. I told her I never remembered lying at school about my father, and she said that song, which she didn't care for any longer, had nothing to do with anyone in our family. But her fans still wanted her to sing it. It was the song that had been on the radio when my mother lost her temper and tried to annihilate the radio.

Had my childhood not been so disrupted by my father's escape, I wouldn't think so much about him, I'm certain of that. My daughter, eighteen now, told me the other day that she is pregnant, and my first thought was that my father might never get to meet his great-grandchild. I was thinking as if he had just left, and could easily return, and he would be pleased by the prospect of becoming a great-grandfather in the same way I had imagined he was pleased each time he had become a grandfather.

It wasn't that long ago, in the middle of the night, I heard laughing. Heard it clear as a bell. The laugh of a man who had lived a full, rich, exciting life. I have dreamed my father's laugh more times than I can count, but the other night it wasn't a dream. I was awake, I know I was awake. I put on my robe, and walked through the house. I searched for the source of that laugh, my mind knowing it could not be my father's. His escape was complete. His cave was never discovered. The country he lives in is far away. But I can still listen for my father's laugh, impossible as hearing that laugh might be. The heart, I know, can sometimes hear things that the ear cannot.

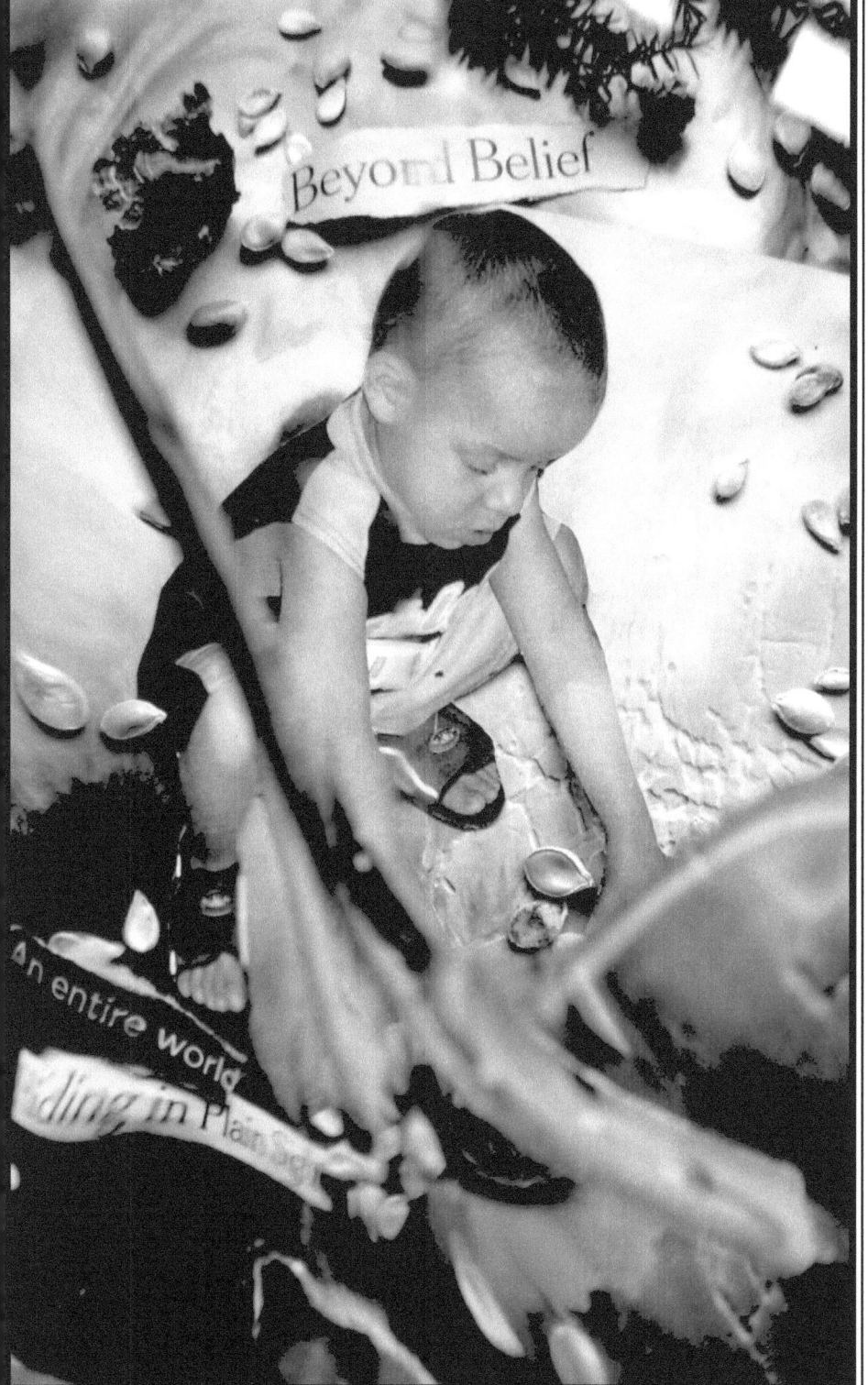

MARA A. COHEN

FAMILY PORTRAIT

The portrait captures the threesome: husband and wife, six-year-old daughter seated between them. Reclining against their bodies, the child smiles broadly and reaches up and slightly back to place a pudgy hand on each parent's face. The couple looks down at her, laughing. Why wouldn't they laugh, blessed as they are with happiness and health, a darling daughter, the means to commission this portrait?

The couple is quite obviously untouched by the sort of domestic dysfunction that drives the darling daughter to slide away from the dinner table and slip down the hall, past the portrait to her tiny playroom to draw and sing, distracting herself from the harsh and desperate tones of her parents' conversation as it builds to a heart-rending crescendo of screams and tears and slamming doors, of parents sleeping in separate beds.

No, it's plain to see the couple in this portrait is the sort that, on a family trip to New York planned around a visit to the wife's ailing grandfather, when she'd forgotten to pack her earrings, the husband had surprised her with a blue box from Tiffany's containing the superior pair of gold earrings she wore to have her portrait taken.

It's inconceivable that the wife of such a doting husband has come to dread the sound of his car pulling into the driveway or that the sound of his heavy footsteps on their hardwood floors would set her on edge. It's inconceivable that the laughing wife regularly lays awake at night, yearning for a gentle word or tender touch. It's inconceivable that the mother with her child's hand upon her cheek often wakes in the morning, despairing of the years stretched out ahead of her, the twisted cycle of serenity and shock continuing without end.

Sometimes on those mornings, the woman forces herself to imagine leaving the sickness and her marriage behind, leaving also the portrait hanging in the hall as a reminder to the husband of what he'd lost.

But those fantasies of hers don't run far. Hope always chases them away. Hope persuades her it's a microscopic distance between her marriage and the one that's framed behind the glass. She knows the ingredients of a homegrown remedy for the dysfunction: acknowledging the other person, treating them with respect, approaching one another with an attitude of friendship, being generous with affection and with apologies when mistakes inevitably are made.

Her seesawing between hopelessness and hope is part of the sickness. So too are her alternating feelings that she has power to improve the relationship followed by her powerlessness when she hears she's "always complaining," "negative," "crazy," or just plain "wrong." Lacking even so much as a name for the malady makes it seem unreal, compounding the pain of his invalidation. Her inability to bring about the desired state exemplified by the family in the portrait makes her feel frustrated and confused and ashamed.

Like the daughter who has learned to slip away when she senses danger, the wife has gradually adapted herself to the disease. Told repeatedly she's too sensitive, she's come to tolerate what would normally be intolerable. Told repeatedly she never listens, she bites her tongue and tries to assume an intent expression of concentration, her heart ricocheting inside her chest, as her husband castigates her. Told repeatedly she cares only about herself, she tries to ask him engaging questions–or leave him to his silence–depending on the subtle nuances she gleans from his body language or his face.

These salves prove ineffective. She's nagged by the feeling there's a larger picture she's missing. But there are no pictures, no physical manifestations of any kind, no bruises or broken bones. So she calls to mind an imaginary chart to hang beside the portrait. Her chart is arrayed with dots, one dot for each disturbing episode. Over time, the dots accumulate and cluster along a curve. The purpose of her mental exercise is not to nurture grievances but to illuminate patterns and correlations, to make predictions in order to sidestep triggers and to reveal a viable treatment.

But the wife is stymied in this exercise, confused about what episodes to include on the chart and what episodes to omit. Should she draw a dot to represent the initial meeting with the contractor when she was jolted by her husband's suggestion she make the man a cup of coffee? Had her husband intended to undermine her with a worker who would be a near-constant presence in their home for more than a year? Had she been thrown because her husband's request implied a hierarchical view of their relationship when she'd assumed they were equals? Or was she reading too much into her husband's gesture of hospitality? Because she is uncertain, the episode goes unmarked. She doesn't draw a dot.

How about the evening when she'd entered their daughter's bedroom to put away clean laundry while father and daughter played with the girl's toy bunnies? At the "tink-tink" of hangers on the hanging rod, her husband proclaimed, "It sounds like peeing in the closet! Mommy, are you in there peeing?" Recalling this incident, the wife remembers her cozy feeling of domesticity and order, cut short—like a rug pulled out from under her. Had her husband, caught up in a moment of play, made a puerile joke that missed? Or in making her the butt of a joke, had he betrayed an "us versus her" orientation and the intent to humiliate her? Recalling the episode, the wife feels embarrassed, and she's not sure if it's for her husband, her daughter or herself. Again, she doesn't know what to make of the episode. Again, she doesn't draw a dot.

She calls to mind other episodes any witness would confirm as clearly out of bounds. Like the drive home after his mother's last holiday party: When the wife told him she had wished he had sat next to her while everyone was unwrapping gifts, he'd pulled the car off the freeway with their daughter in the back seat and raged at her on the shoulder of a dark side street. Had she been indelicate in the words she'd used to express her disappointment? Had she been wrong to share her feelings? What had been her husband's words and how had his anger escalated? She can't remember, and there's nobody she can ask. There are never adult witnesses to incidents like this. Again, she stands in front of the chart. Again, she doesn't draw a dot.

She paces down the hall, past the portrait, to the guest room doorway where the husband stomped off to spend the night after an execrable exchange. The lack of reconciliation had lain heavy as a sledgehammer in the pit of her stomach until she'd crept after him like a dog to beg for scraps.

"Can we just kiss and make up?" she implored.

"You're torturing me!" he bellowed.

It had been her own palms pounding her head in anguish when the husband inquired coolly, "Do you want me to call the emergency room?"

Had he felt genuine concern? Had he been mocking her with his oft-repeated allegation that she's crazy?

Or had it been a threat?

She had known she was acting crazy and that he easily could have had her committed.

The wife doesn't want to remember her fear in that moment of realization. She doesn't draw a dot.

Her imaginary chart arrayed with invisible dots drones with an insistent message. There's an underlying logic to the sickness, subtle and stealthy but real as the documentary evidence of the family portrait, framed and preserved behind shatterproof plexiglass. The sickness causes her to be seen as someone she is not: his adversary.

Her presumption of the sacred bond between husband and wife leads her to dismiss her intuition as absurd. The goodwill radiating out from the portrait reinforces her instinct to seek an innocuous explanation for interactions that upset her. The appalling alternative is unbearable: This is a portrait of domestic abuse.

CARL "PAPA" PALMER

WINNING WAYS

I taught him competition,
always be the star,
play to win,

excel in my eyes,
make dad proud,
best in his class,

stay on top,
maintain that edge,
all this well learned

as he slung those damn darts
at the damn rec room wall,
stomped up those damn stairs

slammed that damn door
kicked at that damn dog
yelled at his damn brother

and stormed out the damn house
when I beat him to the bull's eye
the second time in a row.

HEATED WORDS

I heard my son
shout at his wife
the same words
I yelled at his mother.

Those words I heard
my dad roar at mom
her crying
me covering my ears.

My father never took
his words back.
I haven't either.
I hope my son will.

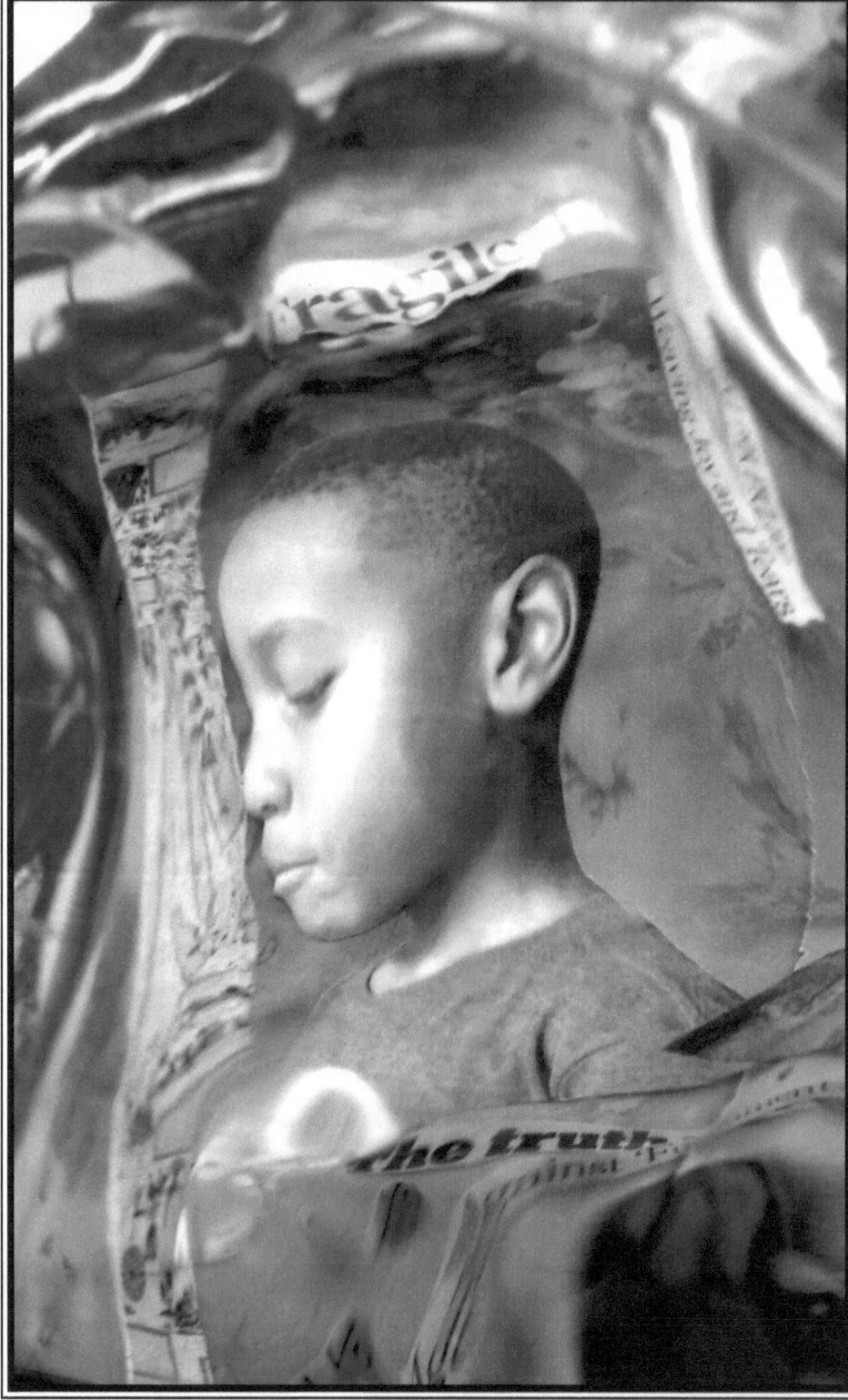

TRAUMA
ಡ್ರಾಮಾ

ALLISON WHITTENBERG

WATCHING JORDAN'S FALL

. . . God, I hate November.
All the hope I had hoped
against hope for Jordan.

Dad beat Jordan, to
straighten him out, to show
Jordan, to silence him.

My brother lived until the next
season, onto the next winter,
very quiet like a fallen leaf.

JAIME GROOKETT

THE LETTING GO

I never remembered him taking off his boots
the way he crept to the side of the bed
pressed his toes gently on rubber heels
sliding them off the soles of his feet
flicking them from the tips of his toes
like plucking off the heads of dandelions
              I never remembered that.

When I was ten, I swung on a giant homemade tire swing,
tread worn smooth like leather.
when the blaze for excitement lit me up
I'd grab the coarse yellow rope
hoist myself onto the worn wheel,
          spinning and swirling,
feet scrambling, slipping then grasping the angry black wheel
my heart drumming the erratic rhythm of my mind
           This is what it means to be alive.

I never remembered him taking off his boots
the casualness of it all
the mundane moment swimming in a deep sea of mundane moments,
          lurched, leaped, snapped, warned
even now, the world will never grasp the magnitude of that moment
that pulls at my pantleg, whispers my name
he walked sock-footed to my side of the bed,
pursed lips parted slightly to gasp
I lurched not far enough away,
        A mouse falling prey
              I never remembered him taking off his boots.

When I was ten,
and perching on the bald tire grew humdrum
I'd climb the rope
bristled threads cut my palms deep as I pushed higher and higher
the world shrinking beneath me
pain of the rope colored the world brighter,
my senses heightening with me.
        This is what it means to be alive.

I never remembered him taking off his boots.
yet now, my fingernails remember
it was the putting on I always remembered
practical lacing of brown laces on worn boots
as he described how he'd kill me if I told
        of the rape
the image of red sputtering from my pale neck
spun in my mind like a crimson web,
        weaving and tangling
naturally, I'd remember the putting on
        but I never remembered him taking off his boots.

When I was ten, and the world slipped far below me
as I hung high on the yellow rope
my thin legs wrapping to lighten the weight
too heavy for my arms to bare
the green earth swirled as my grip slacked from exhaustion.
I held tight as I lowered
        Until one time,
just because I didn't choose to come down,
I stayed
White-knuckled and shaking,
until my will lost
        I plunged deep into the world I dreamed of escaping
fiery pink burns covered my arms, my palms.
fall air scorched my raw skin.
        this is what it means to be alive.

I never remembered him taking off his boots
until one time,
just because I didn't choose to forget,
I stayed.
white-knuckled and shaking
until my will lost
      I dropped deep into the memory I dreamed
          of escaping
      This is what it means to be alive.

THE SEARCH FOR SOMETHING

Spare cheese sits lonely on my porcelain plate
remnants of lunch that left me too tired
to clean up, a chandelier glows above the
table, casting white rings onto worn wood

It twitches, switches on then off again—
it's intermittent glow distracting. A light
bulb needs changing. Or the switch not fully
on, stuck in a no man's land, unsure of its direction

A circuit needs changing, my father would say
he'd hastily make his way to the basement,
flashlight in hand, pants sagging just low enough
to show he had done this for years, a handyman of sorts.

My mother would say it's my grandfather
who comes to her in blinking lights, flickers
to remind her he ever was, apologize
for all he wasn't. It's him she'd say. Your grandfather.

I leave the light, just as it is, its spasmodic
wink creating an aura of mystery to the mundane
summoning the spirits surrounding me
releasing into my kitchen by way of Morse Code.

KATE PASHBY

LETTER TO MY GRANDMA GLORIA

I wonder if you saw dead bodies
every time you closed your eyes
if you ever awoke in a cold sweat
afraid the Japanese soldiers were
about to find you

I still wonder how you escaped
your hometown's massacre
and if you ever went back
before you left the Philippines
for good, never to see your mother
again

certainly you had more than enough
reasons to hypnotize yourself
in the flashing lights of the
dime slot machines
to lose entire weekends to mahjong
to run away from your new home at eighteen
and smoke yourself to death at sixty-five

I could never blame you
for cultivating the seed of addiction
that still ravages this family
you were always the best at growing plants

TEENAGE YEARS

I was always the spitting image of my mother
perhaps that's why she never saw me
did she ever struggle to look in the mirror
like I did? hours spent glaring
at my reflection, longing for a plastic surgeon's knife
applying the scientific method to drugs
counting sleeping pills, counting days
until my next Nair treatment to burn the hate away
kneeling on the cold linoleum floor just to feel
walking half an hour, in the sun, uphill, both ways
on the way to my next high
ecstasy I couldn't feel, pleasure no longer
in my vocabulary
letting boys touch me only as much as they needed
to not leave until I cut them off

HUSTLE

whenever money was tight
I contemplated alternative income

selling used panties or feet pics
or seeking arrangements

but nausea and fear would
form a pit in my stomach

as my body recalled my
so-called daddy issues

so instead my brain would run
hamster wheels of anxiety

every time I saw my grocery bill
or checked my bank account

ASMR

I.
I keep having the zombie dreams
(I tell my therapist)
where I'm fleeing, sometimes alone,
sometimes with others,
from some robots/plague victims/supernatural beings
who are trying to catch us
to make us like them
and I usually wake up right as
they barge into my hiding spot

you know, your dreams are your
brain's way of processing your trauma
(my therapist reminds me,
and I nod)
what do you think
they're trying to tell you?

(I wrinkle my forehead
tree roots to trip my running feet)
I guess
I'm still trying to escape
my parents
even though I haven't seen them in years

II.
I keep dreaming that I'm still dating men
(I admit to a fellow lesbian)
that I'm still with an ex, making out

or some random dude is flirting with me
and I'm flirting back
only last night I remembered mid-dream
that I'm gay
and I thought, oh no, I have to tell this guy
I'm a lesbian!

EEEWWWW
(my friend interrupts mid-way
and we laugh)

III.
Dear Vivian,
(I type in the email to my therapist)
I had another trauma nightmare last night,
but it was different from the others.
I was at my dad's work and he touched
me while I was in the bathroom.
I yelled at him and he
performed his usual "poor me" routine.
I decided I was fed up and told my mom
to not tell my dad
that I was running away
and she actually kept quiet for once
so I met my other gay cousin at a
museum giftshop to purchase last-minute kitsch
before exiting via the giftshop's giant slide.
It started to pour as we prepared to leave town
and I realized my wallet was still in the giftshop
which had closed five minutes prior,
but I was so close to freedom
on the cusp of escape
and then I woke up.

AMBER SOHA

BAGGAGE CLAIM

We're sitting in the car. I can see her, sitting at one of the picnic tables, stubbing out a cigarette in one of those shitty little grills cemented into the ground. She looks sick. She's yellow and gray. Her hair is the same close-cropped cut, but there is none of the color of her youth left—there's no trace of pink in her cheeks or on her lips, and she's stopped bothering to cover it up with bright, gaudy lipstick. She wears those same thick square glasses with the clear frames that make her eyes look ready to bulge out from behind their lenses. She's hunched over, like she's in pain, but she's so hard to believe when she speaks that it's better to observe from afar first.

CRITICAL

I had just finished cleaning the house and stewing on all of my irritations when I sat down to finish reading my book. The kids would be home from school soon, and they were always starving. I wanted to enjoy the fictional world, uninterrupted by the question, "What's for dinner?" or "When's dinner going to be ready?" I needed to finish before the sonic booms and beats carried through the ceiling from the bedrooms upstairs. Nobody in this house can stand music at a volume any less than full blast. I was imagining using all of my strength to push open a bedroom door, as if the sound waves would push back against me, when I got the call.

"Hello, Melody! There's something important I need to talk to you about."

"What could be so important?" I asked.

"I have stage four liver cancer!"

My grandmother, whom I hadn't seen in twenty-one years, was far too happy with a terminal cancer diagnosis after a lifetime of being an abuser and manipulator. The cirrhosis from years of alcohol abuse was finally wagging a karmic finger in her face.

"Don't you see? I'm dying, so everyone has to talk to me."

She had an excuse to reach out to all the family members who had distanced themselves because of her behavior. No apologies or acknowledgments or pleading for another opportunity to demonstrate that she'd "changed" because she's dying—there's no need! The long-awaited excuse to intrude, to insert herself into my life, had arrived.

"That's where you're wrong," I said. We're all *waiting* for you to die so we can have some peace.

"Is that really how you're going to be? You can't have some compassion for a dying old lady?" she asked, just as unapologetically manipulative as ever.

"Why are you calling me?" I asked her, wishing she would just get to the point. "What do you want?"

"I want to see you. I want to meet my great-grandchildren before I die. Won't you grant a dying lady her last wish?"

"I don't think that's a good idea."

"C'mon! Can you really still hold your grudges against me? It's been years." And this almost sounded like pleading, but she was losing her patience and her leverage.

"I'm hanging up," I said, "and don't call me again."

I sat there for a few minutes, wondering if I should indulge the crazy old bat. I was at peace! Did she really have the right to ask me such a thing? My father never forgave her for beating him as a child, or drunkenly telling him that his absent father wasn't really his father anyway; that his real father was some guy doing time for killing his best friend in a drunken rage. Neither of my parents forgave her for the number of times she had tried to destroy their marriage; I remember the screaming matches they used to have when they thought I wasn't listening.

"Don't you see what she's trying to do?" my mother asked, enraged.

"This doesn't have anything to do with her. I want a divorce."

"You can have it. I'm tired of the way you treat me. I don't want to stay married to someone who would take marital advice from a woman whose most steady relationship is with a bottle!" my mother screamed and slammed her hands on the table before pushing her chair away and storming off. I remember feeling a sense of guilt stealing away from the corner I was peeking around so as not to get caught; my dad always told me eavesdropping was impolite, but my grandmother had told me on the phone that keeping secrets was lying, and my parents always tried to keep the scary stuff secret.

At some point, the fighting seemed to stop, and I didn't get to talk to my grandmother on the phone for a while. I didn't know why, but everything was better, and that was enough for me not to notice that the phone calls had stopped. There was one day, after my dad had been on the phone for a while saying something about not getting in the middle of things, he handed me the phone. My parents had let her apologize, and they'd mistakenly hoped she'd treat her grandchildren differently. I remembered this one Easter when I was nine when she slapped me across the face because I was too excited about decorating the eggs. I figured she wouldn't do something like that if it wasn't okay, so I didn't tell my parents. She used to say things like, "Your mother doesn't care about you like I do; she doesn't spend time with you like I do," or she'd tell me things about my father's childhood that weren't true because she didn't raise him, but I didn't know.

She didn't give a shit about the way she's treated people; how could I let her meet my kids? I mean, I was already struggling with their behavior at school—Shawn was suspended last week, and his fourteen year-old excuse for being caught with weed was that he was, "holding it for a friend," and Sarah is so clever, but she doesn't apply herself, so her grades don't reflect how smart she is.

My grandmother was the epitome of what it means to be a horrible human being, but maybe it could be a teaching opportunity. *Hey kids, this is your great-grandmother whom you're only meeting because she's dying. If you're not careful, you'll end up like her.*

☙ℬ)ℭ𝔞℧

The next morning, I called her. "Hello?" she answered, in this nauseatingly sweet voice. It wasn't natural, but she has caller ID, and she knew it was me.

"You still wanna meet my kids? Let's meet in a public place," I said.

"Why? Do you think I'm going to make a scene?" she asked.

"Just meet us at the park. We can talk and go from there. I'll be there at noon."

I warned the kids, "we're meeting somebody I haven't seen in a long time, and they'd like to meet you," and told them to get ready, dismissing the eye rolls and aggressively forced sighs given in return. I stood for a while in front of my closet, perusing the contents: clothes, shoes, old handbags stuffed in the back, picture frames on the shelf collecting dust. I was trying to pick out the perfect outfit—something that looked nice, something that didn't say "you're trying too hard"—but what did I care? I shouldn't have cared, but I did, and I couldn't admit it to myself, so I chose the nicest comfortable thing I owned: a two-toned purple button-down shirt I usually wore to interviews, and my most comfortable pair of jeans.

"Why are we doing this?" Shawn, my son, asked, tearing me away from my internal arguments. He only ever needed reasons when something interrupted what he was doing on that Xbox machine; the "who" didn't matter enough to him to ask. I turned to look at him, this tall, lanky man cub, and I couldn't tell him why because I wasn't completely sure myself. I couldn't bring myself tell him about my damage; the fear, and the anger I have because of the fear; the reasons why I was so over-protective of him and his sister when they were little.

I had run every scenario in my head. Everything that could possibly go wrong. Every turn the conversation could take and my responses. I was prepared. I thought. Dozens of times I've thought about forgiving her, about giving her this opportunity, about allowing her to make her amends in her own way, the way they do in twelve-step programs, and every time I reasoned myself out of it. *She doesn't deserve it. She doesn't even acknowledge what she's done.* But this time, she was dying. This was the only time.

"Can you please just do as I've asked for once?"

ᏣᏠᎠᏣᏑᏠᎠ

"Are we just going to sit here?" Sarah asks, and I stare at her blankly. She realizes she's just interrupted something and shrinks back into her seat. My little goth. Maybe that's not what they call it anymore, but that's what all the dark makeup looks like. Underneath the makeup, I know she's just a kid looking for a place to fit in: the clichéd misunderstood teenager. I did my best to make sure she would never know childhood trauma. Sometimes I worry I've stunted their growth; that my need to protect them was overbearing and misguided; that I tried too hard to do damage-control and ended up being the one to inflict harm.

"Yes. C'mon," and I unbuckle my seat belt, climb out of the car, and adjust my clothes before shutting the door. I look around nervously at my kids before turning back to the old woman at the picnic table and beginning my stride. Confident. *Don't trip.*

My grandmother stands up as we get closer because she recognizes me. I am not the child she remembers, but I do bear a startling resemblance to her son, my father. It's been twenty-one years since I've actually seen her. I have this plan to say something intelligent, something meaningful, but my anxiety gives my plan wings, and it flies away from me, out of my reach, so what comes out instead is, "What the fuck do you want?"

"Mom! What the hell? Do you even know this person?" asks my startled son. He's never gotten away with using that language before, but he's also never heard me use language in this way.

"Do you think I'd talk to a stranger like this?" I snap back, not even turning to look at him. He's stunned, and I've lost control of my emotions.

"I suppose I deserve that," says my grandmother, "Look at you! You're all—"

"Grown up? That's more than you can say for yourself."

"Please, sit down. Hear me out."

"Why should I?" I ask.

"Because you're going to want to hear what I'm about to say."

"And what's that?" The heat creeping into my cheeks makes me feel a little self-conscious—I don't want anyone to think the redness is from embarrassment.

"He's dead," she says.

I stand there, staring at her, stock still. What am I supposed to do with that? What makes her think I wasn't hopefully keeping my eye out for the obituary? Twenty-one years is a long time to wait.

"Who's dead? And who are you?" Sarah's been so quiet that it actually startles me when she speaks. She's moved to stand close to me, arms folded across her chest, leaning heavily on her right hip, her eyes wide and eyebrows reaching toward her hairline. Filled to bursting with sixteen-year-old attitude.

"My husband is dead, and I am your great-grandmother." He was my step-grandfather. At least, that's how I had known him before I turned twelve.

"You stayed with him." It was a whisper, the calm before the storm. "You knew what he did to me, and you did nothing!"

"I know you hate me, but—"

"Hate you? Oh, you are sadly mistaken; do you really think I would allow you that much space in my mind?"

"I know I didn't do the right thing by you, but I didn't have a choice."

"You didn't have a choice?" I asked. My incredulity was blatant.

"I needed a place to live—I didn't have anywhere to go—if I left, I would've been homeless, money-less . . ."

"Why couldn't you get a job?" I asked.

"Well, who would hire someone my age and—"

"No. You're so full of excuses. Don't you think I can see through that? You had one choice, and you didn't take it. Let me ask you something. Why did you do it?"

"What d' you mean?" she asked.

"You know damn well what I mean. You helped him groom me. You didn't do anything to stop him, and you didn't leave. I could understand if he was abusing you, too, but I'm trying to understand why any woman would let that happen to a child."

Shawn drew closer. "Are these your children?" she asked, continuing to avoid my question. Shawn looked at her and cringed. His facial expressions have always been loud—that's how I knew he was lying about the weed.

I looked over at both of my children. Dark hair and dark eyes, my eyes, looking back at me. My eyes began to well up. At that moment, I was filled with love and adoration. Nothing else mattered. My children were my whole world, and I kept them safe. Maybe someday if they became parents, they would understand this, but for now . . .

"Mom . . ."

I shook my head and wiped my tears. My daughter hugged me, and looked up at me before asking, "Can we go get something to eat?"

ഇഇഇ

Later, at McDonald's, Shawn and Sarah were working on burger and French fry combos while I had a salad. It was pretty quiet, with the exception of a small child screaming about a happy meal toy. I closed my eyes and sighed before I started to try explaining what they'd just witnessed, "Listen, I want to apologize for my behavior. When I was a kid—"

"Mom, it's okay," said Sarah, "you don't have to explain." Even though I hadn't spelled it out, my clever girl understood. "I have a friend from school who's in a foster home because of her step-dad; he did stuff to her."

"How come I haven't met her?"

"Well, I was worried you'd think she was trouble because she's in the system."

I was a little hurt. I didn't want my daughter to think I was a judgmental person, but unlike my grandmother, I have plenty of time to show her this, so all I said was, "I just want you to know that you can come to me with anything; don't ever be afraid to talk about anything. I can always help you."

◈◈◈◈◈

A week later I got a call from a number I didn't recognize. "Hello?"

"Hi, uh, is this Melody?"

"Yeah, this is Mel. Who's this?"

"It's uncle Randy. You probably don't remember me."

"No, sorry."

"Well, I don't have a way to reach your father, but I thought he should know that his mother has passed away. We're going to have her cremated and there will be . . ." The unfamiliar voice droned on, but I was miles away. My grandmother really had been dying. It wasn't theatrics, for once. The person I concentrated so much of my blame and anger on was gone. What do I do, grieve? How am I supposed to feel?

I hung up the phone, not bothering with goodbyes, and headed for my closet. I dug around in the back for a gift she had made for me when I was a kid. It was a unique quilted blanket that folded into a pocket to make a pillow. It was made with fabric that was printed with kittens playing with yarn and had a blue and yellow color scheme. It had some tears near the corners where my child-self had been frustrated and stuffed the blanket into the pocket instead of folding it neatly. I don't know why I kept it all these years, but I decided that now was the best time to let it go.

ADDICTION

ങ്ങൊക്ഷ

EDDIE ORTON

LIVING STRANGE

You know, I can still hear the rain? I can still smell it, feel it wriggling on my skin down the back of my neck, in the folds of my clothes and the tattered ends of my shoes. I can still hear the traffic blare, the waves break on the river as I sat alone trying to catch a light, the path empty and dim. From where I was sitting I could see right down to the city, it was sunrise over London but the sky was gray. A roll of thunder overhead and I said to myself, "To see a world in a grain of sand and a heaven in a wild flower, hold eternity in the palm of your hand and infinity in an hour."

I caught a light and looked out at the water, stringing nonsense thoughts together in my head—one for each nonsense boat moored at the dock. I felt like a rabbit. One of those bedraggled, floppy ones you see wide eyed in the headlights, just before impact. Everything was all jumbled up. There were these ghosts, these certain little thoughts like horrors going round and around and around that had me biting my nails, which were already bitten way past the quick, all sore and bleedy looking. I'd been at Fire which is this gay club under the railway, the kind of place where you can smoke crack in the DJ booth or get fucked by saintly bouncers in the men's toilets, but I'd gotten bored and with nowhere to go I'd wandered up to the river, and sat on a bench in the rain. It was torrential, not like London rain at all actually, but more like the monsoons you get in Thailand. I spent a summer there when I was eighteen, smoking grass and just bumming around but what I remember most was the rain. More a force of nature than the dribble we get in England; great hissing, sodden downpours that stung your face and weighted down your clothes, and rose back up again as fog. Only in Thailand it was warm, even in the monsoon season. London was like ice.

Even the pigeons looked cold. This fat brown one with a gimpy leg had hobbled over to roost in the shelter behind my feet. I'd smiled and said, "Hi little man," and it had mooned back up at me as if to say, "Cor, Blimey! Shite weather today mate!" So I gave a nod of assent and pulled on my cigarette sagely. I wished people were as easy. Pigeons don't give a fuck. It's like what Hemingway said about bulls, "Bulls at least are not the greatest stylists in English." I know that he wasn't actually talking about bulls, but he was right. Bulls are shit at English. Pigeons are shit at English too, that's what's so great about them. You don't get any bullshit with pigeons, whatsoever. They just flap around doing their thing, without expectation and I mean, have you ever seen an unhappy looking pigeon? Because I haven't, but I'd challenge you to spot the one happy fucker on the Central Line, eight o'clock of a Monday morning, and then try to tell me that human beings are the superior species . . . When you really think about it, compared to pigeons, people are cunts.

So I guess that made me a cunt. Ipso facto it made everyone I had ever met or could ever meet, nothing more spectacular than: a cunt. Something to bear in mind I guess, but I was still lonely. I felt like the loneliest boy in the world, to tell you the truth and between the ironic weather and that washing machine inside my brain, I just wanted to lay down and die. I'm being glib, but it's the truth. Back then I wanted to die all the time. It was all I thought about and all I could do not to think about it, but I've always found that talking to yourself helps. Lines from old movies, shopping lists or recipes—it doesn't really matter what, it's the act of speaking that's the important thing. It brings you into the moment. So I sang, "*I'm sin-gin' in the rain, just sin-gin' in the rain, what a glor-ious feelin I'm ha-ppy again . . .* " And then I gave it a minute.

No, nothing.

My fag had burned right down to the nub, so I flicked it to the river. It missed and hit the pavement with a spark. I watched it fizzle out, like barnacles receding with high tide and I shuddered. I couldn't just sit there. So I took my phone from my pocket, started scrolling through names and old whatsapp's, L.E.D faces and forgotten; but they were all people who wouldn't want to talk to me, see I didn't really have any friends left. I'd burned a lot of bridges. There were a couple of guys that might but they'd both be asleep and I was wracking my brains with it, firing out texts when I remembered this guy I'd hung out with a few times before all this had happened, but I hadn't seen him in months. His name was Tom. We'd met at NA in the spring and gone for a few coffees. Soho had wilted in the unfamiliar heat. He'd been my most exciting new friend but then things had gotten bad again and I'd kind of faded out. I stopped taking his calls, replying to his messages—everything.

But at the memory of those heady afternoons I felt like I wanted to speak to him more than anyone, so I sent him a text. It went, "Hey, are you awake?"

A moment later, "Yeah man, what's up?"

"Wow," I muttered. I didn't think he'd reply.

So I said, "I really need to talk to someone."

"Are you okay?"

"No." And then I said, "Can you talk?"

"Yeah man. I'm with my girlfriend, give me a minute."

The phone rang.

"Hey man," he said. His voice was warm.

"Hi," I said. "Thanks for picking up the phone."

"It's okay man, I want to talk to you. What's wrong?"

"Everything."

"Okay, well what's everything? Let's narrow it down."

"Everything's just fucked. I fuck everything up," I said, bouncing my knee. "I can't stop using, I've got nowhere to live, all my friends hate me—"

"You haven't got a job," he said.

I grinned.

"Go on man, I'm listening."

"I just feel like there's no way out. It just doesn't end. I can't even top myself. I'm—"

"You tried to kill yourself?"

"Yeah."

"When?"

"A few weeks ago . . . I stopped to think for too long."

There was a silence and then he said, "Joe, you've got to tell me what you need."

I paused, "Just this . . . I just need to talk to someone."

And then the wind changed direction. It felt like a cold slap in the face. He said, "Where are you now?"

"Albert Embankment."

"Where's that?"

"In Vauxhall by the river."

"I'm going to text you my address. Can you get to Barbican?"

"Yeah."

"But do you have any money?"

"No, but I can walk, it's not far."

"It's raining, look text me your account number and I'll send you some money. My girlfriend's here so give me a couple hours. Go somewhere warm and get something to eat."

CRITICAL

Tom lived on Peartree Street in the city, which is this quiet backstreet that you get to from a little alleyway, down the side of a pub on Goswell Road. Tall, narrow and residential with a park running along one side, it's bookended by the trendy cafes and offices typical to that part of London but kind of alien to me. This was a nice place to live. The houses all had window boxes of geraniums and petunias, and great gnarled old oaks stood like sentinels, around a small koi pond in the park. Before everything went sideways, I'd been staying in Shepherds Bush and whatever that place was, it wasn't good. I'd been sharing a room with this guy Eddie, who was a rentboy that I'd run around with for a bit. He used to inject between his toes and he had this thing for turning his clothes inside out every other day, so he never had to wash them, but he was hot so he could get away with it. When you're that good looking you can get away with anything . . . But the room was above an Off License by the tube. It was all blacked out windows and mangy old wallpaper, coming unstuck at the corners; cockroaches and grime. The whole house would shake as the tube trains rumbled past and it always stank of stale cigarette smoke and sex. It made Goswell Road look like Nirvana.

I mean even the fucking weather was better. The rain had stopped and the clouds had all lost that angry gray color, birds were singing in the trees. The place was deserted, silent but for the pigeons and the pad of my shoes, which gave me an enormous sense of wellbeing because I love a bit of it. The quiet I mean (sorry I'm taking the piss again, I can't help it). But this calm hung over everything, like it does in old movies after a shipwreck or something, and the whole top of the street was flooded out, which was kind of cool because the puddles all glimmered with bits of sky; I just walked straight through and got wet. My trousers were fucked anyway.

Tom was waiting for me in the street. He was so beautiful. I kind of glanced at him and then back down at the pavement, until he was standing right in front of me. When I looked up all I could see were his moon eyes.

"Hi poppet," he said.

"Hi," I said.

I tried to smile but I couldn't, and my eyes welled up.

"Come here," he said, pulling me in for a tight hug. It was funny, I don't think I'd ever hugged Tom before and he'd definitely never called me his "poppet." It felt like a strange word for him to use, out of character almost, kind of cloying and overly sentimental because Tom wasn't like that at all. Tom was the kind of guy who thought a bar fight was a good time. He was brilliant.

We stood there like penguins, until I'd eased into it and then he took a step back. He kept a hold of my arms as he looked at my face, at my hollowed-out eyes and sunken cheeks, his mouth ajar as if to say, "Fuck man." It'll sound silly but it was like looking in a mirror because I looked at him and I saw me; or the state I was in, to be more exact. That's usually how it goes though, that thing of other people showing us ourselves. It was kind of a surprise because the guys I'd been going around with didn't really show you anything, accept for just how awful people can be. They were all kind of dead about the eyes. It wasn't that they didn't laugh or smile or anything like that, because they did. But rather that there wasn't any spark of life in there, no semblance of love or hope or kindness—or any of the other qualities which make us human.

There was something gentle about that look, something still. He'd looked shocked. Not in a judgmental way or anything, maybe it would be better to call it a look of concern. It was a kind look, so I must have really looked like shit. The last time I saw him I'd been six months clean, so it was like the gulf between Dr. Jekyll and Mr. Hyde. On the walk up from the tube people had actually crossed the road to avoid me, it was that bad, but Tom had known me when I was a person. As he pulled me in for another hug I let my head drop to his shoulder and I closed my eyes. He smelled of weed and cigarettes.

C3₰CRℜ₰

He led me up a dark staircase, warm and windowless with plush carpet underfoot. His housemate was away and closing the door to his flat I was struck by how kind of warm and cozy it was. "It's so quiet," I said. Everything was white and clean and bright, with floor to ceiling windows and all these crazy abstract prints on the walls.

"They're all mine," he said, beaming. And then pointing to one, "Where do you think that is?"

"The city?" I said.

"No man, guess again."

"I don't know, where?"

"It's Manchester! It's called 'Going to Work,' it's by this artist called Lowry. Oasis put it on an album cover."

"Oh cool," I said, looking harder.

He found me some pajamas and a toothbrush, then took me through to the bathroom and ran a shower. He stood with his hand held under the tap, and made sure that it wasn't too hot while I squirmed, shifting from side to side on the balls of my feet, like an idiot. I hadn't showered in days and the warm water felt like life seeping into my achy bones. I couldn't remember the last time I'd had a shower. Maybe last week, after I fucked that guy in Brixton? Or the one in Earls Court? Everything was kind of a blur. I felt rough, standing up took it out of me and my track mark's all stung with the soapy water, burned like fabulous hot pokers in a cow's backside. Most of them were scarred up but some had blistered into these fat pockmarks running all up my arms and it was starting to give me a kind of limited mobility, because if I grazed one of them or rubbed them up against anything I'd get this sharp searing pain and just have to sit very, very still until it went away. It was horrible. You just couldn't move. I had to sit on the edge of the tub to towel myself dry, careful not to touch my arms.

When I got out he was sitting in his window strumming a guitar, a lit cigarette in an ashtray by his side. It was this cool old cut glass one, round and quite big kind of like a bowl. I'd never seen one like that before and when I asked him about it he said that it had been his dad's. His dad was dead, so that made it seem even more special. It had provenance. He was looking down at the street, facing west toward the pub as he played. He was staring out there really intently which I thought was weird because I'd never sit in front of a window like that, but maybe that's just me? If I was alone and there was a window around, I'd always draw the curtains. Something about people seeing in, I guess. It freaks me out.

I shut the door behind me and sat on the bed.

"Feeling better?" He said.

"Yeah . . . It's so good to be warm," I said.

"I'll put your clothes in the washing machine," he said. "You can keep those."

"Oh, err, thanks."

He looked more like a rock star than a yuppie, all choppie blonde hair and cheekbones—those kind of one-in-a-million movie star good looks. I was a bit intimidated by him which sounds pathetic but it's the truth. He was a real pretty-boy and he knew it. The way he sat there with that guitar, leaning back just a little with his feet propped up. If I'd taken a picture on the spot it would have been perfectly lit and just atmospheric enough to stick on an album cover. Like maybe early Bob Dylan?

"Guess the song?" he said.

"OK, err, oh! I know this one."

He kept playing.

"Err, Err Bowie! Pretty things!"

He didn't look up as he said, "No . . . "

I listened harder.

"Err, Blur?"

"Yeah man. But what's the song?" He grinned.

"Parklife?"

"Yeahhhh," he said.

I moved to lie down, still facing him.

"You should write an album," I said. "You're good."

"No I couldn't."

"Why not?"

"Because of my criminal record. I'd lose my job if it got out."

"Oh."

"And anyway I'm not good enough to write an album yet. There's still a lot I need to learn," he said, frowning. "Like chords and stuff."

He started playing something else.

"Too easy," I said. "Pulp, Common People."

"Got it in one." He sang, "I *wanna live like common people, I wanna do whatever common people do* . . . " And he actually had me smiling. It was incredible. I never thought I'd smile again.

I was nodding off so I fumbled to get under the bed covers, when he said, "Argh man! I just made that!" He'd sounded annoyed, but he didn't make me get out and before long I fell asleep.

ೞಬಛೞ

When I opened my eyes the whole room was spinning. I tried closing them again, but then I felt a lurch in my stomach and I heaved, so I rolled over to the edge of the bed, ready to be sick, but it wouldn't come. I hadn't eaten in days so there wasn't anything to throw up, it was just dry retching and mucus. After it passed I lay there for a bit in the softness of his sheets and his freshly laundered clothes, like freshly mown grass. People were laughing in the street outside his window and the sun kind of sparkled off of the building opposite, which was one of those brutalist Patrick Bateman jobs. I wanted to draw the curtains but I couldn't move, so I just lay there staring at the ceiling. It was a good ceiling, as far as ceilings go. I approved. All in good working order, white and flat and all of that . . . I was alone. I listened out for Tom, who must have cleared out into the next room while I was sleeping. He was in the shower. After a minute, I heard the turn of the shower tap down the hall, soon followed by footsteps to the door; which had been left ajar. He slipped through the gap and flashed me a smile before pushing it to. I saw that he wasn't wearing a shirt.

"Hey mate," he said. "Did you get some sleep?"

"Not very much," I said. "The T hasn't worn off."

"How long does it take?"

"A day or two."

"Fuck man."

He toweled his hair dry and then stuffed it in a drawer demonstrating armpits, the muscles in his back and the hardness of his belly. I sat up, waiting for him to say something and trying not to look, even though I knew he wanted me to. He was teasing me. But then he paused and the air became kind of charged as he lingered over and looked me in the eye. My breath caught in my throat. Was he coming onto me? My heart raced . . . But then, feeling awkward, I looked away. He sat back down in the window and picked up his guitar, without putting on a shirt.

He spoke softly, "You should eat something."

"I'm not hungry," I said.

"You're skin and bones. You need to eat."

I hugged my knees. His fingers found a tune as he watched the street, an echo of laughter and this annoying patter of voices discernible outside. I knew I'd have to leave soon and I was scared. Or not scared, I just really didn't want to leave but then as if he'd read my mind he said, "You need to speak to your mum and ask if you can go home. Then when you're ready we'll go to Euston and I'll buy you a ticket."

"Okay," I said, without even thinking about it. Just okay, yeah, whatever you want.

Then he said, "But we can hang here for a bit, no rush."

He made tea, hot sweet tea which we drank from these cool china cups, all covered in a kind of hazy arabesque. I'd hovered over him in the kitchen, which was a warm dark room at the back of the flat, as he'd taken them out of the cupboard and laid them out on the countertop, one by one while the kettle boiled; and then he told me to pick one. I think I picked the red one. But he was really excited to be showing me these cups, in a self-mocking bright-eyed kind of way and they were pretty cool. They came from a shop on Denmark Street and he said that he collected them. I'd turned one round under my thumbs and I thought of something an old lecturer had said to me, way back when I was like nineteen or something, in my first year of uni. She was incredible—this bisexual, Afro-Carribean, powerhouse of a woman called Nyoka, with a wardrobe full of clothes in tropical colors and a knowing smile. She wrote novels all about love and fate and decadent food and she was one of the most inspiring women I've ever met in my life. But she gave me a piece of advice once and I'll never forget it. She said that personhood is about taking joy in joy. Tom's cups brought him joy, and seeing the happiness that they gave him made me feel pretty happy too. He was just so damn sweet!

We went back to his room and sat on the bed, nursing our mugs of tea. It was going gray again outside, but I didn't mind. I've always thought that tea goes down better on rainy days. It was all kind of desultory chit chat and there were a lot of silences, but they were comfortable silences and when Tom spoke he kind of mumbled, which I liked. It put me at ease, because I mumble. He talked about his girlfriend a bit, told me about how they'd been together for three years and how she was ready to settle down and stuff, but how he wanted to dump her. She was an editor for an art magazine or something. A bit older than him, thirty-one to his twenty-five. Her name was Jaimini, he said. His voice had dropped an octave as he spoke her name, softened as if it were loaded with meaning. He told me about some of the guys he'd been with too (not very many)—a guy up in Leeds where he went to uni, and one back in Kent, which was where he was from. Maybe it was in my head, but they both sounded a bit like me. He said that they both had dark hair and eyes, and when he told me about the one from Kent he'd said, "He'd lived through a war, like he'd done two tours of Iraq but he was just the sweetest person," and then he kind of looked at me, as if he was waiting for me to guess. I don't know. He always kept me guessing.

And we talked about backpacking a bit. He'd taken the hippie trail through Vietnam a couple years before, and he had all these cool stories about giant cows, Jade emperor's and Jade mines. Jade's my favorite gemstone. I only wear one piece of jewelery and I've worn it almost every single day for years—a bracelet of carved Jade turtles (which I didn't actually buy in Thailand, but from a trinket shop behind a bakery in Chinatown) but when he told me his story about the Jade mines, he took my wrist in his palm and started thumbing through the beads. "This is nice," he said, and I smiled.

Then we talked about Stonehenge and UFO's and all kinds of stuff like that. It was one of those slow, winding conversations like a sea breeze, that you can only really have with somebody that you barely know, you know? That you're getting to know.

"Text your mum," he said at last.

"Yeah."

I put, "Hi mum, how are you?"

A moment later.

"Hi Joe, I'm fine thanks. Are you okay?"

"Yeah I'm fine, I'm with Tom . . . Can I come home?"

ᚙ ℬ ℭℛ ℬℴ

We sat near the back of the bus. People had stared as I got on and we made for the first set of empty seats. There'd been this couple sitting across from us and as we sat down they actually moved to stand at the front. I thought, do I really look that bad? Tom had tried to give me some Ray Bans before we left his house, but I wouldn't take them because I didn't know when I'd be able to give them back, but I wished I'd taken them. People were looking and I felt like a prick, but then even the people who weren't looking kind of made me feel like a prick. Why weren't they looking? Tom and I spoke quietly, the beggars and traffic lights of Kings Cross rolling by, out the window.

"I know what I'm doing," I said, speaking slowly. "Like, you go to meetings, you read the literature and you pick up all this stuff—I know where it's gonna end . . . I just don't care anymore."

"You don't care?"

He sounded pissed. His words hung in the air as he looked ahead, his jaw clenched as he said, "I'm taking you somewhere before we go to Euston, somewhere that Colin took me. I want to show you something."

"Where?"

"You'll see, it's not far. Two stops after Euston."

As I looked out at the shifting landscape, newspapers and larger cans tossed to and fro like marionettes in the wind, the scent of his musk and the feel of his body next to mine, I really wished I'd taken those fucking sunglasses.

We got off outside UCLH and the wind howled. We made for the shelter of a high wall and shared a cigarette as people passed oblivious, in the street.

"What are we doing?" I said.

"Just trust me, okay?"

"Okay."

I remember the sinking in my gut. After I tried to kill myself, I'd screamed and screamed because they wouldn't let me leave the hospital and it was the same kind of feeling then, only the sense of relief I had with it this time was new, because I didn't want to be in control anymore. When I was in control it was bad, like living in a nightmare only you couldn't just wake up. You had to wait for it to be over and then when it was, it was only ever a matter of time before the whole sorry thing started over again. I'd had enough. I was sick and tired of being sick and tired so whatever Tom was playing at, it didn't matter. Whatever he wanted me to do, I'd do it. But more than that—I'd have done anything to have a bit more time with him. I didn't want to get the train.

He took the last drag, chucked the butt and led me inside into this huge lobby with a glass ceiling and the sky a few stories above. We sat down on two chairs, side by side in the middle of the room.

"What are we doing?"

"Just watch."

And so I watched. There were all kinds of people milling about, hooked up to machines with wires and tubes. Old women in wheelchairs and men on sticks and walkers; a bald girl in a nightgown bought sweets from the shop. We sat there for a long time, watching them come and go. I didn't know what I was meant to be looking for, but I felt like I could have sat there all day. It was warm and light, and Tom was sitting next to me; and everyone around wore easy, kindly expressions like they do in some country villages on Sundays. It was paradise. I lost all track of time, we could have been sitting there for hours.

After a while he brought something up on his phone and placed it on the armrest between us. He looked dead ahead as he told me to read it. It was a verse from The Bible. I can't remember which one or what it said exactly but it was God speaking to one of his subjects, and God said that he would hold him until the man was strong enough to hold himself. I felt a glow in my belly and I looked to him and after a pause, he turned his head to meet my gaze.

The heavens spoke, "GOD APPEARS AND GOD IS LIGHT TO THOSE POOR SOULS WHO DWELL IN NIGHT, BUT DOES A HUMAN FORM DISPLAY TO THOSE WHO DWELL IN REALMS OF DAY."

We sat there a while longer and then he said "Come on," and got up to walk away. I followed after him, a couple paces behind.

Back out in the street, he turned to me and said, "What did you see?"

"I don't know. They were in a lot of pain?"

"Yeah, what else?"

"Some of them are going to die?"

"Yeah. And what do you have that they don't?"

I paused.

"Err, I don't know. What?"

"You have a chance, Joe."

※☙☜☞☙☜

We walked to Tavistock Square Gardens and found a bench by the fountain. The ground was thick with dew but the sun was finally shining and with it everything had jumped into technicolor. The brilliant green of the laburnums, flowerbeds of vermillions and cadmiums, fuschias and myrtles but mostly him, the brilliant blue of his eyes and the pink of his lips. I felt self-conscious in my battered jacket and in the light of day I found it hard to look at him, which he seemed to like. He'd smile wickedly and narrow his eyes whenever I got shy.

"What's wrong beautiful?" he said.

"I don't know . . . I don't get why you're being so nice to me."

"Joe I'm a scumbag."

"What?" I looked up, surprised. "No you're not."

"Yeah I am Joe, I'm a bad person. You can do better than someone like me."

"No you're not at all. Why do you think you're a bad person?"

There was a pause.

"You aren't a bad person," I said. "You're not."

He just looked at me. A blank, penetrative stare.

And then down to my hands, at the green fly on my thumb.

"Look," he said.

He fished in his pocket for a light and I jumped.

"NO DON'T KILL IT!" I yelled trying to shake it off, but it wouldn't budge.

"I'm not going to kill it," he smiled.

Hesitant, I brought my hand down and offered it to him. He put the lighter gently to my palm, his fingertips brushing the skin along my wrist, until he found it. Our eyes met. He held it there, the touch of his skin on mine until the fly clambered up onto it, and I looked away.

ALISON STONE

BLOOD TIE

One blood test and the future
collapses.
I feel fine (tired,
sure, what mother isn't?) but the
numbers tell a different story.

Blood remembers
everything—every song
teenage hips thrust to, every hunger,
every bent, shared spoon.

Once bodies were safe.
Pam and I knelt beside a twisted
oak. So innocent, we pricked our index
fingers with a pin, then pressed
the bloody tips together, kissed.
Sisters forever.

I swallow mounds
of vitamins, sneak
to a doctor three towns away.
Double bandage each cut.

The present
wobbles.
My sick blood's a secret
that distracts me as I chat with other
moms at pick-up, brush
my daughters' hair. Each untruth
a tiny knife.

NOT ALWAYS BEAUTY

Some truths please the mouth
with sweetness, tangy
pucker, or salty crunch.
Facts to be savored.
Others I choke back
like this virus
with its stench of blood
and back-alleys, its magic trick
of making friends disappear.
Indelible as a rap sheet,
vengeful as a mirror.
Thirty-year dark cloud.
Secret of my sallow skin
and cancellations.
Dry bone always
splintering in the throat.

The Future is Fema[le]

Ghosts Are

without giving anything to our children

What is the sign of a good decision

PERSONAL RESPONSIBILITY
ଔଷ୭ଔଷୠ

KAREN LOEB

THIS WAY OR THAT

l. *Overheard on My Walk*

—the roofer calls in to his boss
If the wood doesn't crumble
under the shingles
she should be good to go
for a long time.

2. *7-19-27*

I still remember the
combination to my first two locks—
the code above for my high school
locker, the one below a symbol
of security when I lost my first. How
easy it was to snap the lock closed
and believe that since everything
inside the metal cavern was safe
that I would be too.
7-34-6.

3. Glass Shattering

He wanted to take
her places with his
cruise-ship smile
then leave her wanting more—
too much—
water-logged and spent
on some deserted isle.

4. I Felt Like I Had

When I visited for a few nights
there were two fives and a ten
in an empty dresser drawer.
I needed change
so I put in a twenty and took
the smaller bills
without telling my friends.
Had I done something shady?

LAUREN CAMP

DISCUSSING DEATH AS A CONSCIOUS ACTIVITY

If you're snug in your life when a man in a red cap jumps
from a bridge to an under story, under a wave or a door
to the ocean, to a torrentless daylight, more prayer,
less phantom, you might not consider the river of children
he leaves behind. But when Merle came by in June
with her two grandsons and they stood on your porch,
tow-headed and particular, you thought of the mother
who couldn't manage her batch of compulsions,
you thought of her strategy, and of course everyone
now assembles to whisper. You thought of the grass
and sky she ripped from those boys, whose gaze
will lift-off and follow any woman they see, who said
please and *thank you* just right. And if, on the screen,
you nibbled the links of a man wearing loss on his head,
the ample rumor of red, you could forgive yourself
the invitation to enter, you were surrounded by news,
and anyway, you looked up, trying to find a way out—
just as a tanager flew toward and peered in your window
with his ebony eyes. Where you might have read danger,
in departure, there remained only feathers, and later,
the perception of roses—not perfume, but stem
and thorn, which made you forgive all the red and not-
red that you've done all your life, and allow even
faint shades of fire. Your friend Lenny said he hates
people who do that—who jump, who swing forward
and don't bring themselves back, and your love claims
it's not what we're here for. It's selfish, he says. You think
about this, but still have trouble turning hysteria
around. You've always been open to hope, and the one
time you traded your spices for pain, even then,

you shook yourself out. Your greatest shelter is pretending
all people will remain hoisted on bridges. Last week
with 61 strangers, you recited 108 six-syllabled
mantras for Kevin whose life neatly folded
around him: *om mani padme hum*. You built a structure
of compassion with your parallel voices, as crimson
beads slipped down a string. Though his life digressed
into cancer, and the body whittled to syllables and bone,
his story went on: *om mani padme hum, om mani padme
hum*. You didn't know what it meant, but you said it
and lifted your head. As many times as it took to be
damaged and returned, he stayed, holding to earth,
and at the memorial, his three-year-old son ran by
with goggles, seeing through generations ghosts
in invisible water—what did not happen, what did;
one man lying beneath the hem of a pylon, the other
pulling open a curtain each morning to let in each
grimace of light. One man perched in the span between
witness and pulse, the other accepting his pardon.
Of the man in a cap who saw only feet of the stars,
do we care? We have cried for smaller things. Sometimes
belief doesn't fit us at all. Sometimes bodies just fall.

FLEXIBLE TRUTHS

—all lines based on actual emails

Dear Lauren, I put all your secrets in the living room under the couch.
Dear Lauren, the cleaning lady moved them and now I can't find them.
Dear Lauren, I am perplexed by my own alienation from the secrets.
Dear Lauren, can I pick something I really want to know about,
    anything at all—and just ask you?
Dear Lauren, let's correspond again about this, then maybe talk tomorrow
    afternoon or Friday morning.
Dear Lauren, tell me what really happened.
Dear Lauren, we need to insist on one day a week, preferably
    in the afternoon, to tell the truth.
Dear Lauren, my first message really sucked.
Dear Lauren, I've got to learn to be positive, I think.
Dear Lauren, thanks for sticking with me on this. I feel better about it already
    for a whole variety of reasons. And I appreciate your honesty.
Dear Lauren, please write soon. I'm surrounded by lunatics
    with classified pasts.
Dear Lauren, everything seems very flexible.
    And now the couch is gone, too.

JANE BLANCHARD

STILL LIFE

A dozen photographs are on display:
all smiling people, grouped or solo in
brass frames, once lacquered, losing shine each day
the feathered duster sweeps the paneled den.

Some images have faded since the sun
drops by most afternoons; the striped drapes close
whenever darkness dares to enter: none
of nearly thirty figures shifts in pose.

Infants stay small; children keep clean; no teen
is ever less than charming; no adult
gets any grayer; no one dies: each mien
suggests that time may pass without result.

Illusions, even limited, persist:
the need for more, for truth, does not exist.

IPSO FACTO

The papers came at last: the deal was done,
tried, juried, judged, recorded, stamped in red—
the dissolution of ourselves as one;
that marriage never happened, so they said.

All went into a drawer. Life resumed,
unshared, a continent apart. No traces
of any former union ever loomed
except in each of our four children's faces.

Now grown, those offspring still negotiate
our separate worlds while trying to arrange
their own. They know a lot and speculate
about the rest; thus, credits, debits change.

Some memories remain: the past can seem
too present in an unexpected dream.

BELATEDLY, A SONNET

Today I took the time to write about
what happened long ago—our brief romance,
its ending too abrupt perhaps, no doubt
the consequence of choice and circumstance.

We run into each other on occasion;
alone or not, we stop to speak and smile,
then soon depart with obvious evasion
of explanations that would take a while.

Mine could be short: I came to realize,
for both our sakes, that we were not a match
in much of anything, that compromise,
or worse, made neither one of us a catch.

If you should ask: Why now? Why write at all?
I guess not doing so, at last, felt small.

LAURENCE SNYDAL

EXCESS

"You never know what is enough unless you know what is more than enough."
—William Blake

Was it the last martini that did me
In? And why did those words so rude, so loud,
Suddenly separate me from the crowd,
Closing a door that could have set me free?
Was it the last bite of lasagna that
Jerked me out of sleep into a dreary
Half-awake, that kept me counting weary
Woes while digits detailed the final flat
Minutes of an early hour? The emailed
Rantings I later regretted, the choice
Of words. And on the telephone my voice
Bitterly recounting the ways life failed
Me. If there were only more time, I could name
More losses, lapses, so many times I
Failed to rein myself in. But that is why
I know Blake understood the sense of shame,
Of judgment. I earned every rejection,
Overflowing, rippling my reflection.

LOST AND FOUND

What have I got to lose? Just everything
I brought to life: the way the lightning strikes
The mountain, sullen sodden mud that likes
To lick my rubber boots, the songs that sing
Themselves. And I remember pathways lost
Long ago that were never found again.

I've been at a loss too often. But then
That's just the wicked way the dice were tossed.
I know it's easier to lose than find.
But you too have found it no surprise
To discover that right before your eyes
Things can appear you've never brought to mind

Choices that you can't remember choosing.
Memories you can't remember losing.

ALONE

*"The you you are with others is not you. To be lonesome
is to be who you most fully are."*
—Frazier, *Varina*

When you're alone and the routine
Of ordinary day has come apart,
There's nothing then between you and your heart.

The barrier that you had raised between
What you know and the real world is just that.
When the midnight mind opens its eyes
It finds the spot where darkness really lies
And all the barriers are fallen, flat.
Maybe it's not too late to learn to trust
Your whole life to yourself. But even you
Might hesitate to trust in someone who
Is so alone. So I suppose you must
Begin to see that we all live this way.
Nobody really knows how things should go
Nor where they're bound nor why. What we do know,
Is only the eternal yesterday.

And when all of those yesterdays are through,
We all discover what we always knew.

TERRI ELDERS

ALL THAT GLITTERS

When Grandma died in 1977, she'd left me her cocktail ring. I thought I'd inherited a fortune. Now I had something impressive to wear on the rare occasions when my husband and I still painted the town.

Decades earlier Grandma had asked her stepdaughter's husband, a jeweler, to design this special ring. Over her lifetime she'd accumulated several pieces of jewelry with a variety of stones, large and small. She'd decided she wanted all of them gathered in one spectacular piece.

"Roy's the finest jeweler in Gardena," she'd reminded us, as if the sleepy Southern California suburb rivaled Fifth Avenue. "He'll do a topnotch job."

The first time she wore Uncle Ray's glitzy creation to a family gathering, Grandma's eyes sparkled even more than the ring when she waved her hand so we could admire it.

"It holds my shiniest memories," she announced. "It has solitaires from my engagement rings from both Joe and Louie, and even the emerald from my daughter's Sweet Sixteen ring."

Mama had nodded and smiled slightly. She'd no longer worn that ring herself, so had offered it to Grandma, thinking that her colorful stone would add some panache to the masterpiece. She'd told me secretly that she'd never liked emeralds, and had hoped for a pearl, which she considered demurer. Mama never went in for flash.

When Grandpa Joe died, I wasn't quite three, but when Grandma got the new ring Mama told me how she'd resented the haste in which Grandma had taken off her first husband's rings, the symbol of a marriage Mama claimed Grandma never seemed to appreciate. Mama had doted on her father, the last blacksmith in South Central Los Angeles. Grandpa also wrote poetry and embedded bits of Grandma's broken crockery into the stone birdbaths, benches, and sundials in the orchard behind their home. Grandma's parents apparently had pressured her to accept a proposal from Joe, their handy man, when she was only sixteen and wanted to finish school.

Mama also disclosed that Grandma had banished to the discard pile an engagement ring she'd received from her second husband, Louie, when she'd learned that it had originally belonged to his first, now deceased, wife. She'd been perfectly willing to stepmother his three grown children, but she'd not wanted to wear what she considered a castoff ring, despite the enormity of its diamond.

As a teenager, I'd been mesmerized by Grandma's new ring. I even asked once if I could try it on, but Grandma had shaken her head. "Not yet," she'd said. "All good things come to those who wait." I'd tried not to show my disappointment.

Later, after her death, when I finally first slid it on my finger, I still believed the ring absolutely radiated glamour, not a term our family previously had used in relation to Grandma. Up until then, she'd always worn modest cotton housedresses, topped by full gingham aprons, decorated with a little rickrack or embroidery on the pockets. Her most extravagant outfit, a poinsettia-patterned frock, embellished with gleaming gold thread, she donned only for Christmas. On birthdays or other special occasions, she might attach a tortoiseshell clip to her silver permed locks, but that was as far as she ever went.

But once Grandma had her cocktail ring, she chose gowns to match its pizzazz. One Thanksgiving she'd swished into Mama's living room, aswirl in lavender velvet. On her eightieth birthday she'd taken her seat at the head of the table at an Italian restaurant, swathed in aquamarine satin. It was if as if the ring had given her permission to be a shade self-indulgent, a tad flamboyant.

Like Mama, and Grandma, until she'd emerged like a butterfly from a chrysalis, I always leaned more towards the sensible than the splashy.

Now, though, at a crossroads when I inherited the ring, I wondered if it could work its magic for me. I figured I could use some color, some shine.

I was halfway through a two-year program leading to a master's degree in social work. My son had started college, and though he still lived at home, I rarely saw him, since he worked nights as a copy boy on the local daily. And my husband of over twenty years still struggled with alcoholism.

For the past several years, Bob had been in and out of ICUs with pancreatitis, in and out of rehab, in and out of recovery. Me . . . I was still *in* the marriage, but I was *out* of love.

After Grandma died and the ring became mine, I wore it with pride for only truly special occasions . . . at the graduation ceremony at UCLA in '78; on New Year's Eve '79, in Times Square when we visited New York City in a half-hearted attempt to put some life back in our dying marriage; and finally, in June 1980, for our twenty-fifth anniversary dinner at the Newport Beach waterfront Villa Nova.

Even Grandma's ring couldn't lend any radiance to that particular evening. Bob believed he had found a recovery program that worked for him. With my MSW, I had landed a job that absorbed all my energy at a facility that housed abused children. We gazed more at the sea than at each other, our conversation consisting of such polite exchanges as "So how did your AA meeting go?" and "How many children were admitted to the nursery this week?" Neither of us really cared. We hadn't even bothered to ask the server to light the candle on our table.

A few months after that last sullen supper, we agreed to divorce. Each morning as I headed north on the San Gabriel River Freeway, I listened to my new tape, John Denver's "Some Days are Diamonds, Some Days are Stone," and nodded knowingly when he sang about cold winds blowing.

I tucked Grandma's ring away in a tiny gold lame sack at the bottom of my jewelry box. I figured it might be a while before there were any other special occasions in my life. For a few years, the cold winds continued to blow.

Finally, in 1987, the winds changed. I'd applied and been accepted by the Peace Corps. In preparation for moving overseas, I sorted through a lifetime's collection of objects. I discarded, gave away or sold nearly everything I owned.

One day I rummaged through my old jewelry box and opened the black velvet bag that housed my rings. I fingered my old engagement and wedding rings, hesitated, and then plunked them in the "sell" pile. I decided to keep a sterling silver ring that Bob had bought for me on a trip to Taxco during happier days. Then I picked up Grandma's cocktail ring. Perhaps my tastes had changed. I slipped it on my finger. How had this rococo clunky ring entranced me? I couldn't picture myself ever wearing it again.

But diamonds were valuable. I decided to sell it. I had no daughters to pass it on to, and the ring could bring a tidy nest egg. During the dimmest days of my marriage, I'd always thought of it as my secret security blanket . . . as something I could pawn or sell in case I ever needed a fresh start. Now I decided that I'd deposit the proceeds from its sale. With accrued interest over the next couple of years, that would help get me started anew once I returned to the States.

That afternoon I visited a jeweler, and we negotiated an acceptable price for my old wedding set. Then I handed him Grandma's ring. "I've never had this appraised," I said. "I wonder what it's worth." I held my breath, prepared to contain my joy if he uttered a figure even larger than I'd imagined.

The man hefted it, peered through his loupe, and grunted. "Not much. I could maybe give you a hundred dollars," he finally said. "Some of the little diamond chips are nice, and it's fourteen karat gold, but both big stones and the emerald are all paste."

"Paste? What do you mean?" I stood there stunned.

"Paste is plain leaded glass that's faceted to look like precious gems."

I gripped the counter to keep from collapsing. I knew in my heart that Grandma's two husbands had given her bona fide diamond engagement rings. Then I remembered Uncle Ray. Like my former husband, Ray always reeked of alcohol. That long dead stepson-in-law must have been the culprit. When he made Grandma's ring, he substituted false stones for the real ones, and Grandma never guessed. She'd had no reason to. He was a relative by marriage, after all. Many times, I'd heard her repeat how blood was thicker than water, and that family always came first. I'd achingly remembered that when Bob and I had first separated, not long after Grandma and my husband's mother had both died.

What chicanery on Uncle Ray's part . . . but at least Grandma had been spared this shocking surprise, and the disillusionment she would have felt knowing her trust had been betrayed.

"Well?"

The jeweler had grown impatient. I didn't hesitate any longer.

"I'll take the hundred," I said.

All these years I'd thought Grandma had left me a treasure . . . and her precious ring turned out to be an illusion, a fake. Even that very day I had thought the legacy would bring me some security in an unforeseeable future.

In the following months as I pursued a new life in another country, I reflected on how much happiness the ring really had brought Grandma, how she had shimmered in its phony glow. Even if Uncle Ray had turned out to be a scoundrel, his workmanship had made Grandma happy. And in willing the ring to me, she'd believed she was passing on something of great value.

Indeed, I decided, she had. I now realized that possessions counted for little in this life. Relationships counted. Adventures, friendships, lovingkindness, memories, generosity, those counted. Objects? Not so much. I remembered how Mama had disdained the showiness of emeralds, wanting something a little more subtle, a pearl. And how willingly she'd contributed her ring to Grandma, knowing her mother set more store in that bright stone than she had herself.

When I'd packed for my Peace Corps assignment in Belize, I'd included the Taxco ring. It might not be glamorous, but it was genuine. More sensible than splashy, it would always remind me that my ex and I had once loved one another. That counted for a lot. I used to wear it on what I anticipated might be a particularly challenging day.

If I'd had a full gingham apron, I likely would have packed that, too, in memory of Grandma who left me a legacy, a valuable lesson about transience and permanence. If all that glitters isn't gold, neither are diamonds always a girl's best friend.

NO WONDER THEY SAY TO FOLLOW YOUR HEART, LOOK WHERE IT LEADS.

YOU ARE NOT WANTED

V
FAITH
ೞಜ಼ೞ಼ೞ

LILLO WAY

HI MY NAME'S HYGEA

—Hygea: Greek goddess of cleanliness and sanitation

I've come to clean your place
    scrub your mind of all confliction
        sweep repressions from under your carpet
            empty your closets of skeletons
                and leave them by the curb

swab your eyes clear of delusion
    feather-dust your heart of particulate pain
        take out the trash I find sleeping in your bed
            remove tarnish from your reputation

on my knees I'll mop your soul
    while humming *cry me a river*
        brush your shards into a pan
            polish each one until it gleams
                transparent as crystal

SARAH BROWN WEITZMAN

THOSE WHO BELIEVED

I was four years old
when I was first told
about God
and I thought it odd
that those who believed
weren't in a big hurry
to live with the Lord.

Unless they lied
to commit suicide
seemed to me
a really good proof of piety.

So it wasn't until
I had the thrill
of my first kiss
that I understood finally
why every one wants to dally.

HEMLATA VASAVADA

PROMISES AND THREATS

Maya read the email message. "If you forward this *mantra* of Lord Ganesh to ten people, you will gain love and prosperity. If you don't forward this message, you will have bad luck."

She blinked and read again. Is this the electronic version of those frightful chain letters from her past with promises and threats?

Maya shook her head and clicked on the next message. "This is a powerful prayer for Saint Therese. You will be richly rewarded if you forward it to your friends and relatives. This is not a joke. One person ignored it and had an accident. Another . . ."

As she thrust her palm in the air, trying to push away the menacing messages, her coffee mug slipped from the desk and splashed on the carpet. She sighed and ran to get a towel.

After blotting up the liquid from the carpet, Maya sprayed a cleaner to remove the stains, slumped on her chair and stared at the computer monitor. The carpet cleaner's smell reminded her of the phenol used to clean hospital floors in India. The computer screen transported her whirling mind to the hot gray asphalt of the driveway of her childhood home in Jaipur.

ೲೞಞೞ

Twelve-year-old Maya's rope slapped the ground in a mesmerizing rhythm under the blazing Jaipur sun. She counted, "Ninety-eight, ninety-nine, one hundred"

She stopped and wiped the sweat with her handkerchief. Now her brother would pass his driving test. Hearing the familiar car horn, Maya dropped her rope and rushed to the wrought-iron compound gate to greet her brother.

Rahul bolted out of the car. "I got my license!"

"Congratulations, Rahul *bhaiya*!" Maya hugged him. Good thing even though she was tired she had continued to skip rope until she reached one hundred. She didn't tell him it was because of her jumping he passed his driving test.

The driver got out of the passenger side and asked, "Should I take the car back to the office for *Sahib*?"

Rahul handed him the car keys. "Gopalji, tell *Pappa* I got my license."

The postman approached the compound gate, and Rahul took the letters from him. Maya followed her eighteen-year-old brother to the drawing room. He set two business envelopes addressed to their father on the center table, then opened the third letter and glanced at it.

"Who sent that, Rahul *bhaiya*?" Maya asked.

"*Aree*, a stupid Krishna *nam* chain letter. They like to scare people, saying if you don't send ten copies with Krishna's name, something bad will happen to you and your family." Rahul crumpled the letter.

Maya covered her mouth with her palm. Her brother had been disrespectful to God. What if Krishna *Bhagwan* got angry and something bad happened to Rahul, or to their parents? "Rahul *bhaiya*, shouldn't we write Lord Krishna's name and send the letters?"

"Maya, these people must have taken an oath to write Krishna *Bhagwan's* names. Instead of writing themselves, they dump it on everyone else. God doesn't reward or punish people for writing or not writing his name. Anyway, as soon as *Pappa* comes home, I'm going to the cinema with my friends. *Mummy* and *Pappa* said if I got my driving license, I could take the car." As he hurried out of the drawing room, to the kitchen, he called their mother, "*Mummy*, I passed my driving test."

Maya picked up the crumpled letter, flattened it on her lap and took it to her room. She vowed to write the chain letters as soon as she returned from the bicycle ride with her friend.

When she returned, her parents were sitting in the drawing room with their tea cups. She sat with them. Mummy said, "Maya, here's your Ovaltine milk."

Maya picked up the glass of milk and took a few gulps. The telephone rang and her father answered it. "What? How? We're coming right away." *Pappa* put the receiver back. "Rahul is in the hospital. A truck hit our car." He paused. "I'll call Sudhir to take us."

When they arrived at the hospital with Uncle Sudhir, the smell of phenol-cleaned floor made Maya sick to her stomach. She couldn't recognize her brother with his face in an oxygen mask, and forehead and eyes covered with white bandages turned pink. Tubes were coming from his body under a white sheet. Nurses hovered around him, fixing the IV bag and checking his pulse. Maya felt a dark hole in her stomach that threatened to consume her. Her father's hands shook as he gripped the foot of the bed. Her mother put her head down on Rahul's bed.

The doctor told them, "His lungs and kidneys have suffered severe injuries. He has lost quite a bit of blood. We need you to bring type O negative from the blood bank." He wrote something on a prescription pad.

Sudhir took the paper from the doctor. "Do you need anything else?"

"Not now. We are trying our best. Maybe your prayers will help."

Prayers! Maya clutched her handkerchief. She'd go home now and write those Krishna *Nam* letters. She grabbed her mother's *sari*. "*Mummy*, can Sudhir *chacha* take me home?"

Her mother glared at Maya with tear-glazed eyes. "How can you think of leaving your brother now?"

She couldn't explain that she had to go home to help her brother.

Sudhir patted her back. "*Beti*, I'm not going home. I'm going to the blood bank across the street."

Maya watched the nurses by Rahul's bed, and waited for her uncle to return so she could persuade him to take her home.

Sudhir *chacha* came back and said, "The nurse will start the blood soon." He took Maya's arm. "Come, we'll sit in the hall."

While they waited in the hall, Maya asked, "Sudhir *Chacha*, can you take me home?"

"Maya *beti*, do you need something?" Sudhir took off his glasses and cleaned them with his handkerchief.

"I need to write Krishna *nam* letters so Rahul *bhaiya* can get well." Maya told him how Rahul had ignored the letter.

"Sometimes we think one thing is the cause of the other." Uncle Sudhir cleared his throat. "In a village, a *pipal* tree was rotting. A crow landed on the tree and it fell. Meanwhile, a sick village elder died. From that day on, whenever the villagers saw crows on any *pipal* tree, they announced that something bad was going to happen."

"But Sudhir *chacha*, I'm not talking about any story. Krishna *Bhagwan* is punishing Rahul *bhaiya*. I must write the letters."

"Maya, the man in the village didn't die because the crow sat on the tree. There is no connection between sending letters in God's name and Rahul's accident. Let's think of positive thoughts for Rahul."

Hearing her mother's wail, they ran back to the room.

Pappa's face was red; his hands still clutching Rahul's bed post. *Mummy* sagged to the floor.

Maya's stomach burned. She could have saved her brother if she had written those Krishna *Nam* letters and posted them.

Summer blended into autumn, then winter and spring, again, and then again. Maya plodded through her days, hoping to bring comfort to her parents. She vowed never to ignore the letters of promises and threats.

Year after year, Maya wrote chain letters in the name of Ram, Krishna, Lakshmi, Ganesh, Sai Baba, Jesus or Allah. She didn't receive any rewards promised in the letters, but she knew she had averted disasters.

When Maya was writing a *mantra*, her mother asked, "Have you thought about what our friends might think when you dump these letters on them?"

"But, *Mummy*, I'm not signing my name."

"Aree, Maya, they know your handwriting."

Soon, Maya started typing the letters and picking strangers' names from the telephone directory to mail the ultimatums.

☙☙❧❧

Blinking at the computer screen, Maya shook her head to cast off the haze of her dreadful memories. After years of writing in fear, it was a relief when the chain letters had stopped.

But now they were back in email form. Maya sighed. She was a thirty-five-year-old woman, living in a suburb of Seattle with her husband and daughter, and she should be able to ignore such "prayer-by-fear" tactics. But forwarding these messages on her email list was so much easier than typing them one at a time, or writing them painfully by hand. Why not do it for the safety of everyone?

She clicked "Forward" but the cursor hovered over the recipient line. To whom could she send such messages? Maya decided to do this later, as she had to get ready and go to her daughter's school where she volunteered in the library.

At the school, the nurse, Carol, came to her. "Mrs. Sen, Reena fell from the monkey bar. She seems okay, but it's better to have her checked by her doctor."

Maya followed the nurse and saw Reena sitting on a chair with a few scratches on her face and hand. The nurse said, "She bumped her head pretty good, so we think the doctor should examine her."

Maya called her husband at his office before going to the doctor.

"I'll meet you there," Ashok said.

She wondered if there was a connection between Reena's fall and her hesitation to forward the prayer messages. It could be a warning.

The doctor examined the six-year-old. "We want to get some X-rays, and we'll observe her for a few hours."

Maya's mind flooded with memories of her late brother. She brought her trembling hands together and promised herself to forward the chain letters as soon as she got home.

In the evening Maya and Ashok brought Reena home. Maya took out leftover chicken curry, rice and spinach for dinner. After eating, they entertained their little girl by playing her favorite Chutes and Ladders board game. Her smile took away Maya's worries. At night, she cuddled with her daughter and fell asleep in Reena's bed.

At midnight, the chain letters popped into Maya's dream, jolting her out of her sleep. She couldn't get to the computer in the bedroom since it would wake up Ashok. She looked at Reena, sleeping next to her. She caressed her daughter's face. Her even breathing calmed Maya's racing heart. Reena was okay, but what about *Mummy* and *Pappa* in Jaipur? Maya went to the kitchen and called them.

"Hello." She heard her father's voice and let out a breath of relief.

"Hello, *Pappa*, how is your health, and how is *Mummy*?"

"We're fine. We just finished our lunch. Your *Mummy* has gone to visit Mrs. Ghosh. But it's one in the morning for you. Is Reena all right?"

"She's fine," Maya assured her father as much as herself. "I couldn't sleep so I thought I'd talk to you. I'll call again when *Mummy* is home."

"*Achha beti,*" Hearing her father's "all right, dear daughter," words, Maya put the phone down.

A lump of relief formed in her throat. She returned to her bedroom, snuggled close to Ashok and drifted off to sleep.

In the morning, the sight of bright yellow and magenta rhododendrons in the yard cheered Maya in spite of the gray clouds. She decided to keep

Reena home and let her sleep in. After Ashok left for work, Maya wrapped her cold hands around her steaming mug of coffee, went to her desk and turned on the computer.

She faced the email messages that promised happiness and wealth, but had caused her agony and fear. How could just forwarding the messages help her or anyone else? Would an omniscient, omnipotent God or Goddess keep score, bless some for forwarding a message, and curse others for not doing so? If she forwarded them to her friends, would their days, too, be marred by anxiety?

She pursed her lips. She highlighted one chain message, then the other and clicked delete, breaking the cycle of promises and threats.

JAN PHILLIPS

THE POWER OF MYTHS

I tell you this because in the course of our lives, every one of us is called to let go of old ideas and make room for the new. It is critical to our evolution, this shedding. What Nature does, we, as Nature, must do as well.

As I matured, I let go of simplistic ideas handed down to me as a child. I took ownership of my beliefs, felt the difference between an inherited thought and original thought.

The letting go starts early, as we recall from our experience with Santa Claus, the Easter Bunny, the Tooth Fairy. But we are young then, and so resilient.

Later, it becomes more difficult. The myths and fables have sunk their roots into our bones by the time we reach puberty. Our identity is grafted to false ideas. We pledge allegiance and give our lives, at times, for the ideas of others. Before we know how to define ourselves, we inherit a belief system they claim is worth our lives.

Catholicism was this to me. It was installed into my cells at an early age. It was mystical, sensual, all-pervasive, flooding into my pores like holy water from a sacred well. I was awash in its wave of wonder.

All my life, Church was something wondrous that happened to me. I was its recipient. Then a day came when I was asked to define my religion, to say what it meant to believe, to consider how I moved in this way, and not that way, because of it. I was asked to create a living faith.

Leaves began to fall from the tree of me.

This is what happened.

—St. Joseph's Provincial House, Latham, New York, 1967

A priest named Father Grabys, a tall, burly Lithuanian, came in three times a week to teach us Theology. The morning he entered the room, we were seated at our desks with our hands folded. The seats were in perfect rows, all facing forward. A crucifix, as always, hung on the front wall. On this morning, he unloaded an armful of books on his desk, then swirled around to face us.

"All right, let's hear it," he said in a thick accent. "Here you are, ready to marry God. Tell me something about this God you love. Someone, stand up and tell me about this relationship of yours."

Right away I didn't like him. How were we supposed to say something about our relationship to God? People didn't talk about that. We knew what we knew from the catechism. We had all the facts, but he was asking about feelings. That was uncharted territory. And I liked it that way.

No one raised a hand.

"Someone?" he barked. "Can't someone say something? You're dedicating yourself to God and you can't say why or what this God means to you?"

One postulant raised her hand, stood up and uttered the familiar words: "God made me to show His goodness and to share his everlasting life with me in heaven."

I nodded my head in agreement, having memorized this years ago just like everyone else in the room. Right out of the Baltimore Catechism.

The priest looked dismayed. He frowned and half-shouted, "That's it? That's all you got?"

"Yes, Father."

"Sit down," he said, looking around for another hand. "Someone else!"

Another brave soul stood up saying, "In God there are three Divine Persons, really distinct, and equal in all things—the Father, the Son, and the Holy Spirit."

I nodded again in the affirmative, and again Father Grabys grimaced. "Is that the best you can do?"

"Yes, Father."

"Next," he yelled, as she took her seat, looking around in wonder. By now, we were all confused, but one more raised her hand. "God can do all things, and nothing is hard or impossible to Him." "Sit down," he barked again.

Rolling his eyes, he crossed his arms and surveyed the whole group of us with a look of disdain. By now, blood was rushing up my neck. Beads of sweat broke out on my forehead. I had my first anxiety attack. A fat tear dripped down my cheek.

Why was he so mean? I wondered. He asked for our ideas about God and when we shared them, he took a sledgehammer and smashed them into smithereens.

Finally he spoke. "You should be ashamed for having nothing more than catechism answers to this question. Are you just a bunch of parrots, repeating everything you've been taught? Hasn't anyone here gone beyond the Baltimore Catechism in your thinking?"

The air was thick with silence. Hands were folded, eyes cast down. A few more tears cascaded down my face. I prayed he wouldn't call on me.

"You must come to know what is true about God from your own experience," said the priest. "If you are to be a religious worth your salt, you have to arrive at a faith that is deeper than your learning—one that rises up from the nature of who you are. Your faith must be rooted in your ultimate concerns."

I had no idea what he was talking about. I'd never heard anything about ultimate concerns before, but Father Grabys insisted we get at the root of ours. He waved his arms in the air shouting about creating a faith for ourselves. I looked up at him, watching spit fly off his Lithuanian lips, wondering how in the world anyone builds a faith for themselves.

Wasn't faith something I was born into? Something I inherited, from the outside? I was a Catholic by default. They told me everything I was supposed to believe. That was the point, wasn't it? As far as I was concerned, I was just lucky to be born into the one true faith. I didn't have anything to *say* about it. That's what infallible popes were for.

Father Grabys was trying to grow us up. Here he was with a class of mostly eighteen-year-olds who believed everything they were ever taught. We never *pondered* our religion. We didn't have feelings or opinions about it. We prayed to the One God, the Holy Trinity, whose only pronouns were he, him, his. Now suddenly we're being asked to share the nature of our relationship—a total invasion of privacy it seemed to me. I raised my hand.

"Father, we've been studying our faith since second grade. We've memorized everything. We know every answer to every question. What you're talking about we never learned," I said. "I don't even know what you mean when you talk."

He towered above us, his brow furrowed. "What you believe, that is religion," he said. "Who you are, what you live for—that is faith. They are two different things, and *faith* is what we're here to explore. Your faith is what you must create and declare—your faith which is and will be the very *essence* of your spirituality." His voice was thunderous, cracking and booming on words like *faith* and *essence*. His thick Baltic accent added to the drama.

"You can let go of religion right now," he added. "Let go of all your beliefs for awhile. Put them up on a shelf for this semester. I will teach you how to create a faith that will see you through everything."

I didn't *want* to let go of any beliefs. They were all I had. And they were enough. I didn't need anything more. As we continued on in the class, the biblical paradox that says we must lose our lives in order to find them began to make sense. We could no longer fall back on ready-made answers. Now that all our memorized dogma and doctrine was on the back shelf, it was unavailable to us. Our religion had been shelved, and our faith was about to make an entrance.

Like an Olympic coach, Father Grabys pushed us beyond our comfort zones. "Think of faith as a plan for action, not a set of beliefs," he shouted, writing it on the board in big white letters: Faith = action (based on commitments); religion = beliefs (based on doctrine.) When we squirmed in our seats, rubbed our heads, stared blankly into our notebooks, he reminded us that *what* any of us believe is not the essential thing.

"Don't look for beliefs! What you believe doesn't matter here. What matters is what you feel strongly about, what you are committed to, what is your ultimate concern."

My stomach churned. My brain ached. What in the hell was he talking about? I was an A+ student, bright as a sunny day, but I couldn't get what he was asking for. I was mired in the software I'd been programmed with. It was a story that I loved, thoroughly believed, would go to my death defending. I was Peter Pan in some kind of Never Land. God was out there in the Heavens taking care of everything.

At night, Father Grabys' words circled in my head like goldfish in a bowl.

"Forget what you have learned."

"Think of what you stand for."

"What is it you care about?"

"To what are you committed?"

Commitments require a sense of self, a sense of purpose, and *even more*, a sense of agency. One needs a feeling of self-authority to act, to say *yes, I stand for this and not that*. This was contrary to what I'd learned. All my life I'd been taught *what* to think, not *how* to think—shaped by *Father Knows Best*, shaped by God the Father, shaped by women earn less, men are the bosses, only boys can be presidents. I didn't have agency. I was no agent of change. I had no sense of authority, and what sense I did have they were trying to beat out of me, it seemed, the whole rest of the time.

He wanted us to create something real from the grist of our lives—to claim what moved us; to be willful; to take our power. His pursuit was to wake us up. His assignment: to involve us in our own spirituality. While our superiors drummed at us about obedience and humility, puncturing whatever sense we had of self-importance, this priest did the opposite: he demanded that we examine our conscience, discern our own values, proclaim out loud our self-created faith.

I don't know how the others were dealing with all this. Even in the few minutes of recreation we did have in our busy schedules, no one ever brought up this situation when we had time to talk. Ask anyone else now who was in that class what happened and they'll never remember it like I do. It was my watershed moment.

I didn't know what I believed outside of what I'd been taught. I knew the church couldn't be right about everything. There was friction, and plenty of it—me being queer and having to hide it; my dad being a non-Catholic and not suitable for heaven; relatives who left the church because they had too many kids and the church said no birth control.

And here I am, in a convent, trying to get my arms around what I'm committed to. According to Paulo Freire, we are *conditioned, but not determined*, and the more people accept the passive role impressed on them, the more they adapt to the *fragmented view of reality deposited in them*. That was exactly where I was, right along with all the other postulants in the room. We had been conditioned, but now we were about to determine something for ourselves.

I was not the only emotional toddler in the room. We had all been infantilized by the church on one level or another. There we sat, a group of thirty young women, wearing exactly the same outfits, pulling a veil out of our pockets every time we visited chapel, reminiscent of some ancient commandment that women cover their heads in church. My superior tells me not to talk to Sister So-and So because she fears our relationship is becoming "carnal," and not one class in our training as religious women focuses on creating healthy relationships. It was a time of blindness and terrible wrong thinking.

Pastors around the world made decisions for Catholic families, bishops had the priests under their thumbs, the pope could not err, thousands of priests around the world were abusing children, and God the Father was out there in the heavens supposedly overseeing everything. Religious authorities told us what was right and wrong, what opinions we should have, what direction to move in morally, spiritually, politically. It made things very simple. All we had to do was abdicate our power.

But Father Grabys had other ideas. Throughout the semester, we avoided the catechism, recited nothing from memory. It was a generative time. A time to create. A time of loss, anxiety, fear. Week after week, I stretched and struggled to let go of ideas that no longer served me. I didn't *want* to let go. I liked how it was—the comfortable certainties, the security of proclamations handed down by popes from generation to generation—Virgin Birth, Immaculate Conception, Perpetual Adoration, Holy Days of Obligation. I worried about being original in matters of faith, but Grabys insisted.

"This is your spiritual life," he'd remind us. "Who better to create it?"

We asked him repeatedly what he meant by ultimate concerns. When we did, he got up from his desk, moved closer to our seats and surveyed the whole room before he spoke, incredulous that this was taking so long.

"What are you *living* for?" he'd shout out, trying to blast inroads in our neural networks. "What means so much to you that you would give your life for it? What *matters* to you? What are you committed to? What will never happen in your presence?"

He hammered at us from every angle—he, Michelangelo, we, his David. He chiseled away at our memorized ideas, our childish concepts, till he carved right into the core of our beings.

Father Grabys' questions were Himalayan and we were barely at the foothills. I tried to remember what Jesus said, thinking I couldn't go wrong with him. I hadn't studied the New Testament, but I'd heard his words in hundreds of Masses:

> *The kingdom of heaven is all around you; it is inside and above you; it is like yeast, like a seed, like a pearl of great price, like a king preparing a wedding banquet, like a man beaten and lying on the street. It is who you are, it is your neighbors and your enemies, it opens its doors to you when you forgive, when you are generous, when you help others; it welcomes you when you believe though you cannot see, when you give praise and thanks; it is visible and invisible, it is like a seed germinating; it is a house built on rock; it is forever, it is yours, you belong; I am in you and you are in me; we are One with the Father; it is like the lost sheep, the lost coin, the lost son, coming home, O! Alleluia! We are the light of the world.*

As I reflected, his words kept coming: "What you have seen me do, you can do and more. . . . Do to others what you would have them do to you. . . . For I was hungry and you gave me food." In the course of this litany, my convictions came into focus.

In order for peace and justice to reign, I myself had to be peaceful and just. In order for light to shine in this world, it had to pour forth from where I was standing. If kindness and mercy were to prevail, it must prevail in *my* life, in *my* thoughts. The pieces started to cohere, eventually rising to the surface. It was as the Hindu Upanishads proclaim:

> *The Self is hidden in the hearts of all*
> *As butter lies hidden in cream.*

The day arrived when I stood before the class and proclaimed my faith, independent of my religion and self-created. I was still a devout Catholic. I still loved the traditions, believed in the doctrines. I had not lost anything at all, but I had gained a life, a spiritual life, which until then I'd never been able to claim. Now that I finally comprehended the meaning of ultimate concerns, this is what I shared:

"I am committed to be a peacemaker and to insist on justice wherever I am.

"I am committed to caring for others as I care for myself.

"I am committed to being a light in the world."

Faith and religion were two distinct things. They took up separate residences in my body: religion in my brain and heart, faith in my gut, my hands and legs. Faith would be my lived-out religion. The faith I shared that day was original and real, born from my body and inseparable from my soul. It was an act of self-revelation, one that I thought of years later when I came upon these words by Audre Lorde in a *Sinister Wisdom* magazine:

> *The transformation of silence into language and action is an act of self-revelation and that always seems fraught with danger. We fear the very visibility without which we also cannot truly live . . . and that visibility which makes us most vulnerable is that which is also the source of our greatest strength.*

As I looked to my life for what I believed, I moved in tandem away from fear, away from silence. As I progressed beyond the creeds I'd inherited and memorized, I felt an energy surge in my innermost being. When asked to give voice to my ultimate concerns, I faced a void I'd never felt. I resisted. I panicked. I had no idea how to think for myself. I cried, but I did not turn and run. Eventually I found words that matched the love in my heart, and a voice that revealed what that love demanded. That was all I needed to create my faith: to see what I loved and to know what I must do to keep it alive.

DAVID LEWITZKY

CAVE WITH FAMILIAR FACES

In this defining moment
This cave holds many meanings for me

My uncertain self, an unsolved puzzle
Isolation, suffocation

Here's my mother on the cave wall
Pushing me. Complaining

Here's my batty father hanging upside down
Playing solitaire. Mumbling to himself

Here's Julie and our children
Imploring me and out of reach

There's a gallery of betrayal here
A display of spleen and spite

The hosts of people who've betrayed me
The hosts that I've betrayed

No one will tell me what's going on here
But I'll have my say

Destiny's a dead end, perception's mere presumption
Fuck Plato. Fuck this cave

THE SEVEN DEADLY SINS
—after Linda Pastan

Avarice
I had a business once
Made a mint of money
Not all that honestly
Trampling clouds and stars

Lost that business
Again, a tad illegally
I walked uneasily
On scorched and naked ground

All that money
Down the tubes
Nada. Gone. Goodbye

I miss
That money

Pride
In the moral conflict
Between pride and self-effacement
Pride's a crème brulee
Self-effacement's jello
Pride parades its weapons
Self-effacement seeks out shadows
Pride's a clerestory
Self-effacement's mud

Gluttony
All my life
From boy to man
To alter-cocker

I've been the noble pig
The valiant over-eater
Lord Never-Enough
The Earl of More-More-More

I can't swallow the universe
And so I weep
My immortal appetites
Will surely make me
Universal

Lust
She has an air of neediness about her
She trusts me
So what

She's bitter from betrayal
She's doing this to punish someone else
I don't care

Although she craves me and adores me
Does everything I want
She'll never matter much to me

This is my preoccupation
My determination to commit
Again, and yet again
This most radiant of sins

Sloth

Sometimes I dream myself
A Medieval cloistered monk
My life laid out for me
Designated hourly devotions
Enthusiastic piety and prayer

Truth is: I'd rather stay in bed
Take a vow of indolence
Skip prayers

I am Everyman
Brother to all mankind

Just let me grab a few more z's

Envy
When my poet friends
Receive awards and the acclaim
That has always eluded me
I support them
Wish them well

But all the time I'm thinking
May their faces become dart boards
Their tongues break out in blisters
Their tonsils
Turn to worms

Anger
Because nobody calls me
Messiah Dave
I'm Nazi Dave
Destroyer of my race

Because I'm not so lovable
I'll walk out on my family
Torch my house
Write my children off
Slander my wife

I'm not so pretty
I declare myself
The President of Ugly

Give myself a hate parade
In the harsh confetti rain
In the familiar streets
I'll run down everyone I can
In my bitter limousine

Such thoughts come to me
Warm me up and comfort me
As I cozy up to rage

DANIEL M. JAFFE

IT'S NOT THAT . . .

From her back row seat, Marla scans the congregation. It's not that she expects to see her parents—they were never ones to attend Friday night services, only Saturday morning ones—but Marla's not taking any chances. It's not that she wishes to avoid her parents *per se*, just their predictable reactions upon seeing her in synagogue: a hopeful look in her mother's eye, "Is Billy converting?" Or Dad's, "Jewishness is part of us; of course you can't give it up, not even for your spouse."

Looking around at the sanctuary's older women with white doily-veils pinned to stiff hairdos, Marla recognizes a few faces, albeit with more wrinkles and cheek sags than she recalls from the last time she attended services . . . ten years ago. None of these particular matrons were ever family friends, just co-presences under God. None of them seem to notice her now. Nor do the assorted men who adjust yarmulkes, the young women who hold black *siddurim*, the children who look up to examine the sanctuary's wooden walls, hand-carved to resemble the Western Wall. No one stares or points at Marla. No one looks at all.

So many new faces in the congregation. Young husband-and-wife faces, tired from a week's work, but here nonetheless. Marla's impressed, not that she thinks services offer a family anything they can't find at home: You want the camaraderie of a crowd on Friday night? Throw a pizza party and dress comfy.

A slight musty smell permeates the sanctuary, as if it's endured one-too-many Noah floods. The hand-embroidered tree of life on the ark's purple velvet curtain is looking frayed at the edges, the royal-blue carpeting is worn and passé. Her seat cushion feels lumpy. All those 1970s refurbishings were undertaken while her Dad was the Temple's Building Committee chairman. She gives a private smirk.

Marla fingers the gold *Magen David* hanging on her chest and joins everyone in chanting the *Barechu*, reciting the *Shema*, singing the *Veahavtah*. She participates softly, in tentative whisper, her tongue thick with resistance. As if these prayers intending communal adoration of God might actually express, for her, some personal heresy. It's not the words that matter, she tells herself. Just concentrate on the melodies, the lilts.

Cantor Weizman on the *bimah* is leading everyone, as usual. A small man with scowling face that always belied his warmth. Does he still widen his eyes in mock surprise whenever children reach into his suit jacket pockets for Israeli hard candies? He used to carry them even on Shabbes when carrying was forbidden. "To instill in children joy while attending *shul*—for such a sin I'll take the risk."

Snippet visions of Cantor Weizman's approving nods beside her as she, in pigtails, practiced the *trup* for her *haftorah* on that very *bimah* twenty . . . thirty years ago. He stood beside her during her actual bat mitzvah, too, whispering over and over, "*yaldah tovah*," good girl.

And behind him now, Rabbi Katz hovers in his standard black robe that Marla always found a tad pretentious, a large gray yarmulke matching his gray mustache. When she asked him, seven years ago, to officiate at her wedding, he shook his head so hard that even his slight jowls wobbled. He's got a full-fledged turkey waddle now, she thinks with satisfaction, and hairs growing out of that ogre-like raised beauty mark on his weak chin.

The day after Rabbi Katz turned her down, Cantor Weizman telephoned, and she expected him, too, to rail against her upcoming marriage; but, he said only: "To attend your wedding would be a joy. Unfortunately, some rules, you know, are like foundation stones—you jiggle them too hard and everything crumbles." He then wished her inner peace and many children. When Audrey was born a year later, she sent the cantor a baby announcement and he replied with a card. Not one saying "Mazel Tov," but "Congratulations." How loud the wail of absent Yiddish or Hebrew.

Tonight Audrey is enjoying a father-daughter evening at the newest Pixar film. Billy's a devoted dad. Marla chose well, in any language.

It's not that Marla planned to attend services tonight. It's not that she's been longing, it's not even that she thinks about services much at all anymore. It's certainly not prayer that she misses, the seemingly endless glorification of a God whose existence she increasingly questions. What kind of God can permit violence in His name? The ancient Hebrews' brutal conquest of the Promised Land. The Crusades. The Spanish Inquisition. Protestant against

Catholic. Pogroms in Russia. Jihad. Sunni against Shiite. Today's fanatical bloodshed on the West Bank, in Gaza, in Israel because God gave the land to this one—no, to that one. No, she hasn't missed prayer.

Not formal prayer, anyway. But those *Fiddler on the Roof* sort of Tevye prayers—direct conversations with God at any time of the day and from any place—those prayers she can respect. If God were all-powerful, then wouldn't He have the time to consider everyone's individual circumstances, to give a sign here and there that He understands one's choices and respects them even if they breach His rules? He is, after all, the One who gave us freedom of choice, isn't He? What kind of parent advocates freedom of choice for his children, only to turn his back when they make a choice he doesn't like? She's a parent, she knows these things. Should God be held to a different standard? Either we're created in His image or we're not.

After she heard Billy drive off this evening, Marla put on a Cyndi Lauper CD, undressed, and set patchouli-scented candles around the oval bathtub. But when she lit them . . . lighting those pillar candles on a Friday night led to old associations and connections like the tug of a lost limb, a vague phantom ache.

Why not? she thought. It'll be a kick. For old times' sake. A hello to Cantor Weizman, a piece of Danish and she'll be home before Billy and Audrey will even know she ever left. Not that Billy would object to her attending services. He'd even let her take Audrey if she wished. No, it's Marla who's chosen to raise Audrey secular, although culturally Jewish (Chanukah, Purim, bagel brunches, klezmer music).

To avoid the inevitable confrontation with parents about an actual wedding—they could tolerate her living with Billy, but marriage?—Marla and Billy eloped to Las Vegas. Plastic chapel, plastic flowers, plastic justice of the peace. No matter how cliché and cheap, the actual ceremony couldn't tarnish her sense of their marriage being sacred in a spiritual-connection-between-two-people sort of way. That's all that mattered.

Gradually their families learned to adapt with only the most subtle of occasional reminders. Like the time after Aunt Roz died and Dad made a point of explaining to Billy why the mirrors were covered, and "by the way, you mustn't use *fleishik* silverware with the dairy noodle kugel." As if Billy would be so stupid. As if Dad explained such basics to the Reform Jewish cousins. And like that time after a wedding mass when Billy's older cousin Phil, with his spider-veined alcoholic's nose, took Marla by the elbow and whispered, "the Host is nothing whatsoever like Jewish matzoh crackers." As if Marla had asked. Or cared.

Marla stumble-hums the unfamiliar version of *adon olam*, then watches as the couples all around exchange "Good Shabbes" handshakes and cheek pecks. Everyone then files out of the rows; Marla moves with the crowd to the auditorium behind the sanctuary for the *oneg* of wine, juice, pastries. She selects a cinnamon *ruggelach*—so flaky and sweet, she can taste the cream cheese, relishes the authenticity of recipe. Children Audrey's age—how cute!—are gobbling chocolate-chip cookies, a group of women on Marla's left chat about their divorce settlements, a group on her right hang on a tall woman's every description of her new recycling company. Marla looks from one woman to another, smiling in case anyone might notice.

Rabbi Katz stands off to the side chatting with Cantor Weizman. Marla stares, hoping to catch the Cantor's eye so that he'll approach her. But she really really really doesn't want Rabbi Katz to spot her, so she turns aside.

She hears Russian, not that she speaks Russian herself. Must be one of the immigrant families. Marla sees a plump short man with gray hair-fringe speaking to a woman with too-red hair and gold crowns. Are they lonely all by themselves? She should go over and extend a "Good Shabbes." But something stops her. She pictures Rabbi Katz spotting her, scurrying over and whispering to the gray hair-fringed man. She pictures the Rabbi ushering the Russian couple away from Marla as if she were some contaminative lump of pork. Or what if the Russian himself were to respond to Marla's greeting with, "Excuse, please, we leave Russia to be good Jews and become part of Jewish collective. But you abandon Jewish identity like old suitcase too heavy to *shlep*."

And so. Finally she gets it. This ridiculous imagining is the reason Marla hasn't attended services in years. This is why she doesn't bring Audrey to temple. Because Marla expects other Jews to show her no flexibility. Because they won't respect her choice to retain Jewish identity deep within herself, privately, in her genes, her angular nose, her memories, her endless questioning. Because she expects fellow Jews to make her feel a stranger in her own tradition. Because . . . *she* expects.

Marla looks over her shoulder at Rabbi Katz and Cantor Weizman, still deeply engaged in conversation and oblivious to everyone around them.

Rabbi Katz looks up. His glance meets hers and he smiles, says something to Cantor Weizman who also looks over and smiles. Both men nod to Marla, wave even.

Could they genuinely be pleased to see her? Perhaps. But most likely, they were rejoicing that Marla couldn't stay away. Or that she came in acknowledgment of having made a mistake marrying a non-Jew. Or that she's now longing to return to the flock. They probably expect her to slink over to them and say she's come to her senses and has returned to her true home, the temple.

Marla nods back at them and waves, beams a broad grin meant to convey inner peace and contentment. She turns, strides out the auditorium door. That'll show them, she thinks. That'll show them.

ALISON STONE

NOT ME, NOT MINE

I. The Writing

Marianne, the paper gleams.
The dark lake of my brain releases nothing.

But you said write it,
So it must be written.
You are old enough
to be my mother.

Each night, a sentence
at a time, I lay my self down.
You ask for everything,
not just pain's dramatic mask.

"List everyone that you resent,
ten things you fear,
two traits you want to change,
at least one page of things you've done
that make you cringe."

I hold the pen in my left hand
and wrestle language,
pushing the past out;
it hurts like a kidney stone.

Each year smudges,
breathing hurts.
Is it the back brace or the words
fighting to be heard?

Prove you love me
I accused a lover once. *Let me take you*
to my mute and ugly girl.
Marianne, he would not know her.

II. The Paintings

I enter and walk up to *Avarice*,
big with blue tentacles.
Sloth touches corners with *Pride*.
In the bedroom *Lust* swirls, dripping crimson.
They are all here, grand and luminous,
every wrong thing beautiful.

Why did your child paint
the names for sin?

Some say language creates desire —
that the gap between an object and its name
grows like a cavity.
But with a name I take
an object's power, hold it with my lips and tongue.
I say *mother's suicide attempts*, I say
methadone, I say *J. testing positive.*

I want to speak with art,
use skill to shape a world.
But when I stare at naked flesh
and carefully charcoal the lines and shadows,
light remains
only in places on the page
where I have drawn nothing.

What I write for you
is not art. For you I write
my dark and messy testament.
I know you do not judge.
You have framed the sins your son made,
spreading vice throughout your house
to greet your guests.

III. The Telling

To overcome illness, a monk taught me—
mentally break down the body; peel
the skin, then place the organs
in a mound. Finally dismantle the odd ladder of bone.
All the while chant: *It is not me.*
It is not mine. It is not myself.

I sit on your bed, holding my life.
Marianne, this stack of words
is just discarded flesh.

Sin
I read once
is to die
without knowing yourself.

I have known myself
nights when the wind growls ancient chants.

You say:
To fail to love your life is sin.
I do not always
love my life.

Marianne,
you are not my mother. You can
love my life as something precious and separate.
You say to be a mother means
to love improperly.
I know this as I know the strange
bend in my finger,
the dull blue of my eyes.

What is forgivable?
I ask you now as we place
each page in the fire
and watch my history burn.
Your fingers tremble as the ashes fly.
I kiss you once, then walk outside
into what is left of my life.

LOWELL JAEGER

A BLESSING

Just noise, the word "soul,"
unless you've paid for it
wide-eyed nights,
stars wheeling and grinding.
The word "god,"
a crumble of dust.

As a kid you longed
to lose yourself in the forest.
An inner compass
led you back to the light
of meadow and hayfield
and onto dirt roads toward home.

O, but how you've been bewildered,
decades gone astray, waking one morning,
an empty shell. Eyes
groping curb to curb
like a blind man's cane.

There's no inner guide
with the flame in your heart
extinguished. Only a wisp
of smoke in the darkness.
Does no good to plead with your "soul"
for shelter. No "god"
reaches and takes your hand.

Best you can do is stay put.
The sun rises at your back.
Then the moon.
Over and over.

You set one foot forward, timidly.
Drag the next after.
This is how words mean.
Thank g-g-god, you stammer. *B-b-bless my s-s-soul.*

AWAKE IN THE MOMENT

Heard myself musing of late
about youth—years risen and gone—in which
my shoes moved merely gristle and bone
while the soul floated patiently aloft
in the ether beyond, tethered to its lost flesh
by some miraculous thread.

Till I woke in the moment my soul landed,
a blind man enlightened,
bemoaning half a life wasted,
yet joyous to have arrived whole
for a singular breath, the next, and next.

Same as last night I rose from bed
to fix a neglected chore holding sleep
hostage. And froze in the yellow glow
streaming through my window,
this harvest moon
come 'round to hold me speechless,
as the black night glittered and flamed,
mirrored in the lake across the road below,
an invisible breeze rippling the moon's reflection . . .

and I stood naked, alone, connected,
one small pulse within the webbed complexity, shivering
to glimpse the mystery and beauty
of how it all fits
into some overwhelming immensity

if anything fits at all.

HOW ARE WE TO BELIEVE GOD IS WATCHING OVER WHERE EVERY SOUL SLEEPS?

An alarming confusion of bees
buzz and nip our wine glasses, testing and tasting,
traversing our tray of cheeses
and spicy meats.

We've chosen a street-side table,
my wife and I, a strategic mistake.
Now the beggar-boy flies up
and hovers over us, an outstretched hand
demanding our attention. No fix

to ignore him or wave him away.
He's quick and resolute in his desperation,
so filthy I cower to his stink.

I'm penning postcards, and . . . while I stand
to dig from my pockets a ransom of pesos . . .
I hand him the card I've freshly addressed.
I don't know why I do this,
just dumb misguided dismay.

Then he's gone. So, too, it seems,
most of the bees. He's smudged
his thumbprint on my postcard. Ruined it.
The wine has soured. My wife complains.

Even the card's outlook has changed.
Behind those manicured hedges along the walkway
beside the convent . . . I suspect
he's hiding and pissing there. Sunshine
has paled on the gardens,
and the cathedral's windows are stained.

NOBODY RIDES ALONE

That's the rule, moving our trucks,
dragging concessions wagons
fairground to fairground.
Of course we break the rule
when a man might need to be by himself
in the cab, time to smoke with no one
joking beside him. Time
to think through what he
hadn't had time to think through.

But never convoy. Just go,
and if we come across one of our own
broke down, we pull over
and do what needs done.
Lots of flats. Busted fan belts.
Fuel filters choked with horserace dust.

Once Teddy pulled off on a side road,
parked his truck in the ditch—
not stuck there, just quit.
We stepped up close enough
to spy him crying behind the wheel,
staring across burned-out sage flats,
his face all screwed with the blues.

We concurred to wait nearby
and worry for a bit—how all of us were lost
one way or another.

When Teddy worked his nerve back up on the pavement,
we followed him, blinking back
ghosts of our own. No
questions asked. That's the rule.
Nobody rides alone.

Intimations, and Imitations

How to understand.

Waiting for Contentment to Bite

CONTRIBUTORS

Patricia Barone is publishing her fifth book, *The Music of this Ruin*, with Taj Mahal Press. Her short stories have been published by Wising Up Press, Peter Lang, Prentice/Merrill, Plume/Penguin, *American Writing,* and *West Wind Review.* She has received a Loft-McKnight Award of Distinction in poetry, a Lake Superior Contemporary Writers Award for short story, and a Minnesota Arts Board Career Opportunity Grant.

Jane Blanchard divides her time between Augusta and Saint Simon's Island, Georgia. She studied English at Wake Forest University before earning a doctorate from Rutgers University. She has published four collections with Kelsay Books: *Unloosed* (2016), *Tides & Currents* (2017), *After Before* (2019), and *In or Out of Season* (2020).

Lauren Camp is the author of five books, most recently *Took House* (Tupelo Press), which *Publishers Weekly* calls a "stirring, original collection." Honors include the Dorset Prize and finalist citations for the Arab American Book Award and the New Mexico-Arizona Book Award. Her work has been translated into Mandarin, Turkish, Spanish, and Arabic.

Mara A. Cohen, PhD has been published in *Eckleburg Review, Trampset, Nervous Breakdown, Litro, BioStories, Mindful Word, Magnolia Review, Mothers Always Write, Hairpin, Alimentum, Chicken Soup for the Soul, Los Angeles Daily News, LA Business Journal, La Opinion, New America Media, National Civic Review, Urban Affairs Review, Political Research Quarterly, Public Opinion Quarterly, Sociological Quarterly, California History,* and others.

Maryah Converse was a Peace Corps educator in Jordan from 2004 to 2006. She has written for publications including *Silk Road Review, The Matador Review,* and *Michigan Quarterly Review.* Maryah works in fundraising for refugees, and teaches Arabic in the New York area. She is currently finishing an essay collection and a memoir.

Terri Elders, LCSW, a lifelong writer and editor, has contributed to 130 anthologies, including multiple editions of the *Chicken Soup for the Soul* and *Not Your Mother's Book* series, as well as in two previous Wising Up Anthologies: *Surprised by Joy* and *Goodness.* A native Californian, she writes feature articles for numerous national and international periodicals.

Jaime Grookett is a poetry and fiction author. Her work is featured in various publications, such as *Across the Margin*, where her short story, "Fine is for Sugar," is listed as Best of Fiction 2020. She is a MFA Candidate at Drexel University where she teaches writing. Currently, she is working on a collection of short stories and a historical fiction novel.

Lowell Jaeger (Montana Poet Laureate 2017-2019) has authored nine books of poems, most recently *Earth-blood & Star-shine* (Shabda Press, 2018). He has mentored young poets for the past thirty-seven years in the classrooms of Flathead Valley Community College, Kalispell, Montana. Jaeger is the recipient of the Montana Governor's Humanities Award for his work in promoting civil civic conversations.

Daniel M. Jaffe is an internationally published, award-winning author, several of whose short stories have been nominated for a Pushcart Prize. His most recent book, *Foreign Affairs*, was selected by *Kirkus Reviews* as one of the Best Indie Short Story Collections of 2020.

Jakob Konger is from Tampa, Florida. He writes short stories about history and reality, and is a graduate of the Michener Fellowship program at the University of Miami.

David Lewitzky is an eighty-year-old retired social worker/family therapist living in Buffalo, New York. He resumed writing poetry in 2002 after a thirty-five-year hiatus. He has published about 125 poems in a variety of literary magazines, such as *Nimrod* and *Passages North*, with work forthcoming in *Seneca Review*, *Slant*, and *Main Street Rag*, among others.

Ellaraine Lockie's recent poems have won the Poetry Super Highway Contest, the Nebraska Writers Guild's Women of the Fur Trade Poetry Contest, and *New Millennium's* Monthly Musepaper Poetry Contest. Her fourteenth chapbook, *Sex and Other Slapsticks*, was released from Presa Press. Ellaraine teaches writing workshops and serves as poetry editor for the lifestyles magazine, LILIPOH.

Karen Loeb was Eau Claire, Wisconsin's writer-in-residence, 2018-2020. Her writing has appeared recently in *Gyroscope Review*, *Pinyon*, *Halfway Down the Stairs*, *Volume One*, and other magazines. Her work has won both the fiction and poetry contests in *Wisconsin People and Ideas*.

Mark Lucius is a writer, songwriter, and speechwriter who lives in Milwaukee, Wisconsin. He has published his work in *Best American Sports Writing, Great River Review, Cowboy Jamboree*, and *FewerThan500*. He has received five Cicero Awards from *Vital Speeches of the Day*.

Linda Maxwell has published work in Eastern Kentucky University's *Chaffin Journal*, UNLV's *Wordriver, The Catholic Digest, Poetry as Prayer, Southern Women's Review*, and *The Litchfield Review*. For the past four years, she has freelanced articles for *The Georgetown Times, South Strand News*, and *Tidelands*. Her poetry was published previously in *The Kindness of Strangers: A Wising Up Anthology*.

Leah Mueller is an indie writer and spoken word performer from Bisbee, Arizona. Her books, *Misguided Behavior, Tales of Poor Life Choices, Death and Heartbreak*, and *Cocktails at Denny's*, were released in 2019. Leah's work appears in *Midway Journal, Citron Review, The Spectacle, Miracle Monocle, Outlook Springs, Atticus Review, Your Impossible Voice*, and elsewhere.

Eddie Orton (pen name) is twenty-six and lives in London. He wrote his first draft of "Living Strange" two years ago, after a breakup (of sorts), and it's taken from his upcoming novel of the same name. Eddie has worked in film and the third sector, but is currently spending a lot of time on the couch. Eddie is three years clean and sober.

Carl "Papa" Palmer of Old Mill Road in Ridgeway, Virginia, lives in University Place, Washington. He is retired from the military and Federal Aviation Administration (FAA), enjoying life as "Papa" to his grand descendants, and being a Franciscan Hospice volunteer. Papa's motto: Long Weekends Forever!

Kate Pashby is a queer Mexican American poet from San Jose, California, who resides in Washington, DC. Kate's work has been published or is forthcoming in *The North Meridian Review, Genre: Urban Arts' House, Embryo Concepts Zine, subTerrain Magazine, Northern Otter Press, The Confessionalist Zine, Rabid Oak*, and many others. Kate was nominated for Best of the Net 2020.

Mark Pawlak is the author of nine poetry collections and the editor of six anthologies. His latest book is *Reconnaissance: New and Selected Poems and Poetic Journals* (Hanging Loose). His work has been translated into German, Japanese, Spanish, and Polish. *My Deniversity: Knowing Denise Levertov*, a memoir, is forthcoming in 2021 from MadHat Press.

Jan Phillips is the author of *No Ordinary Time, Creativity Unzipped, The Art of Original Thinking, Divining the Body, Marry Your Muse, God is at Eye Level, Making Peace, Born Gay, A Waist is a Terrible Thing to Mind,* and *Finding the On-Ramp to Your Spiritual Path.* She has published work in *The New York Times, Ms.,* and *Christian Science Monitor.*

Terry Sanville lives in San Luis Obispo, California, with his artist-poet wife and two plump cats. His stories have been accepted more than 420 times by numerous journals, magazines, and anthologies. Two of his stories were nominated for Pushcart Prizes and one for inclusion in the *Best of the Net* anthology. Terry is also an accomplished jazz and blues guitarist.

Linda A. Vandlac Smith has been writing and publishing poems in small press magazines for many years. Her work has appeared in publications such as *Permafrost, Pontoon,* and *Bellingham Review* and print anthologies that include *Lavanderia* and *Least Loved Beasts of the Really Wild West,* among others. She lives and writes in the Pacific Northwest.

Laurence Snydal is a poet, musician and teacher. He has published more than a hundred poems in magazines such as *Caperock, Spillway, Columbia,* and *Steam Ticket.* His work has appeared also in many anthologies including *Visiting Frost, The Poets Grimm,* and *The Years Best Fantasy and Horror.* Some of his poems have been performed in Baltimore and NYC. He lives in San Jose, CA, with his wife Susan.

Amber Soha is a senior and English major at the University of Maine at Farmington, with minors in creative writing, editing and publishing, and women's and gender studies. When she is not writing, editing, or ascending mountains of homework, she is wrangling children or spending time with her team of ducks.

C.W. Spooner's stories have appeared in *The Storyteller, Spitball, Lost Coast Review, Balloons Literary Journal, Halcyone Review, Sandy River Review/The River,* and an anthology from *Main Street Rag.* He has published two story collections, three novellas, and a collection of essays, memoirs, and poems. He lives and writes in Aliso Viejo, California.

J. J. Steinfeld is a Canadian fiction writer/poet/playwright living on Prince Edward Island. He has published twenty-one books, including both poetry:

Absurdity, Woe Is Me, Glory Be (Guernica Editions, 2017), *A Visit to the Kafka Café* (Ekstasis Editions, 2018), and *Morning Bafflement and Timeless Puzzlement* (Ekstasis, 2020) and stories: *An Unauthorized Biography of Being* (Ekstasis, 2016), *Gregor Samsa Was Never in The Beatles* (Ekstasis, 2019).

Lyn Stevens won the 2014 Saturday's Child Press short story contest. Her stories have also appeared in *Prism Review, Greensboro Review, Eclectica Magazine, Wordrunner eChapbooks, Main Street Rag, the American Literary Review, Santa Ana River Review, Pen + Brush* and *The Saturday Evening Post.* Lyn lives in the Bronx. She is crazy in love with her growing family

Alison Stone has published seven collections, including *Zombies at the Disco* (Jacar Press, 2020), *Caught in the Myth* (NYQ Books, 2019), and *They Sing at Midnight* (2003 Many Mountains Moving Poetry Award). Her work is in *The Paris Review, Poetry, Ploughshares*, and many others. She won *Poetry*'s Frederick Bock Prize and *New York Quarterly*'s Madeline Sadin Award. She created The Stone Tarot.

Johnny Townsend is a climate crisis refugee who relocated from New Orleans to Seattle in the wake of Hurricane Katrina. An ex-Mormon who volunteered two years as a full-time missionary, he advocates now for LGBTQ rights, gender equality, and racial justice both in his former church and throughout society. His latest essay collection is *Am I My Planet's Keeper?*

Hemlata Vasavada's articles and humor essays have been published in *The Seattle Times, Houston Chronicle, Syracuse Post Standard, Northwest Life & Times, Tea A Magazine, Everett Herald, Anthologies of Skagit Writers, India Currents, Khabar,* and the *I Should Have Stayed Home—Food* anthology from RDR Books. Her novel, *The Cascade Winners,* was released in April, 2014.

Nanako Water has published short stories in *Vocal.media,* in *Eastlit Journal,* and translated a Japanese memoir, *Tei, a memoir of the end of war and beginning of peace.* This story comes from her first novel, *Paper Ghost,* about four generations of a Japanese-American family in Japan and California. Other short stories are based on Japanese folklore.

Lillo Way's "Dubious Moon" won the Hudson Valley Writers Center's Slapering Hol Chapbook Contest. Her poems have won the E.E. Cummings Award and a *Florida Review* Editors' Prize. Her writing has appeared in *RHINO, Poet Lore, New Letters, Tampa Review, Louisville Review, Poetry East,* among others. Her collection, *Lend Me Your Wings*, was published by Shanti Arts in 2021.

Sarah Brown Weitzman, a National Endowment for the Arts Fellow in poetry and twice nominated for the Pushcart Poetry Prize, has had poems in hundreds of journals and anthologies including *The North American Review, Rattle, Poet Lore, New Ohio Review, Mid-American Review, The American Journal of Poetry,* and *The New York Quarterly.* Her latest chapbook, *AMOROTICA,* is forthcoming from Main Street Rag.

Allison Whittenberg is a Philadelphia native who has a global perspective. If she wasn't an author she'd be a private detective or a jazz singer. She loves reading about history and true crime. Her novels include *Sweet Thang, Hollywood and Maine, Life is Fine, Tutored,* and *The Sane Asylum.*

Frederick G. Yeager is retired and lives in Sarasota, Florida. He is a graduate of the University of South Dakota and the George Washington University School of Law. He practiced law in Sioux City, Iowa, worked in a Chicago bank, and worked as an international consultant for legal development in Croatia, Armenia, Nepal, Albania, and Moldova.

REFLECTIONS, MEMORIES, CONFESSIONS
Stirs Up Resentment
Exploring the Long Arc
A Better World is Possible!
'Hope Is Over'
CONTEXT IS EVERYTHING
Here's what it means
I AM
A
ACIST
These kinds
of issues cannot
just be left
r another
20, or
ears' time
Skin Deep
Is Still Devouring U
Injustice for All
ect trajectory
Swee
Up Shards

ACKNOWLEDGMENTS

Jane Blanchard's "Still Note" previously appeared in *Rabbit* (2016); "Ipso Facto" in *the Rotary Dial* (2016) and "Belatedly, a Sonnet" in *The Sonnet Scroll* (2015).

Lauren Camp's "Flexible "Truths" was first published in *Found Poetry Review* and "Discussing Death as a Conscious Activity" in *Sweet.*

Maryah Converse's "Sid Ismahan's Brothers and Daughters" first appeared in *Consequence* (2020).

Daniel M. Jaffe previously published "It's Not That . . . " in his *The Genealogy of Understanding* (Lethe Press, 2014).

Ellaraine Lockie's "Airing Dirty Laundry" previously appeared in *Schuylkill Valley Journal of the Arts.*

Karen Loeb's "What Is Discarded" was previously published in *Imagination and Place: Ownership* (Imagination and Place Press, 2010).

Leah Mueller's "Racism and Reasonable Doubt" was first published online in *The Blue Nib.*

J. J. Steinfeld's "The Impossibility of the Escaped Father's Laugh," appeared in a slightly different version in his *Disturbing Identities* (Ekstasis Editions, 1997).

Alison Stone previously published "Not Me, Not Mine" in *They Sing at Midnight* (Many Mountains Moving Press, 2003); "Blood Tie" in *Dangerous Enough* (Presa Press, 2014); and "Not Always Beauty" in *Dazzle* (Jacar Press, 2016).

Johnny Townsend's "This Is All Just Too Hard" was originally published at *BookLocker* (2020).

Photographs by Heather Tosteson.

EDITORS/PUBLISHERS

HEATHER TOSTESON is the author of seven books of fiction, poetry and non-fiction, including most recently the poetry collection *Source Notes: Seventh Decade*, the novel *The Philosophical Transactions of Maria van Leeuwenhoek, Antoni's Dochter*, and *Sharing the Burden of Repair: Reentry after Mass Incarceration* co-authored with Charles Brockett. She has worked in health communications with a focus on communication across disciplines, racism, social trust, and how belief systems develop and change. She has an MFA (UNC-Greensboro) and PhD in English and Creative Writing (Ohio University).

CHARLES BROCKETT has a PhD from UNC-Chapel Hill and is a recipient of several Fulbright and National Endowment for the Humanities awards. A retired political science professor, he has written two well-received books on Central America and numerous social science journal articles and book chapters. With Heather Tosteson, he is co-founder of Universal Table and Wising Up Press, co-editor of the Wising Up Anthologies, and co-author of *Sharing the Burden of Repair: Reentry After Mass Incarceration*.

Visit our website and learn about other Wising Up Press
books, readers guides, and calls for submissions.

www.universaltable.org
wisingup@universaltable.org

P.O. Box 2122
Decatur, GA 30031-2122

www.ingramcontent.com/pod-product-compliance
Lightning Source LLC
Chambersburg PA
CBHW031939010726
47493CB00007B/1999